Bite Me

Bite Me

Food in Popular Culture

Fabio Parasecoli

Oxford • New York

First published in 2008 by
Berg
Editorial offices:
1st Floor, Angel Court, 81 St Clements Street, Oxford, OX4 1AW, UK
175 Fifth Avenue, New York, NY 10010, USA

Berg is the imprint of Oxford International Publishers Ltd.

Library of Congress Cataloguing-in-Publication Data
Parasecoli, Fabio.
    Bite me : food in popular culture / Fabio Parasecoli.
    p. cm.
    Includes bibliographical references and index.
    ISBN-13: 978-1-84520-762-5 (cloth)
    ISBN-10: 1-84520-762-9 (cloth)
    ISBN-13: 978-1-84520-761-8 (paper)
    ISBN-10: 1-84520-761-0 (paper)
    1. Food—Social aspects. 2. Food habits. I. Title.

    GT2850.P274 2008
    394.1'2—dc22

                                                    2008024329

British Library Cataloguing-in-Publication Data
A catalogue record for this book is available from the British Library.

ISBN 978 1 84520 762 5 (Cloth)
ISBN 978 1 84520 761 8 (Paper)

Typeset by JS Typesetting Ltd, Porthcawl, Mid Glamorgan
Printed in the United Kingdom by Biddles Ltd, King's Lynn

www.bergpublishers.com

Contents

Acknowledgments   vii

Introduction: Pop Culture Drama: Food and Body Politics   1

1   Hungry Memories: Food, the Brain, and the Consuming Self   15

2   Of Breasts and Beasts: Vampires and Other Voracious Monsters   37

3   Tasty Utopias: Food and Politics in Science Fiction Novels   61

4   Quilting the Empty Body: Food and Dieting   85

5   Jam, Juice, and Strange Fruits: Edible Black Bodies   103

6   Tourism and Taste: Exploring Identities   127

Afterword: A Plea for Pleasure   147

References   153

Index   165

Acknowledgments

This book is dedicated to all those who helped me become who I am as a human being, a writer, and an intellectual. You know who you are.

My first thanks go to my family in Rome, for their unflinching love and sustenance despite my wandering and restlessness.

Thanks to all my coworkers at *Gambero Rosso* magazine and Città del Gusto, and to the *direttore*, Stefano Bonilli, who allowed me to explore food culture beyond what was expected from a feature writer.

A special thank you to Doran Ricks, who, besides guiding me through the intricacies of the English language, encouraged me to keep on writing when I was ready to drop everything and go lie on a beach.

Many friends and colleagues helped me in different ways with specific topics and chapters: for the introduction, Krishnendu Ray; for Chapter 1, Fritz Allhoff, Dave Monroe, and Miguel Sánchez Romera; for Chapter 2, Kyla Wazana Tompkins; for Chapter 3, Warren Belasco; for Chapter 4, Lisa Heldke, Alice Julier, and Laura Lindenfeld; for Chapter 5, Myron Beasley, Shelly Eversley, Jennifer Morgan, Robert Reid-Pharr (who also introduced me to the men's health literature and to the amazing work of Samuel R. Delany), and Psyche Williams-Forson; and for Chapter 6, Rachel Black and Lucy Long.

Much affection and gratitude to everybody in the Department of Nutrition, Food Studies, and Public Health at New York University, especially Judith Gilbride, Marion Nestle, Jennifer Berg, Amy Bentley, Lisa Sasson, Domingo Piñero, Anne McBride, Damian Mosley, Sierra Burnett, Kelli Ranieri, and Andy Bellatti.

Thanks to my fellow foodies in academia for their continuous encouragement, inspiration, and feedback, especially Ken Albala, Arlene Avakian, Anne Bellows, Charlotte Biltekoff, Janet Chrzan, Carole Counihan, Julia Csergo, Mitchell Davis, Netta Davis, Jonathan Deutsch, Darra Goldstein, Annie Hawk Lawson, Jean-Pierre Lemasson, Khary Polk, Elaine Power, Maryl Rosofky, Richard Wilk, and everybody in the Association for the Study of Food and Society.

I could not have written this book without the stimulation from my students both at New York University and at the Città del Gusto school in Rome, who really taught me how to get my ideas through.

A final thank you to Kathryn Earle, Julia Hall, Julene Knox, and Kathleen May at Berg, who made my work a real pleasure. Also thank you to Justin Dyer, who turned the usually tedious process of copy editing into a constructive moment!

Portions of Chapter 1 were published in "Hungry Engrams: Food and Non-Representational Memory", in *Food and Philosophy* (Oxford: Blackwell 2007).

Portions of Chapter 4 were previously published in "Low-Carb Dieting and the Mirror: A Lacanian Analysis of the Atkins Diet," in *The Atkins Diet and Philosopy* (Chicago: Open Court, 2005); and "Feeding Hard Bodies: Food and Nutrition in Men's Fitness Magazines," in *Food and Foodways* 13(1–2), 2005: 17–37, Special Issue "Food and Masculinity," edited by Alice Julier and Laura Lindenfeld Sher, reprinted in *Food and Culture*, ed. Carole Counihan and Penny Van Esterik (London: Routledge, 2007).

Portions of Chapter 5 were previously published in "Bootylicious: Food and the Female Body in Contemporary Pop Culture," in *WSQ: Women's Studies Quarterly* 35(1–2): 110–25 (Spring/Summer 2007).

Portions of Chapter 6 were previously published in "Identity, Diversity, and Dialogue," in *Food: Identity and Diversity in Culinary Cultures of Europe* (Strasbourg, Council of Europe, 2005; 50th Anniversary Publication).

Introduction: Pop Culture Drama
Food and Body Politics

Food is fundamental, fun, frightening, and far-reaching.

Rozin 1998: 9

No one can escape the conditions of naturality, of eating and drinking and domestic life with which still-life is concerned. ... Whether to see it as trivial, base and unworthy of serious attention, or to see it otherwise, is very much a matter of history and ideology

Bryson 1990: 13

Excessive Food

The obsession with food that in the past few decades has taken large sections of many Western cultures by storm apparently will not subside any time soon. In Europe, despite the panic created by looming epidemics (mad cow and such) and the tensions within the European Union about food security and hygiene protocols in certain traditional production methods, artisanal food is more and more popular, becoming a hot topic in a slate of publications, TV shows, and even Internet podcasts. America has apparently recovered from (and quickly forgotten) about the E. Coli scare – the last one in a long series of food-borne disease outbreaks – related to packaged fresh spinach that at the end of 2006 caused vegetable sales to drop dramatically, more or less at the same time as the New York City and Chicago health authorities were debating whether they should introduce a legal ban on the use of trans-fats in restaurants.

The public at large, bombarded by the media with results from scientific research mixed with folk remedies, has a hard time making sense of new findings of the day, such as the supposedly beneficial effects of low-calorie life-long diets on aging, or the anti-inflammatory and life-prolonging properties of the natural compound resveratrol, found in grape skins and various berries. Free radicals and phytonutrients are battling to conquer consumers' imagination, while the food industry is busy making claims on all sorts of nutrients to market new products and boost sales. The Food Network in the U.S., UKTV Food in Britain, and the Gambero Rosso Channel in Italy have become mainstays for TV audiences, providing a daily feed of food-themed shows and recipes . The Scottish-born Gordon Ramsay, one of the many chefs who have become media stars, has had multiple shows on different TV channels on both sides on the Atlantic, from *The F- Word* and *Ramsay's Kitchen Nightmares* on Channel 4 in the UK and BBC America to *Hell's Kitchen* on Fox in the USA. Numerous chefs have become public figures, exerting their influence at different levels. The Food Network star Rachel Ray has her own daytime talk show, while the English *enfant terrible* Jamie Oliver has stirred the UK authorities to improve school menus after a series of shows where he uncovered the horrors of canteen eating and its toll on the younger generations of Britons. The Spanish chef Ferran Adriá has managed to make a name for himself all over the world with his innovative – some say gimmicky – creations, while the new trend of molecular gastronomy, spearheaded by scientists such as the French Hervé This or the American Harold McGee and chefs like the above-mentioned Adriá and the British Heston Blumenthal, is changing the way high-end restaurants manipulate, prepare, and even conceptualize food. Besides writing best-selling books, famous chefs have themselves become the topic of books, TV segments, radio shows, and magazine feature articles. Even academia is taking an interest in them, as a part of the new discipline of food studies. Following the *gurume* (gourmet) revolution that swept the country from the late 1980s, food-centered series have appeared in Japanese *manga* comics books, while marketers in China have figured out that exotic products (wine, anyone?), foreign cuisines, and fancy restaurants may constitute an outlet for the new spending power of a growing portion of its huge population.

White truffles from Italy, Pata Negra ham from Spain, shark fins from the South Pacific, Argan oil from Morocco, cru chocolate beans from Venezuela or Ecuador, Blue Mountain coffee from Jamaica, though actually consumed by few, have acquired a special status in the collective imagination of the ever-growing cohorts of food aficionados all over the world. The food industry, marketing and advertising firms, political lobbies, academic institutions, and last but not least the media seem to have realized that recipes, delicacies, food-related traditions, and even daily shopping all play a role that goes well beyond the economic and material aspects of consumption.

Food is pervasive. The social, economic, and even political relevance cannot be ignored. Ingestion and incorporation constitute a fundamental component of our connection with reality and the world outside our body. Food influences our lives as a relevant marker of power, cultural capital, class, gender, ethnic, and religious identities. It has become the object of a wide and ever-growing corpus of studies and analysis, from marketing to history, from nutrition to anthropology. Yet, food reveals many other layers of meaning that are often left unexplored when it comes to phenomena that fall squarely under the heading of pop culture, especially the "low brow" or even "trash" kind. Intriguingly, these phenomena may reveal interesting aspects of our relationships with the body and, more specifically, with eating and ingestion.

Although at times we would rather not come to terms with it – and when we do we prefer to assume an aloof and critical stance – we cannot deny that we live in what the French philosopher Guy Debord, originally writing some four decades ago, defined as a "society of the spectacle" (Debord 1977). If the grand meta-narratives of modernity are actually dead, as François Lyotard affirmed in his infamous postmodern manifesto (Lyotard 1984), citizens of Western and also non-Western societies are increasingly relying on narratives to make sense of their everyday lives. As anthropologist Arjun Appadurai noticed, imagination and fantasy have become a fundamental social practice, playing an important role in shaping everyday life for many people all over the world: "In the past two decades, as the deterritorialization of persons, images, and ideas has taken on new force ... more persons throughout the world see their lives through the prisms of the possible lives offered by mass media in all their forms" (Appadurai 1996: 53–4). Pop culture happens to be the arena where new narratives, changing identities, and possible practices become part of a shared patrimony that participates in the constitution of contemporary subjectivities. By creating projections about the future, by picturing alternative realities, and by prompting all sorts of interests, attachment, and aspirations, collective imagination can become a basis for agency and social mobilization. In this sense, imagination is deeply political, since it comes to constitute an organized field of social practices and discourses, and a space of negotiation that is "neither purely emancipatory nor entirely disciplined" (Appadurai 1996: 4)

And here is where food is relevant, since it deals with those crucial aspects of the human experience that hinge on the material, the physical, and the body. We all realize how fraught and complex the relationship between lived bodies and imagined realities often is: desires, fantasies, fears, and dreams coagulating around and in the body deeply influence our development as individual subjects. From where do many of these imaginary elements derive? I believe that pop culture constitutes a major repository of visual elements, ideas, practices, and discourses that influence our relationship with the body, with food consumption, and, of course, with the whole system ensuring that we get what we need on a daily basis, with all its social and political ramifications. How has the *Iron Chef* show, a very culturally specific product of Japanese TV, become a solid hit in Western countries? What is it that keeps audiences glued to the screen, even if they have no intention to cook, ever? Is it the voyeuristic appeal of gastroporn or the glamour of celebrity chefs (Adema 2000; Cockburn 1977; O'Neill 2003)? Is it the practical matter-of-fact approach of Rachel Ray, the sensual expressions of Nigella Lawson, the puckish enjoyment of "the Naked Chef," a.k.a. Jamie Oliver, the macho attitude of Emeril Lagassi, the brash adventurousness of Anthony Bourdain, the sexy braggadocio of Rocco Di Spirito, or the bubbly worldliness of Giada De Laurentis? At the same time, as food scholar Krishendu Ray pointed out, many Americans (including intellectuals) have a veneration for Julia Child, who, with her TV shows, introduced large American audiences to French cuisine and, above all, to a different, more relaxed and fun-loving relationship with cooking and with unfamiliar foods that were often considered high-end and inaccessible (Ray 2007: 51).

The Labyrinth of Pop Culture

Whatever it is that pop culture does to reach it goals, it does it right. It is a spectacle that works, building on dreams and desires. And food is pervasive in contemporary Western pop culture, influencing the way we perceive and represent ourselves as individuals and as members of social groups. However, the ubiquitous nature of these cultural elements makes their ideological and political relevance almost invisible, buried in the supposedly natural and self-evident fabric of everyday life. Meanwhile, our own flesh becomes fuel for all kinds of cultural battles among different visions of personhood, family, society, and even economics. For these reasons, developing an accessible analytical framework to handle these topics is an important task to achieve a deeper, even if somewhat unorthodox, comprehension of our twenty-first-century globalized consumer society.

First of all, it is necessary to give at least a working definition of how the expression "pop culture" will be used in this book. It will refer to any form of cultural phenomenon, material item, practice, social relation, and even idea that is conceived, produced, distributed, and consumed within a market-driven environment.

Of course, pop culture has always existed, although historically it was neither acknowledged as creative and original, nor admitted in the established canons of culture. Things have changed in the past decades. Received ideas about what culture is have deeply altered, following the counterculture movements of the 1960s and 1970s, the crisis of the project of modernity that hinged on the ideal of progress and often coincided with the goals of Western white males, the end of the old-style Cold War and the crisis of traditional political ideologies, the beginning of new cultural wars (including the so-called "War on Terror"), the crisis of the post-colonial model of international relations, the complex and ever-shifting dialectics between globalization, national boundaries, and empire, and many other factors that go beyond the scope of this book. Western societies have witnessed the crisis of the grand narratives that sustained the rift between what was deemed valuable enough to be admitted to the pantheon of culture (especially national culture) and what was often considered as amusement for the masses or as a reflection of the less dignified aspects of our societies (including food).

The duration and the "shelf life" of pop culture items have evolved, making their observation and cultural investigation even more complicated, if not frantic. In the past, they were limited in number, and their appearance on the market was less frequent, with the consequence that they probably had a more stable, more uniform, and less debatable meaning for most users. A hit song would stay in the charts for long periods, and an Academy Award-winning film would fill the theaters for months. Starting with the development of new media such as photography, radio, movies, magazines, and then TV, CDs, DVDs, the Internet, the iPod, mobile phones, and hand-held computers, more and more elements are added by the minute to the big, bubbling cauldron of pop culture. While many consumers are rediscovering traditional produce, ingredients, and dishes, which often become objects of fads in their own right, food industries are always developing new products to boost their sales, while elaborating marketing strategies that translate into new communication, advertising, tastes, cultural and visual elements.

It is increasingly more difficult for scholars to keep up with current occurrences, trends, and customs. Although transitory, or maybe precisely because of their fleeting quality, the present contingencies need to be taken into account, understood, and put into perspective to achieve a better grasp on contemporary events. Anthropology, sociology, economics, cultural and gender studies have certainly offered new and stimulating approaches through which to analyze our own cultures, each discipline with its specific set of tools and conceptual framework. However, they are removed from the sensitivity and the perception of society at large, often unable (and sometimes unwilling) to translate into a layman's language not only their insights and conclusions, but also the very objects of their inquiry. On the other hand, the common public and media perceptions of what culture is, and especially of what high culture is, have changed dramatically. The distinction between "high brow" and "low brow" appears increasingly blurred. It might be useful to elaborate a new approach to pop culture, allowing the analytical instruments and the general theories behind it to become accessible to readers and citizens outside academia.

This book does not pretend to be definitive or to encompass all the existing expressions of pop culture, precisely owing to its inherent complexity. The choice of subject matter can come across as quirky. I must admit I have followed my personal interests and tapped into those aspect of pop culture that I enjoy the most as a consumer. Living between the US and Europe has allowed me to "compare and contrast" – as my students love to say – different cultures, allowing me to notice aspects that are maybe too mundane and common to be taken seriously. Besides, I do enjoy looking at things from unusual angles: they often grant unexpected revelations. All the topics focus on the main argument of the book: that our bodies, including our crucial relationship with food and ingestion, are represented in pop culture as a reflection of wider cultural, social, and political debates among various and diffused agencies, trying to influence the way we perceive ourselves and our world, and they way we operate in it. I believe that analyzing and uncovering certain practices, ideas, and discourses hidden – or, it would be better to say, made to look natural and neutral – in the way pop culture deals with food and eating, we can adopt a more critical and constructive stance as citizens, and not only when it comes our choices about what to put on the table and in our mouth.

Even if the main subject of this book is food, we cannot limit ourselves to observe those aspects of pop culture that are directly connected with it: shopping, eating trends, marketing, advertising, packaging, and nutrition, just to mention a few. To attain a more comprehensive understanding of the imaginary and of the perceptions of consumers and of the way they reflect them in their social and political attitudes and decisions, we have to access other media, products, and practices where food appears, such as movies, books, comics, songs, music videos, websites, slang, and all kind of performances, even when their connection to our central topic may not always be readily apparent.

However, there is also a more theoretical reason for touching on aspects of pop culture that would seem totally unrelated: a deeper comprehension of their mechanisms can grant us a better grasp of the concept of cultural change, updating and expanding it.

In the worldwide, instantly connected, and overexposed contemporary pop culture, it is likely that apparently distant elements actually influence each other, surfacing in the most unexpected contexts. For instance, the photo of a celebrity acquires different cultural meanings when it is printed in a magazine, it is broadcast on TV and posted on a website, or it is used as a reference or a visual citation in a commercial or in a video. The same image further acquires new life when some stand-up comedian makes fun of it in a skit, a rapper mentions it on a new track, a fashion designer winks at it in a collection, a group of young people adopts a certain gesture or embodies it in its physical appearance, and most of all when some pop culture pundit starts a debate about it on a blog. The same dynamics seem to operate in the world of food. A given ingredient can be analyzed by scientists and nutrition-ists, whose research is picked up in bits and pieces by newspapers, magazines, TV talk shows, and blogs, influencing consumers' expectations and behaviors, creating fads and fashions, prompting changes in distribution chains and in shopping habits, while at the same time interfering with the industry development of new foods, which translates into nutritional claims, advertising, and marketing campaigns that in turn interact with consumers' perceptions and with scientists' research.

To achieve a comprehensive grasp of this multifaceted and complex reality, we need to update the old and maybe find new tools for what theorists call "synchronic analysis," that is to say the study of a given phenomenon at a specific moment in time. In our case, we need to uncover the connections, the mechanisms, and even the malfunctions in that extensive, intrusive, and all-encompassing web of meanings, practices, and language that is contemporary pop culture, especially when it comes to food and ingestion. As we will see, this will allow us to develop our understanding of how these webs change over time, achieving what is called "diachronic analysis" and actually integrating the two dimension of our inquiry.

The French theorists Roland Barthes and Jean Baudrillard wrote extensively on these topics, most of the time in a very critical voice. Barthes developed the concept of "myth" as a special kind of "sign." In the terminology of semiotics, the discipline that studies precisely signs, a sign is an element of communication composed of a physical expression (image, sound, or other, known as "signifier") and various meanings arbitrarily attached to it (its "signified"). The "myth" is a sign that in its entirety becomes a mere signifier for another sign, being given a different meaning. Writing in the late 1950s, Barthes used the famous example of a magazine cover picture representing a young black man in a French uniform saluting, with his eyes uplifted, the French flag. The basic meaning of the picture, the content that all viewers more or less share (its "denotation"), is just that: a black soldier saluting a flag. However, different meanings (or "connotations") can be given to this picture depending on the context. It can be used as a symbol of nationalism, of French pride, of the attachment of the colonized to the colonizer, and so on (Barthes 1972: 109–59) This shift of meaning can become even more noticeable if the media also change, for instance if that same picture becomes a poster, or a record cover. Something similar happens, say, when a slice of certain ripe cheese is shown by a farmer to a visitor from out of town, and then later when the same slice appears in the counter of an upscale gourmet shop, on the table of a famous star in her last movie, in the hands of a political lobbyist defending local agriculture, in the pages of a diet book, and last but not least in the logo of an association.

What happens when this transmutation from media to media and from context to context becomes as fast and intense as in today's pop culture? Baudrillard advanced the hypothesis of a reality based on "matrices, memory banks, and command models" that can be reproduced for an infinite number of times and where real and imaginary are blurred into a new dimension, the hyperreal, totally unanchored to reality.

> The age of simulation thus begins with a liquidation of all referentials – worse: by their artificial resurrection in systems of signs, a more ductile material than meaning, in that it lends itself to all systems of equivalence, all binary oppositions and all combinatory algebra. It is no longer a question of imitation, nor of reduplication, nor even of parody. It is rather a question of substituting signs of the real for the real itself. (Baudrillard 1983a: 4)

In this process, certain signifiers bounce around, reflected and distorted, acquiring different and even controversial meanings. However, their presence or omnipresence as signifiers, as elements of communication regardless of their actual sense, is reinforced. Their life might be shorter, but their temporary interaction with the rest of the communication network is much more intense: the ripples travel faster and wider in the global meaning pond. And signifiers take on new connotations, sometimes even denotations, in every culture that receives them in order to embrace them, tweak them to meet its needs, or refuse them. The use of signifiers coming from another culture can turn out to be extremely creative. What can be the impact of Madonna's sexualized avatars, say, in Vietnam, India, Zimbabwe, and Bolivia? What would happen to the slice of ripe cheese we mentioned when exported to China, where consumers are not very used to cheese in the first place, to appear later in the menu of a fashionable Tokyo restaurant and in a food show in Thailand?

Signifiers *will* acquire different meanings when they are integrated in different cultural, economic, social, political, and even material contexts.

How do these dynamics work? How can signs change their meanings? Since its heyday, semiotics has tried to give answers to these questions. The first to recognize in each element of communication, or sign, a material element and a meaning (a "signifier" and a "signified") was the Swiss linguist Ferninand de Saussure, whose teachings were collected and edited by his students (Saussure 1983). Others, like the American Charles Sanders Peirce, included in the theoretical model of the sign also the object to which the sign itself refers to, the "referent" (Peirce 1966). Since Saussure, signs have also been analyzed within a context, as parts of a "system," where each element's role is somehow defined by the other elements in the system. The anthropologists, social scientists, and theorists known as structuralists actually pushed this argument to claim that no element in a system has any meaning in itself, but it is defined by what actually the sign is *not*, in relation to the other elements. What counts, on the other hand, would be oppositions and differences. Following this approach and basing his analysis on his therapeutic experience, the French psychoanalyst Jacques Lacan affirmed that the signifier is actually more stable than the signified: the material element of a sign stays the same, while its meaning can shift, determined by the other signs connected with it, which he called a "signifying chain." Lacan actually talked of "an incessant sliding of the signified under the signifier" through the mechanisms of metaphor and metonymy (Lacan 2002: 145). In the case of food, this element is quite intuitive: a slice of a given type of cheese tends to remain the same wherever it ends up, even when the meaning its consumers give to it can change dramatically. The meaning of a dish can change over time, even if the recipe and the ingredients stay roughly the same: a dish of chitterlings meant certain things in antebellum America, during the reconstruction, when it was brought by immigrants to New York City in the roaring 1920s, when it was contested by the Black Panthers as slaves' food, and when it appears on the menus of contemporary soul food restaurants.

Despite the slippery nature of meaning, subjects need points of reference around which they can build their mental universe and their communication tools, lest they become victims of psychosis. Lacan calls these stable components "upholstery buttons" or "button points," and they are constituted by the repressed elements of subjects' conscious experience, such as the notion of the father, the desire for the mother in the Oedipal complex, and the incest taboo. Just like upholstery buttons make sure that the stuffing of a chair or a sofa does not move around and stays attached to the framework of the furniture, these elements give meaning to the whole system of communication of the subjects (Lee 1990: 61–2).

As stimulating as the structuralist model was, it was criticized because it could only used as a device to explain a system at a specific moment, as a totality with its internal relationships, oppositions, and differences. However, it could not explain the transformation of a system into something different; history and change are difficult to corset into static structures. Sticking to our soul food example, what made the meaning of chitterling change in time and space? What elements remained the same to keep the recipe recognizable, and what changed? What significations attached to the meaning were stable, and what developed over time?

Pop Politics

The answers can be found in the work of two political theorists, the Argentinean Ernesto Laclau and the Belgian Chantal Mouffe, who based their analysis on some Lacanian concepts and the theories of the Italian Antonio Gramsci.

Gramsci was a leader of the Italian Communist Party who, imprisoned by the Fascist regime for most of his adult life, used his time in jail to reflect on the political and social situation of his country, the clutch that the Fascist party had on the people, and the role of culture in those dynamics. Despite his Marxist background, he felt he could not dismiss culture (including politics) as a "superstructure," a mere consequence of the economic structure with no influence on social and political life. What were the ideological resources of Fascism? How could this totalitarian regime get so many to adhere to its tenets and practices? The answer Gramsci gave was that the Fascist party had gained hegemony, in that it had transcended the interests of the specific sectors that it represented and created a political and social culture that met the interests of most subordinate groups, thus ensuring its dominant position in Italy (Gramsci 2000: 205). Taking advantage of the incapacity of Italian intellectuals, especially the ones in the Left, to create a lively and productive relationship with the people, due to their status as a separate caste, Fascism had been able to talk to the imagination, the dreams, and the actual material and immaterial needs of the masses, shaping the beginning of a "national-popular" culture which influenced their mentalities and behaviors (Gramsci 2000: 365–70). In Gramsci's thought, pop culture becomes a field were political, social, and ideological battles are fought among different groups of interest to establish their hegemony over society at large. He specifically discusses serial novels, mostly foreign and from the nineteenth century, and opera as examples of popular entertainment: two genres that nowadays sit comfortably in the "high brow" categories.

Ernesto Laclau and Chantal Mouffe used the Gamscian concept of hegemony to explain changes within a system still considered as a relational network of differential positions, as in classic structuralism. However, these networks and their composing elements are far from static. Laclau and Mouffe describe them as incomplete, open, and politically negotiable, transferring Lacan's analysis of the sign as composed of a stable material element (signifier) and an ever-changing and shifting meaning (signified) to identities, concepts, and practices, which can all be interpreted as signifying networks, webs of meaning enveloping reality. Laclau and Mouffe defined certain elements within these signifying networks as "floating signifiers" whose meaning and place within the larger cultural system are fixed and determined by the emergence of new centers of interests. This implies that cultural elements are constantly submitted to an ongoing negotiation among various forces in a specific society (Laclau and Mouffe 1985: 93–148). Nevertheless, these negotiations require some stable anchorage that protects society from implosion and eventual destruction: some nodal points, which Laclau and Mouffe describe as "partial fixations," become the equivalent of the upholstery points described by Lacan in his work on psychoses, providing stability to the social discourse as a whole and to the ever-mutating networks of meaning (Laclau and Mouffe 1985: 112)

For instance, in most Western societies, values such as freedom and democracy are shared by most components of the social and political body, even if diverse social and cultural segments interpret them differently. Others, such as the free market or the environment or sustainability, are much more contentious, and their meaning is subject to wide debate. In time, though, certain sections of society might be able to use these values to gain hegemony over larger parts of society by articulating their meaning to make them acceptable or even desirable to other segments of the political body.

Laclau and Mouffe's work is relevant to this book because it offers great analytical tools for the study of pop culture, including food. First of all, it rejects the distinction between linguistic, behavioral, and material aspects of social and political practice, since they all are part of the dynamics that produce meaning in any give society. We can interpret pop culture as an all-embracing signifying network that includes elements such as values, practices, ideas, and objects, whose meaning is determined by their reciprocal influence within the network as a whole and by the negotiations taking place among its users. Going back to the examples we used, both cheese and chitterlings become the objects of ongoing negotiations within the communities that produced them, the larger bodies of which those communities are part, the different social strata and political groups within them, with their specific agendas, the media that use those elements in different ways according to their editorial needs, the consumers and their sense of who they are and what they like (or supposed to like). Certain dishes and street foods that until a few years ago had low-class connotations are now recognized as part of cultural heritage under a changing social and political climate that nurtures different sensibilities. The same slice of ripe cheese that until a few years ago might have been considered with disdain in comparison to neatly packed, hygienically made, and ready-to-serve slices of industrially produced cheese is now perceived as an embodiment of culture, tradition, know-how, prestige, gourmet expertise, and even political resistance.

Ingestion constitutes an important layer, based on our own physical presence, in the interconnected webs of signification that constitute pop culture. The meanings of our own bodies change over time for ourselves and for society, and in turn they determine and influence other factors in food production, distribution, and consumption processes. When it comes to eating, many contentious and negotiable elements become weapons in a struggle within various cultural and political interests to gain hegemony in our societies.

The Long and Winding Road

Food has only recently become a respectful object of interest and research in academia. The mass media had long before uncovered its relevance and its appeal to large audiences. Food can be approached from many points of view: first of all, we can focus on its interaction with our body (nutrition) and our inner wellbeing (psychology and psychoanalysis). We can analyze its material elements, such as ingredients, flavors, techniques, and dishes (culinary practice and education). We can learn how certain foods changed over time, how they traveled from place to place, and how they influenced changes in specific societies (history). We can examine food's meanings and practices within a specific community and their relations with its culture (folklore, ethnology, and anthropology); its production, distribution, and consumption patterns according to census, class, sex, gender, age, and cultural level (sociology and economics); and its weight in contemporary political debates and administrative practices in Western countries (political science). We can consider the many ways food becomes part of social communication (media studies), of performances of identity and subjectivity (performance, cultural, and gender studies), of artistic expressions of all kinds (literary and art criticism). We can investigate the impact of food's production, distribution, and consumption on water, land usage, and air pollution (environmental studies). This perfunctory list of possible approaches indicates that food studies are intrinsically interdisciplinary.

This book will mainly employ the theoretical framework and the tools of semiotics and media studies, but other disciplines will be evoked when necessary, depending on the topic at hand. Throughout its pages, I will try to illustrate the "working tools," that is, the analytical instruments introduced in each chapter to deal with specific aspects of the presence of food in pop culture, in a plain and accessible language without diluting their content and complexity. Despite the supposed abstractness of these concepts, I think an attentive audience can understand and apply them without excessive difficulty if all the explanations and the examples focus on the topics that most interest us and relate to our daily experience. Starting from concrete and familiar occurrences, it is easier to introduce concepts that otherwise would require long explanations and lots of reading. I will integrate the topics with theoretical contributions from authors such as Foucault, de Certeau, Bourdieu, Gramsci, Laclau and Mouffe, Žižek, and Butler. Again, when applying their theories to concrete cases and examples, I am sure that readers will have no problem grasping the most complex concepts. It is a question of breaking down theory to make it closer to experience. As a result, I hope this book will be not only a fun foray into pop culture but also an introduction to strains of contemporary critical thought whose influence too often remains limited to academia and intellectuals. Once again following

Gramsci, I do believe that also general audiences should be provided with effective intellectual weapons to better comprehend and deal with our contemporary reality. As with any other weapons, these also need practice and familiarization. Could there be better targets than food and pop culture, in which we all are immersed, more or less willingly? The goal is to integrate different styles of cultural analysis to tackle a peculiar subject – food – that is so encompassing to the point of being daunting. I have chosen to concentrate on certain aspects that are accessible and experienced by many in Western societies, often using elements of the U.S. pop universe as examples because of its pervasiveness and its influence on cultural production all over the world.

Chapter 1 analyzes the role of food in memory, representation, and the construction of the subject from the point of view of brain processes. According to recent research in neuroscience, rational processes, hinging heavily on memories, cannot be isolated from what is traditionally considered irrational, physical, and instinctual. We will see how pop culture uses eating and ingestion to naturalize and make acceptable different visions of what a human being is, particularly when it comes to the relationship between mind and the senses, memories and the body. These visions are far from neutral: they represent contrasting approaches to sexuality, gender, and social interaction. Furthermore, a better understanding of how our mind works will lay the foundations for a more effective grasp on our participation in pop culture, from shopping to gadgetry, from advertising to marketing.

Food also plays a major role in our psychological development and existence as individuals. Chapter 2 is dedicated to the relationship between ingestion and our wellbeing as functioning subjects. Many psychoanalysts have individuated hunger and the desire for incorporation, even at the price of the destruction of the desired object, as a necessary and constitutive dimension for individual growth. Of course, these destructive drives and cannibalistic desires are not culturally acceptable, being the negation of all appropriate social interactions and negotiations, which in turn constitute the basis for power structures. Yet these desires exist, emerging here and there despite all attempts at foreclosure. Pop culture mainstays such as vampires and other horror characters, always popular in the imagination of the West (yet not exclusively), constitute suitable expressions and engaging metaphors for otherwise unacceptable drives such as limitless hunger and desire for continuous incorporation. This multi-layered discourse acquires further complexity when analyzing metaphors that describe the state and any sort of political power in terms of devouring entities.

The political aspects of the metaphors about the body and ingestion also point to the material foundations of power and its structures. The ways we choose, store, prepare, cook ingest, digest, and excrete food are inherently political, yet we are taught to perceive our body as natural.

The maneuvers to hide the clutch of power on the body are not always successful: traces of the attempted concealment seep through narratives and non-discursive elements. It is often the case in science fiction, the main focus of Chapter 3. As a literary genre, sci-fi constitutes an intrinsic critique of the status quo in that it creates alternatives to present realities. It forces readers to face the fact that the world in which they live is not natural or absolute, enticing them to political and social reflections. In this chapter, I will focus on how food can enhance the critical power of the genre, both when nourishment is at the forefront of the narration and when it constitutes a secondary subplot.

Hunger and desires for ingestion also interact with the construction of the subject's body image, building the foundation for the adult obsession with figure, shape, and dieting, which is analyzed in Chapter 4. Health and exercise have become a constitutive element of contemporary pop culture in affluent countries. Our bodies frequently bother us, to the point where we end up perceiving them as some external burden imposed on our real self, that inner self that does not succeed in shining through the obtrusive flesh. The questions that I will address in the chapter deal with body images and their emotional power over our inner lives, the way they are created and maintained in our cultures and their influence on our eating habits and on our relation to food. Using the Atkins diet and male fitness magazines as examples, I will show how visual images and cultural elements interact to create new eating patterns with the aim of controlling our biological requirements (hunger) and psychological needs (desire), both for men and for women, also changing concepts of masculinity and femininity, and the power structures related to them.

The connections among food, body, and politics are also closely associated with race issues, the core of Chapter 5. Soul food, for instance, is identified with the African American community. Yet it is enough to dig a little deeper to find several layers to essentialist discourses. Blackness is after all a cultural construct with powerful political corollaries. Yet is perceived as a natural element, and metaphors used to describe the black body are smoothly included in the texture of pop culture. Chocolate, licorice, and cinnamon are only the most common metaphors for edibility, often used with sexual subtexts. The black body as a source of nourishment and even as an edible substance in itself is a topic made even more intricate by a strong ambivalent element of sexual attraction and repulsion, danger and fascination. The chapter will explore the re-emergence of food metaphors to describe black bodies and to inscribe them in mainstream cultural politics. I will look at representations of female bodies, which pay particular attention to the derrière, also known as the "booty." I will try to show how the connection between food and the booty, for centuries often used to debase black women, has become part of the re-evaluation of the black female body also as a locus for sex and passion, not in a negative sense but in a positive, self-affirming fashion. I will also analyze the cultural and political implications of the complex relationship between food and the black male body in contemporary America, from the Chocolate Salty Balls of *South Park* to Nelly's Pimp Juice.

The political, social, and cultural relevance of food is particularly evident in one of the most common leisure activities of affluent societies: tourism, the main topic of Chapter 6. During a trip abroad, or even to another region in one's own country, the differences in culinary systems have to eventually be addressed, in a more or less conscious fashion. These dynamics imply that travelers, endowed with a specific culinary competence, are forced to acknowledge and take into account the existence of different food codes. Examining travelers' behaviors can shed a new light on the semiotic character of food and its role in constituting stable identities, a trait that acquires particular relevance in an age or globalization and swift technological changes. Foreign foods are captured in a network of symbols, images, practices and beliefs that occupy an important space in pop culture, generating at the same time a whole industry with important revenues. A deeper awareness of the political, non-neutral nature of processes defining codes and communication modalities can help us to shift our location as tourists not only physically, but also culturally.

–1–

Hungry Memories
Food, the Brain, and the Consuming Self

It is the same for our past. We would exert ourselves to no result if we tried to evoke it; all the efforts of our intelligence are of no use. The past is hidden outside its realm and its range, in some material objects (in the sensation this object would give us) which we don't suspect.

Proust 1984: 59

What is the role of food in pop culture? Why does it seem to crop up everywhere we look? What are the mechanisms that determine its influence on how we chose, buy, consume, and enjoy ourselves? After all, one could say, eating and drinking are mere reflections of biological necessities and functions. As a matter of fact, they are usually perceived as purely "natural" aspects of our lives. If this were actually the case, how could they ever become an arena for competing political projects, ideological approaches, and deep beliefs and principles? If food were only a matter-of-fact, mundane requirement with which all humans need to cope on a daily basis, just like breathing or sweating, how could it acquire such weight and become the expression of multi-layered and intense attachments? The answer is quite straightforward: precisely for its key role in our survival since infancy as physical beings, eating is charged with very intense and complex emotional significance. In the following chapters we will see how this basic fact has found expression in different aspects of pop culture. In fact, hunger and the desire for incorporation and appropriation, together with sexual drives, are arguably at the origin of consumption in all its expressions. It is definitely the case for contemporary consumerism, which lies at the core of Western society as its propelling engine, filtered through social and economic structures and dynamics. After all, it was the desire for goods and commodities that prodded Europeans to travel, explore, and colonize (Braudel 1982; Wallerstein 1980; Welch 2005).

Nevertheless, as modern Western consumers, we are definitely more complex than a simple bundle of drives and impulses. We are far from being defenseless victims of marketing and political maneuvers. We think, we evaluate, we decide, basing our choices and actions on values and goals. Although crucial, the emotional and physical influences of hunger and ingestion on our day-by-day choices and behaviors are not sufficient to explain their impact on our perceptions and on the ways we categorize reality and deal with it.

However, we cannot revert to the opposition between rationality and the soul, on the one hand, and matter, the flesh, and feelings, on the other. In the following chapters I will address the possibility of a different resolution of the contrast between reason and emotions, spirit and body. To do this, we have to plunge into the complex and often still mysterious processes of the human brain, in order to acquire a better understanding of how our minds work.

Food will provide us an unusual point of entry into the functions of the brain, emotions, and memories. It is enough to pause and recall our liveliest memories related to taste, smell, and sensual pleasure to realize that they do not simply mirror past events. Instead, they are vivid, profound, and emotional. Our bodies almost seem to relive these moments. We are all more or less acutely aware of this. How does that happen? As a matter of fact, as we will see, most scientists now seem to agree that sensations and emotions heavily influence not only recollection, but also rational processes. According to recent research in neuroscience –exciting but developing and open-ended, like all scientific endeavor – memories turn out to be not fixed once and for all, but rather the result of an ongoing dynamic interaction between different activities in the brain and the information we receive from the senses. That is to say, the brain re-creates memories in different ways every time they are recalled, depending on emotional and sensory stimulations. Memories are alive and a fundamental part of who we are and of how we experience our lives. Gustatory and olfactory ones are especially intense. Their power over our functionality, even if often unconscious, enhances our experiences of desire, pleasure, pain, our emotional states and motivations. Our body appears to be involved in all cognitive processes, including rational ones. We cannot disregard its relevance for our participation in consumption and pop culture.

Let flavors and scents guide us in exploring our brains and bodies. And could there be a better muse than a chef who is also a scientist?

The Neurologist and the Chef

"Let me introduce myself: I have been a neurologist and a neurophysiologist for twenty years, and a chef for six." This is the matter-of-fact statement that opens *La Cocina de los Sentidos* (Cooking with the Senses), the first book by Miguel Sánchez Romera, chef and owner of the renowned restaurant L'Esguard in Sant Andreu de Llavaneres on the coast of Catalonia, Spain (Sánchez Romera 2001). Now in his 50s, Sánchez Romera has worked for many years in hospitals and scientific institutions, focusing particularly on epilepsy. He was always passionate about cooking and food, but the turning point in his career was his 40th birthday dinner, when he cooked for 50 people together with his friend, the famous Catalan chef

Ferran Adriá (Bolasco 2000: 117–26) The dinner turned out to be such a success that the gatherings at the Sánchez Romeras became a tradition. It was only in 1996 that the neurologist decided to open a restaurant, namely L'Esguard, receiving a good deal of attention throughout Europe and, more recently, all over the world. When Mr. Romera, together with David Bouley, presented his work at the French Culinary Institute in October 2003, he attracted daring young New York chefs such as Wylie Dufresne and Sam Mason from WD-50 and Jonnie Uzini from Jean-Georges.

In *La Cocina de los Sentidos*, Sánchez Romera's diverse interests meet in the most intriguing and stimulating fashion (Parasecoli 2003a). I will concentrate on Sánchez Romera's theories regarding the senses, the mind, and memory. Being both a successful chef and a respected scientist, he is in a privileged position to analyze the connections between cognition and recollection in the realm of food and flavors. His whole argument, which also influences his cooking style, is based on the concept that memory and mind activities, at least in the case of food, are closely connected with emotions through the senses, the body, and its most basic needs, hunger and thirst.

> The sensory being is born from the sensations that its own brain reproduces under a determined stimulus, as this stimulus provokes a chain of reactions in different parts of the brain itself that go and come through electrical impulses. Nevertheless, the spirit and the degree of ability to feel sensations depend exclusively on the individual. The only necessities that the body recognizes from the brain are, in gastronomy, hunger and thirst. The necessity is to stay alive in some way or another: all stimuli from our brain end up transformed into emotions, and these emotions are part of our lives. ... Everything depends on sensations; then memory and remembering take us to the world of analysis, from which a state of wellbeing and happiness, as well as its contrary, can derive. (Sánchez Romera 2001: 38–9)

When they eat and drink, individuals find themselves at the juncture between biological necessity, the world of drives and instincts, the inputs from the outside world, and the tremendous landslide of sensations, feelings, and emotions resulting from uninterrupted brain activities. In a similar way Sánchez Romera, as a chef, is at the crossroads between the material world of edible products and culinary arts, a creative experience that connects human physiology to culture. His work enhances the notion that food is at the frontier between the biological and the cultural.

No other organ in the human being embodies the complexity of this frontier better than the brain itself, where electrical and chemical signals become the texture of perception, memory, thought, creativity, and emotions. Already in the seventeenth century, the French philosopher Descartes identified the pineal gland – the small endocrine organ located in the center of the brain that is responsible for the production of melatonin – as the contact point between *res extensa* and *res cogitans*, that is to say, between body and soul, the material and the spiritual worlds (Descartes 2003:

19). In Western culture, following Plato's split of reality between the world of matter and the intelligible world of ideas, these domains have often been kept separated, even as knowledge about our mental processes and the physiology of the brain itself were making spectacular advances. Sánchez Romera, both as chef and as scientist, spearheads a different approach. The fact that he focuses on food and its appreciation – that is to say, pleasure – is particularly relevant since taste and smell are the least studied senses, whose importance and impact on mental processes and especially on memory have been almost neglected (Classen 1994; Rouby et al. 2005).

In *La Cocina de los Sentidos*, which is also an unconventional cookbook (it does not give precise measures for the ingredients for the recipes), Sánchez Romera delves into the most recent findings of neuroscience research about sensations, emotions, memory, and rational processes. While highlighting the connections between food and memory, he states: "Remembering is first of all a dynamic process, and not only a trunk of memories or a library of experiences lived once, which can be later evoked according to the circumstances. It is something as lively and nimble as our own self, since … individuals create memories in connection to many personal necessities" (Sánchez Romera 2001: 220). In Sánchez Romera's work, food ushers in a conception of the mind that clashes with traditional conceptions of knowledge as representation. These theories consider the senses and memory as faculties that limit themselves to mirror nature, and their contents as more or less precise reflections of the external world. For the Spanish chef, recollections are rather the result of an ongoing dynamic interaction between different properties of the brain and the stimuli deriving from the senses. In this process, memory is not fixed once and for all, but, rather, a creative and vibrant faculty that allows human beings to relive the past each time in different ways. Furthermore, memory depends heavily on the body, not only because most of the material the mind elaborates is derived from the senses, but also because the body and the emotions connected with it (pleasure, pain, fear) influence the way memories are maintained and eventually recalled. The necessary conclusion is that rational processes, heavily depending on memories, cannot be totally isolated from what is traditionally considered irrational, physical, and instinctual. Many activities, such as eating, cooking, having sex, dancing, singing, and exercising, place themselves beyond the mind vs. body split that has informed much of Western thought. In certain quarters, these activities are still not considered theoretically relevant because they intrinsically erase the separation between inquirer and inquired, the subject and its object, and because they are not concerned with truth, with the eternal and the immutable, but rather with "the transitory, the perishable, the changeable" (Heldke 1992; Onfray 1995: 223–58).

Using food and eating as points of departure, we will approach alternative theories concerning sensations, memory, and emotions, and more generally the relationship between body and mind. We will see how pop culture employs food-related images and concepts to reflect on these issues, endorsing different theories and making them popular with the general public in the form of more or less natural assumptions about how our minds function, the role of feelings and sensations, and the appreciation of our own bodies.

Computers and the Flesh

Let us start with memory. Several science fiction narratives are based on an understanding of this function as a storage device where pieces of knowledge, actions, and even emotions are stored in neat equivalents of computer bytes, ready to be retrieved and, if necessary, mechanically substituted with electronically originated elements. Mnemonic materials are considered discrete, composed of recognizable, circumscribed, interchangeable, reproducible components that can also be disposed of. Memories can be easily transferred from a human being to a machine: they share the same physical nature and structure, which allows them to travel freely from one medium to another.

This theme plays an especially important role in sci-fi movies such as *Johnny Mnemonic*, *The 6th Day*, *Strange Days*, and many others. The plot of *Johnny Mnemonic* (1995) is built on the premise that huge amounts of data can be saved in special chips implanted in the brain of so-called "messengers," who remain totally human even with a trifle of cyborg in them. Just plug a computer in and upload. The information that you need will be safely and unassumingly stored in the memory of a professional.

The same concept underlies the three movies in the *Robocop* series (1987, 1990, and 1993), where the policeman Murphy, killed in service, is transformed into an invincible semi-human android that shares the dead agent's memories and capacities, obviously enhanced by a never-ending array of gizmos. In *Robocop 3* the antagonists try to deprive Robocop of the emotional content of his memories, in order to transform him into a stupid but efficient killing-machine. A good-hearted scientist compelled to implant into Murphy's brain a device that would serve that goal actually discovers that certain mnemonic elements are triggered by clues that apparently have no connection with the event that created the original memories. Interestingly, the scientist can view Robocop's recollection on a monitor connected with the cyborg's brain, implying that mental activity can be easily televised once neural signals are transformed neatly into electric impulses through a computer. The theme of the cyborg, which usually is employed to undermine the concept of a unified, Cartesian subject, here denies the complexities of the mental life of human beings.

In the 1995 visionary movie *12 Monkeys*, by Terry Gilliam, the character played by Brad Pitt, the schizoid founder of an anarchic organization trying to destroy humankind by spreading a deadly virus, finds himself wondering how his ex-psychiatrist managed to discover his plot.

Six years ago I had not thought about the 12 monkeys. ... When I was institutionalized I was interrogated, I was X-rayed, I was examined thoroughly. They learned everything about me, and they put that into a computer where they created this model of my mind. Using that model, they managed to generate every thought I could possibly have in the next, say, ten years, which they then probably filtered through some probability matrix of some kind to determine everything I was going to do in that period. So they knew everything I was going to do even before I knew it myself.

In *The 6th Day* (2000) the personal memories of the main character, played by Arnold Schwarzenegger, are extracted through the optic nerve, saved on disk, and then transmitted to his clone, without suffering any damage. During the movie both the main character and the clone share the same personality, the same sensibility, and the same set of memories, up to the point where they were extracted. Once again, memories appear to be easily encoded into bits and bytes, kept in some artificial device and used when necessary, without any change even if the person who uses them is not the same who produced them in the first place. A similar instrument constitutes the main theme of *Strange Days* (1995) by Kathryn Bigelow, starring Angela Bassett and Ralph Fiennes. At the dawn of the third millennium a machine has been created which is able to record everything a person experiences, sees, and feels, when connected with the surface of his or her head. Stored on diskettes, these memories can be replayed, allowing another individual to relive them, with all their emotional charge and the sensations connected with them. Needless to say, the memory diskettes become a very popular device with the porn industry ...

These similarities between humans and machines appear to be so widely spread and accepted that contemporary culture often refers to computers to create metaphors for our brain. Political scientists Michael Hardt and Antonio Negri affirm:

Just as modernization did in a previous era, postmodernization of information today marks a new mode of becoming human. ... Today we increasingly think like computers, while communication technologies and their model of interaction are becoming more and more central to laboring activities. ... Interactive and cybernetic machines become a new prosthesis integrated into our bodies and minds and a lens through which to redefine our bodies and minds themselves. The anthropology of cyberspace is really a recognition of the new human condition. (Hardt and Negri 2001: 289–91)

Nevertheless, some science fiction movies seem to put forth different concepts about the nature of memories and, as a consequence, a different appreciation of the role of the body in their construction, storage, and retrieval. Intriguingly, they use eating and ingestion to make their point.

Let us start with *The Matrix* (1999), a motion picture that at the turn of the century became an instant cult for the wired, Internet-oriented, dot.com-employed, Nasdaq bull-riding generation. In the year 2019 or so, machines dominate the world.

To do so they exploit human beings as a source of heat and electricity (which is to say, food): living creatures are fed with the liquefied remains of the dead. To keep humans under control, the machines have created a digital virtual reality, directly transmitted to their victims' brains, which is a perfectly functioning image of the world like it used to be before the machines took power. In reality, humans are kept in a state of suspended animation within cocoons, deprived through wires and pipes of their life force, while dreaming of a normal life. A group of men, aware of the situation, decide to live outside the illusion and to jeopardize the whole system to free humanity. Although the main tenet of the movie is the intrinsic similarity between the human brain and computers, there are two back-to-back scenes that appear to undermine these assumptions. Interestingly enough, both scenes focus on food.

The first one takes place in a restaurant located in the virtual reality projected on the human mind. One of the rebels is cutting a deal with an envoy of the machines to betray the rebel leader. All he wants in exchange is to be sucked into the matrix and to abandon the sad reality of the dehumanized world, though he is fully aware the whole move is a delusion. The two characters talk over a steak.

> *Rebel*: I know this steak doesn't exist. I know that when I put it in my mouth the matrix is telling my brain that it is juicy and delicious. After nine years, you know what? [He chows on a chunk of meat, sighing with delight] Ignorance is bliss.

The other scene happens in the rebel warship, in the grim reality outside the matrix. Since the crew have to nourish themselves, they have recourse to an artificially processed aliment that "looks like snot."

> *Rebel 1*: Tastee wheat. Did you ever eat tastee wheat?
> *Rebel 2*: No, but technically neither did you.
> *Rebel 1*: That's exactly my point. Because you have to wonder, now. How do the machines really know what tastee wheat tasted like? Maybe they got it wrong. Maybe what I think tastee wheat tastes like actually tasted like oatmeal or tuna fish, that makes you wonder about lots of things. You take chicken, for example. Maybe they could not figure out what to make chicken taste like. Which is why chicken tastes like everything.
> *Rebel 3*: Shut up, Mouse
> *Rebel 4*: It's a single-celled protein, combined with synthetic aminos, vitamins, and minerals. Everything the body needs.
> *Rebel 2*: No, it does not have everything the body needs.

The dialogues point out that machines cannot possibly know what real food tastes like, and above all that they cannot convey the actual sensations that flavor memories elicit. The Matrix algorithms are not able to give the same depth and emotional value as real food recollections to neural perceptions of taste and smell, although the system is able to re-create them, and also to activate the connection between food and sex. In the second episode of the Trilogy, *The Matrix Reloaded* (2003), the Merovingian, an embodiment of the computer system, is able to give an orgasm to a woman through a slice of chocolate cake. Despite the virtual world created by the machines, however, the body seems to reaffirm its own autonomous, specific memories – in particular, gustatory and olfactory ones.

The same theme emerges in *The Island* (2005), starring Ewan McGregor as Lincoln 6 Echo, a cloned human being. In the not-too-distant future, a biotech company finds a way to ensure longer lives to all those who can afford it, providing them with organs developed from their own tissue that can substitute aging or damaged ones. During the development of the projects the scientists realized that organs could only thrive and grow as part of bodies. As the manager of the project states: "Without consciousness, motion, human experience, without life, the organs failed." The body/mind split sounds like a souvenir from the past. As a matter of fact, as the plot unfolds, Lincoln 6 Echo discovers he is able to ride a high-speed motorbike or to drive a boat simply because, as a clone, he was developed from the tissue of his original donor: the whole body developed from that tiny portion of tissues carries all the physical experiences of the donor. As they say, once you learn how to ride a bike, you never forget. At least in the movie, you do not forget your food preferences either. In one of the first scenes, Lincoln 6 Echo craves bacon at a breakfast counter, where a very unfriendly canteen lady tries to impose the foods that have been chosen for him by his creators in order to ensure his health. He is actually mirroring the likes and dislikes of the person from whom he has been cloned.

Canteen Lady: You have a nutrition flag.
Lincoln 6 Echo: In that case, I'll have two eggs, over easy, not too runny; a side of sausage and a French toast maybe. And a little powder sugar.

The power of these bodily and sensual memories is so strong that the new clones need to be conditioned with new memories in order to avoid any resurgence of the past. It does not work, though. The body still remembers, if not consciously, in the form of dreams. It is actually after dreaming of driving a boat that Lincoln 6 Echo starts having doubts about his situation. Again, in a visit to the doctor, he expresses his malaise in terms of food, the only communication tool he can still master.

Tuesday night is tofu night, and I ask to myself: who decides that everyone here likes tofu in the first place? And what is tofu anyway? Why can't I have bacon? I line up every morning and I can't have bacon for my breakfast … I want answers, and I wish there were more.

Fuel for the Brain

Despite the exceptions we mentioned, which interestingly use food to get their point across, most science fiction movies, books, and comic books are particularly attuned to theories that assume a fundamental similarity in the ways computers and human brains operate. As a matter of fact, contemporary pop culture often references computers to create metaphors for our brain. Outside the realm of fiction, many scientists seem to share a similar take on mind and memory that developed into a new branch of research – cognitive psychology – during the second half of the twentieth century. As Ulrich Neisser stated in 1966, "the term cognition refers to all processes by which the sensory input is transformed, reduced, elaborated, stored, recovered, and used" (Neisser 1966: 2). Cognitive psychologists are not primarily interested in analyzing the mind at the physiological and neural level, understanding its structure and function starting from the cell level up. Their goal is rather to assess the brain's unconscious processes in functional terms. In an introductive book to cognitive science, oddly enough, kitchen recipes are used as metaphors to describe how the brain operates.

> Readers who have never written a computer program but have used cookbooks can consider another analogy. A recipe usually has two parts: a list of ingredients and a set of instructions to the ingredients, just as a running program results from applying algorithms to data structures such as numbers and lists, and just as thinking results from applying computational procedures to mental representations. The recipe analogy for thinking is weak, since ingredients are not representations and cooking instructions require someone to interpret them. (Thagard 2005: 12)

As this example demonstrates, one of the main tenets of cognitive psychology is that information functions according to patterns and rules constituting a formal logic that is totally independent from the actual medium that carries it out (LeDoux 1998: 27). As psychologist Jerry Fodor elaborated in 1983, brain operations would be based on modules, each focusing on a specific function, e.g. face recognition, speech, and numbers (Fodor 1983). These modules would constitute a sort of "architecture of the mind," another metaphor that suggests stability, if not a static condition.

The medium within which these modules can operate can be indifferently a brain or a machine. As a matter of fact, terms that are widely used in information studies, such as "code," "signal," "processing," "transformation," "processor," are employed in other fields connected with the human mind, such as neuroscience, semiotics, and psychology. The relevance of the research on Artificial Intelligence (AI) can be attributed to the spectacular advance of this discipline and to the fact that modern computers and robots are symbol-using entities, based on formal systems. Furthermore, AI reinforces the choice of cognitive psychologists to concentrate on the software of the mind rather than on its hardware (Flanagan 1984: 222). To a certain extent, humans and computers are different manifestations of the same phenomenon: they are thinking engines, based on systems organized like computers, which function using signals (Haugeland 1981: 31).

According to these theories, the long-lasting mind vs. brain opposition becomes irrelevant, since the mind is virtually disembodied, for all research purposes. Furthermore, the logical and rational aspects of the mind take over its emotional side since emotions are closely connected with the body and its responses to external stimuli, even if under brain control. Nonetheless, with the enormous development of neuroscience in the last 20 years, many scientists have turned their attention back to brain structures, trying to come to terms with the new discoveries about the relevance of their physical functions and dynamics (Thagard 2005: 170). Joseph LeDoux noted in his seminal work *The Emotional Brain* (1998) that it is not possible to separate cognition from the emotional elements of the mind. Furthermore, LeDoux argues, the hardware, the actual structure of the brain, is non-secondary in understanding the mind, especially when it comes to emotions (LeDoux 1998: 41: LeDoux 2002). It is not an easy task. As biologist Steven Rose points out, "the brain is full of paradoxes. It is simultaneously a fixed structure and a set of dynamic, partly coherent and partly independent processes" (Rose 2005: 4). At the same time, "the mind is wider than the brain" (Rose 2005: 88). That is to say, we cannot approach the brain's hardware and its functioning in the same way we would dissect the internal wiring of a computer.

One of the most influential voices in this field is the Nobel Prize recipient Gerald Edelman. In his book *A Universe of Consciousness* (2000), written with Giulio Tononi, he underlines the features of the brain that point to fundamental differences with computers. Since no two brains are identical, the overall pattern of connections in a brain can be defined in general terms, but the microscopic variability of these connections in different individuals is enormous because of their developmental history and their past experiences. For instance, when it comes to food, although children of the same family might be genetically similar and are likely to be exposed to the same dishes, they all show their own likes and dislikes, different tastes, sometimes even diverging memories concerning the same events. Synaptic connections change, die, are created every day, and vary in each individual, affecting the way things and events are remembered (Edelman and Tononi 2000: 47).

Of course, computer simulations of neural networks reveal that a man-made system can develop exceptional complexity in a short time if it is programmed to develop patterns that are beneficial to the goal it is created to carry out. Nevertheless, the inputs the brain receives from the external world are not an unambiguous series of signals, as in the case of computers. The brain has developed functions aimed and filtering and organizing perceptions into categories, which are instrumental to our interaction with the world. Furthermore, our perceptions and the categories we use to give them order are not neutral, impassionate, and impartial. In fact, the brain has developed several mechanisms called "value systems," that is to say, dynamics aimed to evaluate the relevance (also called "salience," meaning "to stick out") of all sensory inputs. These dynamics are regulated by organs – sometimes defined as the limbic system – located outside the cortical areas in charge of rational thinking. The evaluation of relevance is also determined by substances (e.g. neurotransmitters, hormones and even peptides, a specific kind of protein) that respond to emotional stimulation and that travel through our body through all kinds of fluids, including blood. These facts all indicate that neural impulses cannot be compared to computer information in that they travel following many alternate routes and that their flow is not linear, going from A to B, bur rather "parallel, recursive, feedforward, and feedback" (Cytowic 2003: 156).

All these elements influence the strength of synapses (i.e. the contact points between neurons) because neurons that "fire together, wire together," using the expression modeled after Canadian psychologist Donald Hebb's theory (Hebb 1949). In other words, repeated neural activity involving two or more neurons strengthens the connection between them, under the influence of "value systems" (LeDoux 1998: 214). These dynamics have a great impact on learning, categorizing abilities and adaptive behaviors. Because of these factors, human memory differs from a computer's in that it is selective. Not every item is retained in the same way, or always retrieved in the same way.

As biologist Steven Rose pointedly noted, "Dynamism is all. The brain, like all features of living systems, is both being and becoming, its apparent stability a stability of process, not of fixed architecture. Today's brain is not yesterday's, and will not be tomorrow's" (Rose 2005: 147).

Flavors and Memories

If memories are anchored to our sensual and physical experiences, we can easily understand how the connection between body and mind, and in particular between memory and food, with its flavors and smells, has become a center of interest for sociologists, anthropologists, and ethnographers, both as topics of research and as methodology (Geurts 2002; Howes 2003; Sutton 2001). Outside academia, too, these themes frequently appear in various forms of pop culture all over the world.

Memory seems to play a key role especially in contemporary movies that revolve around food, a theme that in the past few years has become central in all sorts of film genres, following the growth of general interest towards food and eating in Western societies. The evocative potential of moving images acquires a particular depth and power when cuisine and ingestion are used to convey feelings and emotions that would otherwise be difficult to express visually or verbally.

It is often when women are involved that food and cooking reveal their deeper connections with memory, especially with activities that involve meal preparation, nourishing, and nurturing. Needless to say, these chores are identified with a bodily dimension that has been historically considered not very intellectual, since it deals with the sheer survival of individuals, families, and communities, rather than with personal achievements and spiritual aspects of life.

When the lead characters are women, movies often shift towards genres such as biography, memoir, sentimental journey, and romantic exploration, where visual and narrative elements concur to put viewers in touch with the more emotional and mundane aspects of life: pleasures and sorrows, affections, memories, and the joys deriving from activities such as cooking.

This aspect is particularly strong in the so-called "magic realism" novels by authors like Gabriel García Márquez (particularly *A Hundred Years of Solitude* and *Love in the Time of Cholera*) and above all Jorge Amado, who has dedicated the novels *Gabriela, Clove and Cinnamon* (*Gabriela, Cravo e Canela*, 1958) and *Dona Flor and Her Two Husbands* (*Dona Flor e Sues Dois Maridos*, 1966) to smell and taste. Both novels were adapted for the big screen as amusing and touching movies, starring the sensual Brazilian actress Sonia Braga and directed by Bruno Barreto respectively in 1983 and 1976. The character of Dona Flor in particular finds in food a conduit through which she can express her sensuality and also develop her business expertise, affirming herself as an individual. She actually manages a cooking school, while her husband Vadinho, a gambler who is nevertheless capable to keep her sexually happy, spends all their money. When he dies of a heart attack during Carnival, Donha Flor marries the town pharmacist, a very decent man who lacks passion and sexual appetites. She soon finds herself desiring Vadinho so much that she begs a Candomblé priestess to bring his spirit back. Eventually Flor keeps them both, one to satisfy her sexual and bodily appetites, the other to give her respect and to make her a lady. Food plays a more crucial role in the book than in the movie, but also on film some scenes remain unforgettable. Right after the death of Vadinho, she relives their passion by thinking of one of his favorite dishes, the *moqueca de siri mole*, a soft-shell crab stew with coconut milk and red palm oil, and the memory of the sensations that punctuated their sexual bliss carry her back to the first night after the wedding, when his mouth tasted like onion, one of the main ingredients of the recipe. During one of her most lonely moments, she compares herself to a hot, steaming dish that no man consumes and enjoys.

Spanish actress Penélope Cruz plays a similar character in Fina Torres's *Woman on Top* (2000), a movie where exotic food and sensuality are used to wow Western audiences, supposedly disconnected from these fascinating but ultimately primitive aspects of life. Isabela Oliveira (Cruz) is a very talented chef who is deeply in love with her husband Toninho. They own a restaurant in Bahia where she cooks while her husband works the front of the house, taking all the merit for the success of the establishment. When she discovers him in bed with another woman, she runs away to visit a transvestite friend in San Francisco, finding a job as a teacher in a cooking school. One day, while preparing a *moqueca*, the smell of the *malagueta* pepper brings back memories of Toninho, of how he would rub some chili peppers on her lips to arouse her. That is when she realizes she has to free herself of those memories, and also with the intervention of a Candomblé priestess she manages to set herself free. That is when her career as a chef takes off. The flavors and scents of her dishes, reminiscent of Brazil, make her famous as a TV celebrity chef, able to excite and stimulate both men and women with her cooking.

Emotions and feelings are actually incorporated into food in the novel by Laura Esquivel *Like Water for Chocolate* (*Como Agua para Chocolate*, 1989), which in 1992 became a movie by filmmaker Alfonso Arau, Esquivel's husband at the time. Tita (actress Lumi Cavazos), brought up in the kitchen by the Indian cook Nacha, is condemned to celibacy in order to take care of her mother in her old age. Her love interest Pedro (Marco Leonardi) decides to get married to one of her sisters so that he can be close to her. During the preparations for the nuptial banquet, the tears of sorrow of Tita for her lost love end up in her sister's wedding cake, provoking desperation and stomach upset in all those who taste it. Later on, Tita's passionate feelings, concentrated in a bunch or roses Pedro gives her, end up in a dish of quails with rose petals, which has such a potent effect that one of her sisters has to run to an outdoor shower to calm herself. The passion unleashed by Tita's dish is so potent that her sister ends up burning the whole wood shack where the shower is located, attracting with her scent a revolutionary soldier who takes her away naked on horseback.

In the 1999 novel by Joanne Harris, *Chocolat*, brought to the screen by Lasse Hallström in 2000, chocolate brings back to life a whole village suffocated by the traditionalism of the local mayor and other oppressive characters. Vianne, an independent woman traveling around with her young daughter, is a descendant of the Mayas, and she has inherited the faculty to be able to use chocolate to treat any emotional trauma. The sweet substance comes to embody all that is passion, body, and sensuality, able to transmit feelings and recollections. Chocolate, probably for its supposed effects on women, appears in many movies, novels, and also TV commercials as the favorite substance in the fight against feminine depressive states.

However, other foods also would seem to have the power to revitalize women and the men around them: in the 1985 Japanese movie *Tampopo*, the eponymous character, a young widow with a child, finds herself in the quest for the perfect ramen noodles. Her research for taste, texture, and technique, with the help of a cohort of unusual male friends, helps her focus on who she is and her goals as a professional, although often it seems that it is the men who know better and are more aware of what she actually needs than herself.

Not all women in the kitchen appear to be so defenseless and in need of guidance. In the 2007 Walt Disney animated and Oscar-winning blockbuster *Ratatouille*, the story of the rat Remy and his culinary achievements in one of the most successful restaurants in Paris, the female chef Colette shows her male coworkers that she doesn't need anybody's help in the kitchen. Her encounter with the sweet and disaster-prone Linguini mellows her out a bit, but she remains in charge. In a world dominated by men, Colette shows how skills and determination are necessary for a woman to succeed, despite the movie's motto, "Everybody can cook."

We cannot proceed without a short mention of *Babette's Feast* (*Babette Gaestebud*, 1987) by the Danish filmmaker Gabriel Axel, based on the tale of that name in Karen Blixen's collection *Anecdotes of Destiny* (1958). Babette, a French refugee in a Danish Protestant village, decides to spend all the money she won in a lottery to offer a memorable dinner to the villagers, whose faith makes them impermeable to any sort of sensual pleasure. The only dinner guest who actually is reanimated by the fantastic dishes and the spectacular wines is a general whom Babette's flavors transport back to his youth as a soldier in France. In the dinner, Babette's mysterious past is translated into actual sensory elements, a communication that most guests are unable to decode. She does not care: her generosity and her desire to express her gratefulness towards her hosts knows no limit.

In all the movies we mentioned, women appear to have access to a special connection with food, which allows them to translate their sensuality and their emotional world in pleasurable – and socially sanctioned – ways.

It is very interesting that when science fiction and action movies, frequently perceived as masculine or at least as favored by young men, focus on food and eating as narrative elements, they seldom refer to nurturing and caring. They project this approach also on women: more and more often science fiction comics and movies present hot babes ready to kick ass, such as Charlize Theron in *Aeon Flux* (2005), originally an action-packed, anime-influenced cartoon series broadcast on MTV, the above-mentioned Angela Bassett in *Strange Days*, or the black mutant Storm in the *X-Men* comics and in the movie trilogy under the same name (2000, 2003, and 2006), with Halle Berry playing the role of the weather-controlling hero. Their nurturing role is either secondary or totally absent, even in Storm, who is supposedly a teacher of younger, more insecure mutants. We could hardly imagine the tomb-raiding Lara Croft (2001), played by Angelina Jolie, as a cooking woman. In the 2007 *Mr. & Mrs. Smith*, Ms. Jolie plays a killer who leads a double life, playing the devoted housewife to her husband, played by Brad Pitt, who is also an undercover killer. Of course, the two are unaware of each other's true identity. In various scenes, dinners turn into tense confrontations: knives and all kinds of kitchen elements (including the oven) become deadly weapons, to the point where one crucial fight between the spouses turns into a violent and systematic destruction of their house, starting precisely from the kitchen. Could there be a better metaphor for the instability of domesticity?

Men in the Kitchen

Food apparently threatens masculinity in action and sci-fi movies. When man are represented in nurturing roles, like Arnold Swarzenegger in *Kindergarten Cop* (1990) and Vin Diesel in Disney's *The Pacifier* (2005), it is only for comical purposes, and at any rate their femininization is only temporary, used as a decoy or as an emergency measure. By the end of the movie, the main characters have forgotten all about stoves and dishes, and they are back to their tough, criminal-punishing selves. Food definitely does not constitute a significant part of their world.

In other genres, though, men can express themselves freely through cooking and dishes when they are chefs or cooks. The professionalization of food preparation safeguards their masculinity, allowing them to express feelings and connect with memories that otherwise would not be acceptable. We can find examples in movies from all over the world. In Roland Joffé's *Vatel* (2000) Gérard Depardieu plays the role of the eponymous chef and master of ceremonies working for the Prince of Condé. While scrambling to prepare the most spectacular banquet for the king Louis XIV, on a visit to his employer at the Chantilly castle, he falls for Anne de Montausier, a fascinating dame played by Uma Thurman. Unable to convey his passion any other way, he prepares a beautiful sugar composition with flowers for the object of his longings. For political reasons, the woman cannot accept his courtship, and the chef eventually kills himself. The movie leaves it to the viewers to decide if Vatel took his life for love, or because he was distraught by the fact that his mentor had lost him to the King during a game of cards, or because the fish he was expecting for the banquet had not arrived, as the tradition relates.

Not all movie chefs are doomed to such a gloomy destiny. Through food, cooking men often find ways to express themselves and get in contact with their loved ones. The main character of Ang Lee's *Eat Drink Man Woman* (*Yin Shi Nan Nu*, 1994) and of its American remake by María Ripoll, *Tortilla Soup* (2001), is a widower, estranged from his three daughters, with whom the only tie seems to be Sunday lunch. In both movies, the magnificent opening scenes picture the chefs preparing sumptuous banquets (Chinese in the Ang Lee version, Mexican in the American remake), where no virtuosity is spared and unusual and exotic techniques and ingredients are displayed. The meals, despite their goal to nurture ailing family feelings, are definitely works of art and the achievement of professionals. Once again, the chef is represented as a masculine role that struggles with its emotional overtones. Viewers soon realize that the artist has lost his sense of taste: his connection with his memory and his identity risks being lost forever. Only when he falls for his younger neighbor and starts preparing school lunches for her daughter is he able to recover his sensual abilities, while reconnecting at the same time with his inner, most delicate feelings. The final sequences, where the older man declares his love for the young woman who had secretly shared the same feeling, reassures the viewer of the chef's masculinity and potency. Despite his age and his ability to connect with his sensory memories and to express nurture and love through food, he is still undoubtedly a man.

Male chefs are also safely allowed to use food to express their longings for their far-away homelands. Curiously, two of the most renowned emigrant chefs in recent films are Italian: Mario, played by Sergio Castellitto in Sandra Nettlebeck's *Mostly*

Martha (*Bella Martha*, 2001), and Primo, played by Tony Shalhoub in Campbell Scott and Stanley Tucci's *Big Night* (1996). Despite the different plots and characters, the two chefs are both interpreters of a culinary tradition that is described to viewers as full of care, passion, and sensual involvement. The memories of flavors and dishes from their childhoods give both a sense of direction in a new land, respectively Germany and America, where not everybody is able to appreciate their skills. Though food, Mario is able to restore the *joie de vivre* of his female head chef, Martha, and to give hope to her little niece, distraught by her mother's loss, while Primo re-creates the protective womb of the family where his Americanized brother Secondo finds refuge when all his hope and projects to become a successful businessman miserably fail.

The comedy genre protects masculinity, when goofy chefs – and the movie's main characters – reveal all their weaknesses and food becomes a security valve for their emotional needs. This is the case for a romantic Adam Sandler in *Spanglish* (2004) and the surreal Hong Kong movie star Stephen Chow in *God of Cookery* (*Sik San*, 1996). Sandler plays an award-winning chef who rediscovers his passion for cooking and his skills, almost forgotten because of the stress of fame and his failed marriage, through the straightforward sensuality of his home caretaker, played by Paz Vega. The celebrity chef played by Chow falls into disgrace and manages to get back to the top only with the help of an ugly, but effective woman, who creates a new sort of meatballs that become all the rage and with whom he eventually falls in love.

Of course, when gay men cook in movies all bets are off and masculinity is no longer an issue. With them, food preparation reveals all its nurturing and poignant undertones. The Turkish filmmaker Ferzan Ozpetek often deals with gay characters whose emotional lives and memories are expressed through food. In *His Secret Life* (*Le Fate Ignoranti*, 2001), Michele (Stefano Accorsi) is the center of a whole community of unusual characters, including gay men, a transsexual, a prostitute, and an AIDS victim, who gather every week around the table, and for whom cooking and feeding each other constitutes an act of resistance and a declaration of love for life. When his deceased lover's wife Antonia (Margerita Buy) discovers his existence, it is by inviting her to join the cooking and by preparing her morning coffee that the two manage to create a relationship built on respect and affection. In *Facing Windows* (*La Finestra di Fronte*, 2003), Giovanna (Giovanna Mezzogiorno), an aspiring baker, meets an old man suffering from amnesia who turns out to be a Holocaust survivor whose suffering was compounded by his repressed homosexuality. The man turns out to be a expert pastry chef who, by making cakes and desserts with the younger woman, succeeds in reconnecting with his past and his memories, even if only briefly, while giving to Giovanna a new sense of herself and of her femininity. In another of Ang Lee's movies, *The Wedding Banquet* (*Xi Yan*, 1993), it is through food that an interracial gay couple convey their emotional attachments and their mutual love. Wai-tung (Winston Chao) a successful and career-driven

Taiwanese businessman, and his American lover, Simon (Mitchell Lichtenstein), have to fake a wedding with a Chinese woman and organize a massive banquet to appease Wai-tung's parents, visiting from the mainland and unaware of their son's sexual inclinations. Despite the difficulties, Simon reaffirms his nurturing qualities by cooking for his partner's parents, who eventually show acceptance by enjoying his food, even if it is not Chinese.

These works focusing on food, although from different genres, share a model of human being where the body and the mind are not separated, but integrated in a functioning whole. Emotions and sensations are not considered as better or worse than rational faculties, just as a different, complementary dimension of human inner life. They propose a totally different position from the computer-related movies we analyzed previously, where the body is a mere material support for higher functions that – autonomous from the flesh – can be easily shared with machines and computers. This deep contrast between two different conceptions of the human experience emerges in different instances of pop culture, which we know plays an important role in disseminating and naturalizing concepts and ideas, values and anxieties. The presence of diverging, even contradictory, approaches to food points to the fact that an ongoing negotiation is taking place among different ideologies to assert their take on human life, the mind, and its connection with the body. The political and social implications go well beyond pop culture.

Sell It to the Brain!

A new branch of neuroscience is being developed in collaboration with sociologists, anthropologists, psychologists, and philosophers: the neuroscience of human behavior, which focuses on the interaction of the brain with the social environment (Adolphs 2003). Some researchers have pointed to the existence of brain functions, defined as "emphatic," that are tuned to perceive and react to another's pain (Singer et al. 2004). Others are studying the so-called "mirror neurons," which allow individuals to imitate another's action by stirring in their brain the same areas active in other persons (Frith and Wolpert 2004; Meltzoff and Prinz, 2002). This link connecting different brains would also explain the capacity swiftly to synchronize and harmonize people's movements, body postures, and vocal intonations as they interact with other individuals (Goleman, 2006). These studies could throw new light on the dynamics that take place around the table, on the emotional relevance of the act of sharing food, and on the desire to adapt to other people's eating habits. Other scholars are working on the new field of "neuronomics," which analyzes the dynamics of the brain in behaviors related to economic choices, and the relevance of the emotional and values systems in risk-taking and decision-making (Camerer 2005; Cassidy 2006). Social relations are still to be fully analyzed from the point of view of neuroscience: for instance, how do humans read intentions out of a fellow human's actions (Blakemore and Decety 2001)? This line of research is crucial to understand any collective behavior, including food consumption. For instance, it could allow new insights into how children are socialized into eating, how likes and dislikes develop, and how we try to experiment with new ingredients or dishes.

We also witness the rise of a new interest in the emotional dynamics of the brain to assess the relations that humans build with the objects they acquire and employ in everyday life. Design, marketing, and advertising are paying new attention to this dimension of human psychology and culture. Donald Norman, a cognitive scientist, is at the forefront of these studies both as an academic and as a businessman, having served as vice-president of Apple Computer's Advanced Technology Group and having co-founded the Nielsen Norman Group, a consulting firm that focuses on human-centered products and services. In his books, Norman puts forth the intriguing hypothesis that appealing things, able to elicit intense and positive emotions, actually work better (Norman 1989 and 2004). He often uses kitchen design objects as examples, but the same line of reasoning can be applied to food packaging, arrangements of food on dishes, and produce itself. Norman argues that design and use of objects are influenced by strong emotional components. He actually identifies three different aspect of design, each of them responding to a different brain dynamic: the visceral, concerning appearances and related to immediate, almost mechanical reactions; the behavioral, connected with enjoyment and usability and corresponding to routine performances and learned skills; and the reflective, regarding intellectual and rational aspects (Norman 2004: 38).

The three levels also differ in their relations to time: while the first two are all about the present, about "now," the third level is not so much about immediate use as about the long run, the memories that objects solicit, and the future satisfaction derived from their possession. At this level, self-esteem and identification processes play a key role, as do customer service and interpersonal interactions.

Kitchen objects and tools can shed some light on these matters. They may be bought just because they are cute and then never be used. This is often the case, for instance, with copper pots and pans, which usually end up as decorations because they are hard to keep clean and in good condition. At the same time they satisfy intellectual needs: the owners' desire to show their refinement and their taste, a nostalgic connection with the past, or just the will to display expensive objects. On the other hand, expensive pots and pans can be bought for their functionality and usability. In this case their quality not only satisfies behavioral requirements, but also ensures durable enjoyment for people who actually cook and can use them with pleasure over and over. Many Western kitchens are full of gizmos of all kinds, either received as presents or actually bought, whose main value is definitively reflective. It relates to the pleasure of owning something unusual or designed for very specific purposes, underlining the owner's expertise.

The relevance of these factors on food consumption is evident. If a product is meant for impulse buying, for instance a candy bar placed at the check-out of a supermarket, its packaging will above all be alluring, stimulating, and able to catch the shopper's attention. Its format and size should interact with the behavioral habits of consumers, without challenging but sending clear messages about its content and its use. Everyday products should more or less fall in this category, underlining their utility, their easy usage, and their performance.

The same category of products can play on different levels. For example, bottled water can be very straightforward: small transparent bottles can be kept in a pocket on the go, while larger bottles, usually in packages of six, underline convenience and practicality. On the other hand, certain exclusive and refined bottles are sold only in restaurants. In this case the aesthetic pleasure is paired with the reflective enjoyment of something supposedly rare. Luxury products have to appeal at a very intellectual level to be successful. Because of their rarity and their high prices, they need to entice consumers' sense of taste and their connoisseurship; in other words, they relate to the consumer's sense of self, reflecting their sense of distinction. Very often the consumption of these products presupposes some sort of acquired taste: caviar, truffle, or foie gras have unusual flavors, whose appreciation is frequently associated with refinement, high social status, conspicuous consumption, and other values perceived as positive. Other high-end products also require knowledge: wine or cheese may not be necessarily expensive, but expert consumers tend to know what they like, are eager to try new products, and willingly share with other passionate consumers their thoughts and their latest discoveries. Furthermore, a certain amount of information – regarding origins, fabrication techniques, and the correct mode of consumption – is necessary to distinguish one product from another. The reflective aspect of this kind of enjoyment is obvious. In this case, visceral and behavioral values are not relevant, since consumers are not primarily attracted by the appearance or the usability of the products. Connoisseurs would not pick their wines or cheeses based on packaging or labels. On the other hand, a supermarket shopper would probably be influenced by these elements and also by other factors such as price and convenience.

Similarly, good advertising must be able to get in tune with our brain dynamics if it wants to prompt us to buy particular brands (du Plessis, 2005). Advertisers try to find the best ways to access the emotional functions that determine value and action. Emotions, we have seen, feed into and mold our thoughts, including the conscious ones that we like to consider completely rational. Since emotions solicit our attention, advertisers have to find ways to stimulate our interest, and to do so they attune the communication tools precisely to those mechanisms that in our brain control attention, excitement, and pleasure. So doing, advertisers also ensure that memories they create are durable and positive. We have seen how the value systems in the brain are able to reinforce and stabilize synaptic connections, increasing the strength of certain memories because the neurons involved become more likely to fire under future similar stimuli. But this is not enough: ads need to be more than memorable; they must aim at reinforcing the recollection of the brands they promote.

We use our existing concept of the brand (our memory of the brand, if you prefer) to help us to decode this advertisement; and in turn, our decoding of the advertisement has an impact on our existing concept of the brand. So (provided the advertisement is not so disastrously obscure that it fails to evoke the brand concept at all …) there is a direct connection between our memory of the advertisement and our memory of the brand. (du Plessis 2005: 171)

In commercials directed to children, their favorite cartoon characters often promote certain products, creating a pleasurable connection between the positive feelings about the beloved character and the product itself. For example, if a child is emotionally attached to Mickey Mouse and Mickey is shown together with a certain brand of cereal, the child is likely to attach positive feelings to that cereal. Commercials directed to adults often work on the same principles. Hence the abundance of more or less explicit sexual undertones in advertising: we all recall seeing girls promoting certain brands of beer in bars. First the sexually charged image captures our attention, and then the arousal that it provokes helps to reinforce the memory and the pleasurable feelings connected to it. Other products and brands target more behavioral and reflective levels of memory, to use the terminology we have already introduced. This is the case for commercials that depict lifestyles that are perceived as positive and desirable. This strategy goes well beyond the printed ad or the TV commercial: events, shows, and happenings are organized to attract the attention of the media and reinforce the strength of the brand. For instance, alcoholic beverages often throw A-list parties in fashionable bars or clubs to accentuate their hipness.

Of course, consumers cannot be considered as helpless dupes without defense against the shrewd promotional techniques of advertising. As marketers are well aware, myriad elements interact with the actual effectiveness of commercials: social and cultural values, monetary constraints, personal likes and dislikes, historical contingencies. On the one hand, products are created for certain segments of the market, supposedly characterized by a defined set of preferences determined by social status, cultural capital, engrained and acquired habits, and desire for distinction (Bourdieu 1984). On the other hand, consumers continue to show an unbridled creativity in negotiating their relationship with markets and products, even when they appear to have no power. As French scholar Michel de Certeau pointed out:

Culture articulates conflicts and alternately legitimizes, displaces, or controls the superior forces. It develops an atmosphere of tensions, and often of violence, for which is provides symbolic balances, contracts of compatibility and compromises, all more or less temporary. The tactics of consumption, the ingenious ways in which the weak make use of the strong, thus lend a political dimension to everyday practices. (de Certeau 1984: xvii)

Whatever the relations of power in the marketplace, designers, marketers, and advertisers can rely on a stable element: the desire for ever-growing consumption, which has become one of the main characters of contemporary Western society. We have examined different aspects of the role food plays in the complex relationship between mind and body, as reflected in pop culture items such as movies and advertising. We get a picture of human subjects whose rational function and memories are closely connected with sensations and emotions, practices, and desires, and whose mental and physical processes are more related than we would care to admit. Actually, we have noticed how this approach, leaning on contemporary research on the brain, is still contrasted by forces that refer to a disembodied human spirit or alternatively to similarities between the mind and machines. In the next chapter we will proceed beyond the brain, analyzing psychological dynamics to achieve a broader overview of the cultural negotiations surrounding food and the body in pop culture.

–2–

Of Breasts and Beasts

Vampires and Other Voracious Monsters

> It is the very nature of this world that all things are devoured and time is a mouth as bloody as any other.
>
> Rice 2000: 292

> Everything which is eaten is the food of power
>
> Canetti 1984: 219

Imagine to find yourself traveling at the end of the universe, and to realize suddenly that you are starving. Where would you go? It is definitely not an easy situation.

> The History of every major Galactic Civilization tends to pass through three distinct and recognizable phases, those of Survival, Inquiry and Sophistication, otherwise known as the How, Why and Where phases. For instance, the first phase is characterized by the question How can we eat? The second by the question Why do we eat? And the third by the question Where shall we eat? (Adams 1995: 215)

This predicament is the premise of *The Restaurant at the End of the Universe* (1980), the second book in the series *The Hitchhiker's Guide to the Galaxy* by Douglas Adams, whose first installment has been turned into a movie in 2005 by Garth Jennings with a screenplay by Adams himself. Zaphod Beeblebrox, the two-headed, three-armed president of the Galaxy, decides to take Arthur Dent, the only survivor from Earth, and the rest of his crew for a quick bite at the Restaurant at the End of the Universe. What ensues deserves to be quoted extensively.

> A large dairy animal approached Zaphod Beeblebrox's table, a large fat meaty quadruped of the bovine type with large watery eyes, small horns and what might almost have been and ingratiating smile on its lips.
>
> "Good evening," it lowed and sat back heavily on its haunches, "I am the main Dish of the Day. May I interest you in parts of my body?" It harrumphed and gurgled a it, wriggled its hind quarters into a more comfortable position and gazed peacefully at them. ...
>
> "Something off the shoulder perhaps?" suggested the animal. "Braised in a white wine sauce?"

"Er, *your* shoulder?" said Arthur in a horrified whisper.

"But naturally my shoulder, sir," mooed the animal contentedly, "nobody's else's is mine to offer." ...

"What's the problem, Earthman?" said Zaphod ... .

"I just don't want to eat an animal that's standing there inviting me to," said Arthur. "It's heartless."

"Better than eating an animal that doesn't want to be eaten," said Zaphod ...

"Look," said Zaphod, "we want to eat, we don't want to make a meal of the issues. Four rare stakes please, and hurry. ..."

"A very wise choice, sir, if I may say so. Very good," it said. "I'll just nip off and shoot myself."

He turned and gave a friendly wink to Arthur.

"Don't worry, sir," he said, "I'll be very humane."

It waddled unhurriedly off to the kitchen. (Adams 1995: 115–17)

The goal of this scene is, of course, to poke fun at all those carnivores who require that animals are treated more humanely, especially when slaughtered. We will not get into this debate, which is actually quite sensitive and deeply fraught with ethical issues. Instead, we will try to understand why the dialog makes us subtly, but undoubtedly, uncomfortable. Since the environment in which the scene unfolds is all in all quite familiar, despite the location at the end of the universe, it is easy for us to recognize it and to relate to its dynamics. At the same time, presumably none of us has ever witnessed a meal presenting itself and inviting us to consume it. By addressing the guests, the animal reveals feelings like patience and pride. Suddenly, the divide between what devours and what is devoured turns out to be quite blurred. The bovine acts like a human being, while some of the human-like characters, ready to eat a sentient and speaking creature, appear to be at least partially devoid of what we would consider human traits. The strange intensity of this apparently funny scene and its troubling effect on the reader requires some explication. Why is it so powerful in its simplicity? We know that humor is often able to reach deep into us, allowing us to deal with issues that otherwise would bother or even frighten us. Why does the bovine make us laugh and shudder at the same time? I believe that the speaking animal embodies one of deepest, primal fears of all humans: the dread of being eaten and the correspondent anxiety that we might end up eating somebody.

One of the contemporary masters of horror, Stephen King, allows us to face these fears in the short story "Lunch at the Gotham Café," from the novella collection *Everything's Eventual* (2003). In a restaurant, a maître d' suddenly goes bonkers, and starts stabbing the patrons.

The maître d' brought his left hand out from behind his back. In it was the largest butcher's knife I have ever seen. It had to have been two feet long, with the top part of its cutting edge slightly belled, like a cutlass in an old pirate movie ...

"Eeeeee! EEEEEEE!" the maître d' screamed, and swung the butcher-knife flat through the air. It made a kind of whickering sound, like a whispered sentence. The period was the sound of the blade burying itself in William Humboldt's right cheek. Blood exploded out of the wound in a furious spray of tiny droplets. They decorated the tablecloth in a fan-shaped stipplework, and I clearly saw (I will never forget it) one bright red drop fall into my waterglass and then dive for the bottom into a pinkish filament like a trail stretching our behind it. It looked like a bloody tadpole. ...

If there had been a paralysis in the room – I can't actually say if there was or not, although I seem to have seen a great deal, and remember it all – that broke it. There were more screams and other people got up. Several tables were overturned. Glasses and china shattered on the floor. (King 2003: 414–16)

The tale strikes and unsettles us because it overturns the usual situation of a restaurant. The patrons get butchered and bleed over white tablecloths. The roles are inverted, and the illusion of a safe, stable reality is shattered, as the broken glasses and china aptly symbolize. The patrons, usually the eaters, end up dead and in pieces, metaphorically ready to be ingested and consumed.

Restaurants appear also in horror movies and TV shows. In Robert Rodriguez's 1996 *From Dusk Till Dawn*, written together with Quentin Tarantino, a family is taken hostage by criminals but they end up in a road-side café that at night turns into a vampire den, where occasional and unknowing clients end up on the menu. In the Season 6 episode "Doublemeat Palace" in the hugely successful series *Buffy the Vampire Slayer*, the blonde monster-killer gets a job in a fast-food joint where employees keep disappearing. In the end, nobody is actually being turned into hamburgers, but the unpleasant doubts linger.

These stories bother us because they show the fragility of what we consider as normality. In a heartbeat, ordinary people turn into men-eating monsters. Where do these unsettling fears come from? Why are we afraid of being killed and ingested? Why are we fascinated by characters that express their limitless hunger at all costs, to the point of dismembering and consuming human beings? Horror stories are mainstays in fiction: flesh-eating monsters and evil witches ready to cook us crowd our imagination from childhood. They cannot just be an instrument used by adults to impose discipline on their offspring; if this were the case, we could not fully explain why icons such as vampires, cannibals, and other monstrous characters have always been popular, and not only in Western cultures.

Using examples taken from contemporary pop culture, I will argue that these scary creatures express drives and desires that we would find otherwise unacceptable, like the unbridled hunger and the single-minded longing for ingestion that seem to define us as infants and later on – in sublimated and controlled ways – as adults. As newborns, all we want and need is to be fed, but our source of nourishment happens to be a human being. However, in the opinion of many psychologists, even at that young age, we cannot fully accept those drives, so intense that they would not stop until full satisfaction: the consequence is guilt, which has to be addressed and relieved. For this reason, every culture seems to find ways to deal with what we can define as cannibalistic desires, despite the ethical and social refusal to acknowledge their very existence and to accept them as a constitutive part of normal dynamics in the development of autonomous individuals and the functional dynamics of social communities. Certain civilizations apparently codified and limited the expression of these drives to very specific situations and conditions of ritual cannibalism. Otherwise these instincts are perceived as a threat and as the ultimate negation of all proper social interactions and negotiations.

Yet they exist, occasionally emerging both at the personal and at the social level, despite all attempts at denying them. Refused and stigmatized, cannibalistic desires resist against the social and cultural rules that condemn them by assuming different qualities under various historical conditions. For instance, since the emergence of absolute kings and nation states in Europe, they have surfaced as political metaphors to describe political power in terms of a devouring entity. Political science, philosophy, but also popular culture have often employed these food-related images to critique invasive governments and controlling authorities of all kinds. Thomas Hobbes, one of the first thinkers to analyze the absolute power of the state, considered human beings in their natural condition as willing to destroy each other as famished beasts; in his opinion, centralized governments set up by social contract to control these destructive tendencies had to be as powerful as a Leviathan, the voracious and vicious sea monster that the Judaic-Christian tradition often identified with absolute Evil (Hobbes 1982).

Where does the strength of these images come from? What kind of chords do they strike at the individual level? And what social and political mechanisms do they uncover, making them visible and understandable in very immediate and direct way?

Embodied Appetites

In the previous chapter, we analyzed the development and the functions of the brain to achieve a better understanding of why pop culture has such a compelling grip on us: recent developments in neuroscience seem to indicate that emotions, passions, and pleasure constitute essential elements in all mental processes, including the ones we would like to believe to be totally rational – a fact of which marketers have long been aware. We have also illustrated how pop culture perceives the mind, describing it at times as a computer completely independent from the body, at times as a mix of memories, feelings, and sensations heavily dependent on physical experiences. We can now proceed to analyze the main engine of market-oriented pop culture: consumption – and, in the case of Western affluent cultures, uninterrupted and all-encompassing consumption. Food, as the primary and primal form of consumption, cannot but play a fundamental role in this discussion.

Once again, it can be useful to begin from the basic mechanisms that seem to regulate our bodies and our inner lives. We need to go back to our time as newborns to start this journey into our fears and dreams, and to understand how they relate to food and ingestion. Infants' need to be nourished constitutes the motivation for one of the first connections to the reality outside their own bodies: eating. These contacts with the world aim at absorbing all the elements that provide the energy necessary to survival and growth. When the source of nourishment disappears, or it is not able totally to satisfy the hunger, infants experience their first frustrations and disappointments, often expressed as crying and wailing, as all parents, infancy professionals, and anybody who has been around a newborn know very well.

Being one of our first interactions with the external world, it is likely that the feeding experience somehow determines the modality of our relation with reality at large, not only limited to the physiological mechanisms of nutrition, but also regarding emotional and rational aspects. Our dependence on food is after all "one of the most common and pervasive sources of value in human experience" (Curtin and Heldke 1992: xiii).

Hunger and the desire for incorporation – although inherently destructive – are a constitutive dimension of human life, stubborn, and for this reason scary. The irrepressible instinct for ingestion and the guilt that comes with it needs to be managed to ensure the emotional stability of the individual; the result is often unconscious denial.

Psychoanalysts such as Sigmund Freud, Melanie Klein, and Jacques Lacan located the source of this process – known as repression – in the early phases of our development as autonomous individuals. As a matter of fact, it could be considered as an inevitable byproduct of our growth process and of the simultaneous acquisition of language, which also marks the introduction into the world of culture and sociality outside the protective and caring boundaries of the immediate family. The painful process of learning rules and practices whose sense often escapes us and that aim to regulate body functions like eating, defecating, and even moving cannot but be perceived as a deprivation and as a fall from the full satisfaction of our emotional and biological needs that the relationship with our parents seemed to ensure.

These experiences, according to most psychoanalytic theories, remain emotionally effective and active at a subconscious level, even when most of us are totally unaware of them. To cope with them, we create defense mechanisms protecting our conscious processes and, above all, our self-esteem. One of the most effective among these mechanisms is to project the feelings connected with distressful experiences outside of ourselves, so that we can deal with them more easily. These dynamics create a pattern that we can apply, later on, to any disturbing event in our adult lives.

Sigmund Freud was the first therapist to work on the hypothesis that unconscious fears, uncontrollable drives, and unacceptable desires, otherwise unmanageable by the conscious self, are often expressed – at the individual level – in the forms of dreams, involuntary verbal expression and actions, psychosomatic symptoms, and, in the worst cases, paranoia and full-blown neurosis. Nevertheless, the forms that individuals choose to externalize these inner demons are not random or whimsical. On the contrary, the modality of their expression is deeply embedded in culture and society; after all, even our subconscious needs languages and codes to express itself. These behaviors also apply when it comes to eating. We are all fully aware of the key role that food, ingestion, and body images play as an outlet for these kinds of disturbances. Conditions such as anorexia and bulimia have been acknowledged as dangerous social plagues, and new neuroses such as the excessive fixation on physical exercise and orthorexia, the compulsive need to eat correctly, i.e. healthy, nutritionally balanced food, are on the rise. These neurotic expressions are not arbitrary and unsystematic, but rather they seem to articulate themselves in predictable and classifiable forms. Individuals seem to choose from a predetermined set of possible expressions in a bodily and performative language that can be communicated and understood. In other words, they have recourse to culturally determined codes and expressions to convey their most intimate fears and desires. The same fears and desires, repressed at the personal and communal level, become part of shared narratives that cultures create to neutralize any disruptive element that could become detrimental to its smooth functioning. Legends and tales, mythical figures and historical characters, traditions and customs all seem to fulfill this purpose as acceptable modalities of expression and representation of memories, feelings, and experiences that determine our development as infants and that we tend to suppress or even foreclose in adult life.

In vampires, cannibals, and various monsters – cruel but fascinating characters – we can externalize the elements of our inner life that most haunt and scares us, by giving them life and flesh (blood included, of course) (Dundes 1998: 159–75). We make them into autonomous agents with a life of their own, for whose actions we carry no responsibilities. As a matter of fact, in the fictional worlds we create we ourselves are at risk of becoming the victims of their ungodly instincts. Our innocence is safe.

This would explain why Anne Rice, arguably the most popular vampire-story writer of today, often connects – more or less patently and consciously – children's attitudes, food, and the vampires' craving for blood. Here is a passage from the first book of her most famous series, *Interview with the Vampire* (1977), where the vampire Louis tells the story of his first feeding: "I drank, sucking the blood out of the holes, experiencing for the first time since infancy the special pleasure of sucking nourishment, the body focused with the mind upon one vital source. ... How pathetic it is to describe these things, which can't truly be described" (Rice 1977: 19). The parallel between the vampire's blood sucking and the infant's suckling is so obvious that it is not even necessary to linger on it. Describing his body as absolutely concentrated on the feeding act, the vampire re-enacts the instinctive, stubborn, single-minded hunger of infants, who from birth are able to identify their source of nourishment. Furthermore, it is an experience that cannot be expressed in words. This is another important clue to the constitutive similarity between the monster and infants: they are both placed in a world beyond language, a world that does not know culture and symbols, laws and rules. It is a fantasy world where pleasure can be accessed directly, without the mediation of words, enjoying total bliss.

The parallel between infants and vampires becomes even more manifest in one of the most disturbing characters ever created by Anne Rice, the young vampire girl Claudia, stuck in an eternal present as a child by her transformation into a destructive monster. She is described as extremely obstinate in all her manifestations: "For little child she was, but also fierce killer now capable of the ruthless pursuit of blood with all a child's demanding" (Rice 1997: 98). The obnoxious, stubborn, and almost mindless repetitiveness of the vampire's killing and sucking activities is striking, as Anne Rice herself points out: "What truly lies before you is vampire nature, which is killing. ... You will be filled, Louis, as you were meant to be, with all the life that you can hold; and you will have hunger when that's gone for the same, and the same, and the same" (Rice 1997: 83).

For vampires, killing is not only the inevitable outcome of a need for nourishment and survival. It appears to constitute their whole reality, the nature of their inner selves. Sucking blood reflects unbridled drives beyond simple hunger, pointing to some fundamental experience that all of us share in some measure. Otherwise, how could we explain the never-ending success of books and movies dedicated to these creatures of darkness? Their analysis can reveal interesting elements not only about the structure and dynamics of society (at least the Western, consumerist one), but also about the psychological mechanisms of individuals (Žižek 1992).

Condemned to feed on blood, vampires cannot share their repasts with humans. Just as the experience of feeding on blood cannot be expressed in any structured language, it cannot be organized in any structured meal. Yet the sensuality of food as experienced by mortals often reveals connections with the vampire's hunger. Both share the same sensual nature, even when they are placed on the opposite sides of culture.

> I moved silently over the narrow street and met the thick aromas of the kitchen rising on the air past the gate. The slightly nauseating smell of cooking meat. ... She stirred the mixture in the kettle. I caught the sweet smell of the spices and the fresh green of marjoram and bay; and then in a wave came the horrid smell of the cooking meat, the blood and flesh decaying in the boiling fluids. ... The juices of the pot foamed on the lip and pit in the glowing coals below. Her dark odor came to me, her dusky spiced perfume, stronger than the curious mixture from the pot. (Rice 1977: 155)

Being an aspect of culture, prepared meals seem revolting to vampires, who position themselves beyond the distinction between the raw and the cooked that anthropologist Claude Lévi-Strauss presupposed at the base of every culinary culture (Lévi-Strauss 1968).

Furthermore, vampires can only move at night, when the rest of humankind (or at least its respectable parts) is asleep; they exist outside the human collectivity in a dimension where neither culture nor nurture has any meaning. Vampires are the undead, surviving beyond the limited life of humans. These elements reinforce the non-cultural character of the vampire experience, revealed by the impossibility for words to express it. The vampire's urge to feed on humans cannot be an object of knowledge; it cannot be symbolized, and become part of culture.

Nevertheless, humans and vampires share the same enjoyment in satisfying their hunger, as the follow passage hints.

> "Your slave," Armand whispered with a deep intake of breath that was passionate. And he watched, as the boy drank deeply. I could see him savoring the wet lips, the mobile flesh of the throat as the wine went down. And now the boy took a morsel of white meat, making that same salute, and consumed it slowly, his eyes fixed on Armand. It was as though Armand feasted upon the feast, drinking in that part of life which he could not share any longer except with his eyes. (Rice 1977: 252–3)

Here the human shows utter bliss in eating his food, mimicking the vampire's sensuality and transport. Vampires' victims seem to experience a deep and uncontrolled pleasure in becoming food themselves, revealing a profound ambivalence towards devouring and being devoured.

> I saw the mortal boy watching me, and I smelled the hot aroma of his flesh. ... Never had I felt like this, never had I experienced it, this yielding of a conscious mortal. ... He was pressing the length of his body against me now, and I felt the hard strength of his sex beneath his clothes pressing against my leg. A wretched gasp escaped my lips, but he bent close, his lips on what must have been so cold, so lifeless for him; and I sank my teeth into his skin, my body rigid, that hard sex driving against me, and I lifted him in passion off the floor. Wave after wave of his beating heart passed into me as, weightless, I rocked with him, devouring him, his ecstasy, his conscious pleasure. (Rice 1977: 231–2)

This element is also evident in the forefather of all vampire tales, Bram Stoker's *Dracula* (1867). Here is the description of the encounter between the young Jonathan Harker and the three vampire women living in Dracula's castle.

> There was something about them that made me uneasy, some longing and at the same time some deadly fear. ... I could feel the soft, shivering touch of the lips on the super-sensitive skin of my throat, and the hard dents of two sharp teeth, just touching and pausing there. I closed my eyes in a languorous ecstasy and waited – waited with beating heart. (Stoker 2003: 43–4)

Several literary critics have noticed these sexual undertones. "Dracula is the symptom of a wish, largely sexual, that we wish we did not have. The effect of repression is to turn a hunger into horror; the image of a repressed longing as it appears in a dream or a fiction is a sinister shape that threatens with what it promises, that insinuates the desire beneath the fear" (Stade 1982: vi).

In the moment of the embrace, followed by the fatal bite, victim and monster temporarily lose their individuality; as a matter of fact, they seem to experience sensual pleasure precisely because they get lost in a sort blurring of their boundaries, a feeling that provokes both bliss and panic.

This move is excluded from Western culture, at least from its components based on the Greco-Christian oppositions of desires and emotions vs. reason, of body vs. soul, of matter vs. spirit, where humans are considered as absolutely autonomous and individual selves with clearly distinct – though arbitrary – borders (Bordo 1993: 1–42; Foucault 1988: 133–44). Vampires, feeding on others, blur these boundaries: they are inherently relational, unable to separate themselves from their prey. Their survival depends on the existence of others, even if the others become their victims, in a conundrum that opposes limitless hunger and destruction of the source of nourishment.

Because of their insatiability, vampires could also be interpreted as representations of certain aspects of our bodily experience, associated in many traditional Western cultures to the image of women as "hungering, voracious, all-needing and all-wanting" (Bordo 1993: 160). Since the Middle Ages, women's association with the preparation and serving of meals seems to have given rise to men's fear about feminine control over ingestion and consumption. Building in part of this connection between food and the feminine, medieval theologians tended to relate women to matter and the body, while men were equated to the spiritual and the rational (Bynum 1984 and 1987). Since the spiritual had pre-eminence over the physical, this dualism also led to the attribution to women of traits such as unruliness, lack of self-control, and unbridled appetite, in terms of both food and sex. Besides other philosophical implications, these elements could also be interpreted as the rationalization of the infant's fear regarding the end of the limitless access to the mother's body, and "the terrifying erotic independence of every baby's mother" (Dinnerstein 1976: 62). In other words, we can detect a strong ambivalence when it comes to the endless, unspeakable, and symbiotic source of nourishment that the mother constitutes for the infant: it can be the origin of infinite pleasure, but also of fear and potential starvation when denied.

The consummate science fiction writer Octavia E. Butler reflected on these troublesome issues in her last full-length novel, *Fledgling*, published in 2005, one year before her death. Approaching vampire stories from the same feminist point of view that made her voice unique in science fiction writing, she imagined a world where vampires actually live in symbiosis with humans, who are given the choice to voluntarily become a part of families where humans, both men and women, provide blood and the vampire, does not matter whether male or female, ensures pleasure, love, longer spans of life, and protection. The novel's protagonist, the young female vampire Shori, has lost her memories and only slowly she realizes her true nature when she bites a male human.

> He tasted wonderful, and he had fed me without trying to escape or to hurt me. I licked the bite until it stopped bleeding. I wished I could make it heal, wished I could repay him by healing him.
>
> He sighed and held me, leaning back in his seat and letting me lean against him. "So what was that?" he asked after a while. "How did you do that? And why the hell did it feel so fantastic?"
>
> He had enjoyed it – maybe as much as I had. I felt pleased, felt myself smile. That was right somehow. (Butler 2005: 18)

All boundaries of sex, gender, class, and even victim and victimizer, are completely blurred. Humans do not become vampires when bitten; and vampires, who live much longer than humans, suffer deeply every time one of their symbiotic partners dies of old age: "Once I had tasted them, they enjoyed the way I made them feel. Instead of being afraid or angry, they were first confused, then trusting and welcoming, eager for more of the pleasure that I could give them. It happened that way each time" (Butler 2005: 32). In Butler's novel, the enjoyment that humans sense in the vampire's embrace uncovers the subtle identification of viewers and readers with the monsters at which previous narratives had only timidly hinted. The recurrent theme of the bliss found in the vampire's bite seems to point to the uncomfortable revelation that somehow, deep down, we want to lose our individuality and that we all could find the monster in ourselves.

What makes vampires really scary is that they confront us with what we could become if we let go, if we gave way to instincts and drives that we are afraid might be buried inside us. It would not take much for us to turn into monsters; this fear is metaphorically expressed in the fact that once bitten, the victims become themselves vampires. It is something that spreads easily and fast, like an infectious disease. This theme acquires greater relevance and political undertones in modern stories such as *I Am Legend* by Richard Matheson. In this 1954 novel, becoming in 2007 a movie starring Will Smith, the protagonist Robert Neville is the last human being in a world where everybody else has turned into vampires. Every night he has to endure the unrelenting siege of his home, while during the day he wanders around killing monsters and trying to figure out how to stop the contagion. Neville lives in what seems to be middle America, yet one where reality seems to have gone mad. Or has it really? During one of the long nights, Neville gets to think about the reason why the vampire is so hated:

> Are his needs more shocking than the needs of other animals and men? Are his needs more outrageous than the deeds of the parent who drained the spirit of his child? The vampire may foster quickened heartbeats and levitated hair. But is he worse than the

parent who gave to society a neurotic child who became a politician? Is he worse than the manufacturer who set up belated foundations with the money he made by handing bombs and guns to suicidal nationalists? Is he worse than the distiller who gave bastardized grain juice to stultify further the brains of those who, sober, were incapable of a progressive thought? (Nay, I apologize for this calumny; I nip the brew that feeds me.) Is he worse than the publisher who filled ubiquitous racks with lust and death wishes? Really, now, search your soul, lovie – is the vampire so bad?

All he does is drink blood. (Matheson 1995: 32)

After all, Matheson seems to warn us, we are all vampires. Or at least it would not take us much to turn into monsters. A generation later, in 1975, Stephen King again gave voice to these dreads. In his novel *'Salem's Lot*, two vampires under the aspect of businessmen move into an old abandoned mansion in a small American town, which in a short time turns into a sort of ghost town where more and more citizens are turned into vampires. The novel is frightening because it shows a bunch of peaceful middle-Americans becoming monsters through slight changes in their daily routines, especially in eating and drinking. As one of the vampires explains:

The folk here are still rich and full-blooded, folk who are stuffed with the aggression and the darkness so necessary to ... There is no English word for it. *Pokol*; *vurderlak*; *eyalik* ... The people have not cut off the vitality which flows from their mother, the earth, with a shell of concrete and cement. Their hands are plunged into the very waters of life. They have ripped the life from the earth, whole and beating. (King 2000: 256)

It is enough to dig a little deeper to find energies and drives that only need to be set free to express themselves in ways that terrorize us. This unbridled vitality, the voraciousness and the wild craving for ingestion that vampires awake in 'Salem's Lot's citizens is the same that we often recognize in infants, especially in hungry ones.

Hunger and Development

The connection between vampires and infants can be approached from different points of view. As we mentioned, the representations of vampires' victims in pop culture hint at both their fear of being destroyed, and their wish to lose themselves in the monsters. When the creatures of the night bite, their targets seem to lose their individuality and pleasurably abandon themselves. At the same time, vampires' prey are terrified by the bites from the monsters, which are dangerous and deadly. This ambivalence can be explained if we assume that we readers somehow can identify not only with the prey, but also with the hunters. In other words, the constant success of vampires in Western pop culture makes sense if we can find some trait of the undead bloodsuckers in ourselves, particularly in our fantasies and in our drives.

At this point, it might be useful to explore what psychology and psychoanalysis have to say about these issues, to achieve a better understanding not only of vampires, but also of ingestion and, more broadly, of the consumption drives that constitute the back-bone of market-driven pop culture.

As a matter of fact, traditional psychoanalysis tended to limit the impact of eating and ingestion, and hence consumption, only to the development of the early phases of life, with little or no consequence once the individual reaches adulthood. An inherent contradiction seems to haunt Freud's approach to hunger. He definitely acknowledges its importance, to the point that, in his three seminal essays on the theory of sexuality, originally published in 1905, and specifically in "The Sexual Aberrations," he resorts twice to hunger as a metaphor for the libido.

> The fact of existence of sexual needs in human beings and animals is expressed in biology by the assumption of a "sexual instinct," on the analogy of the instinct of nutrition, that is of hunger. Everyday language possesses no counterpart to the word "hunger," but science makes use of the word "libido" for that purpose. (Freud 2000: 1)

> The normal sexual aim is regarded as being the union of the genitals in the act known as copulation, which leads to a release of sexual tension and a temporary extinction of the sexual instinct – a satisfaction analogous to the sating of hunger. (Freud 2000: 15)

The psychoanalyst describes hunger as a drive, and an extremely powerful one, that needs satisfaction just like the sexual instinct and that anybody can understand, since it is familiar to any human being. As a matter of fact, in "Infantile Sexuality" Freud argues that the first stage of the sexual development of infants is closely connected to eating and food.

> The first of these [phases] is the oral or, as it might be called, cannibalistic pregenital sexual organization. Here sexual activity has not yet been separated from the ingestion of food. ... The sexual aim consists in the incorporation of the object – the prototype of a process which, in the form of identification, is later to play such an important psychological part. (Freud 2000: 64)

> The child's lips, in our view, behave like an erotogenic zone, and no doubt stimulation by the warm flow of milk is the cause of the pleasurable sensation. The satisfaction of the erotogenic zone is associated, in the first instance, with the satisfaction of the need for nourishment. To begin with, sexual activity attaches itself to functions serving the purpose of self-preservation and does not become independent of them until later. No one who has ever seen a baby sinking back satiated from the breast and falling asleep with flushed cheeks and a blissful smile can escape the reflection that this picture persists as a prototype of the expression of sexual satisfaction in later life. (Freud 2000: 47–8)

It is significant that the passage is part of a section on autoerotism. Freud seems to emphasize that in his opinion there are no external objects of pleasure, and he stresses this concept several times in the essay. On the other hand, Freud also makes the assertion that the breast is the first sexual object, previous to autoerotism. In "Transformation of Puberty," he affirms: "A child suckling at his mother's breast has become the prototype of every relation of love. The finding of an object is in fact a refinding of it" (Freud 2000: 88). Later on, in "On Narcissism" (1914), he appears quite unresolved, stating that the child has originally two objects, himself and the mother who feeds him. As it has been noted, this is no secondary matter, since it engendered the competing psychoanalytic theories based on the mutually exclusive assumptions that the libido is originally pleasure-seeking (inward) or object-seeking (outward) (Chodorow 2000: xv–xvi)

Freud argues that fantasies of devouring are particularly disturbing, because they are based on the earliest pleasure drive: oral gratification. Developing children desire to consume their parents, and these unacceptable longings inspire fear of retaliation. It is not by chance that bedtime stories and children's tales, such as the brothers Grimm's Hansel and Gretel or Little Red Riding Hood, are full of cannibalistic acts.

Whatever importance Freud gives to hunger and nourishment in infancy, he seems to underestimate their role in later stages of the sexual development of the human being, unless in the form of "hysterical vomiting" following repression and disgust about food (Freud 2000: 48). How can the influence of an activity that remains crucial during the whole span of life become so negligible in classic psycho-analytical theory? Do human beings stop eating, or experiencing pleasure or disgust through food?

Freud let many issues open to further examination, some of which were addressed by child psychologist Melanie Klein in the 1920s.

Her point of departure was the narcissistic attitude of newborns, that is to say, their exclusive focus on themselves and their needs, whose satisfaction brings pleasure. "Children form relations with the outside world by directing to objects from which pleasure is obtained the libido that was originally attached exclusively to the child's own ego" (Klein 1987a: 58). From the earlier stages of her career, she understood that the psychoanalytic methods developed by Freud were based on language, a skill still not fully mastered by young children. This realization led her to develop a new approach that she called "play technique": this consisted in observing children play with toys and objects to analyze their behavior, which she assumed was a reflection of their inner world. Following this intuition, she moved towards the study of object relations, considered as the ego's earlier mechanisms of defense.

Now, the first object to which infants relate is their mothers' breast (or any substitute for it), on which they depend for the pleasurable satisfaction of their vital needs. When babies are content and well fed, they feel one with it. But if they sense that their needs are not met, then the breast is experienced as a separate entity, becoming their first psychological object and a cause of anxiety. The withdrawal of the breast probably constitutes the infant's first experience of object loss, which can be exorcized by games such as peek-a-boo and hide-and-seek, re-enacting the loss but reassuring the child about its positive ending with the finding of the lost object (Frankiel 1993).

At this point, infants end up perceiving the breast as split into a good part, which they identify with themselves and which provides hallucinatory pleasure, and a bad part, which becomes the object of the oral-sadistic, or cannibalistic, desires of the infant. In these phantasies (in Klenian language, phantasies are the representations that allow babies to relate psychically to the conjunction of their inner and outer world), children bite, devour, and ingest the breast, but as a consequence of the guilt provoked by this desire they dread a punishment corresponding to the offense. The object of their attack becomes a source of danger because infants fear similar retaliatory attacks from it. This early oral-sadistic phase will be overcome only when, with the beginning of the genital phase, the children's ego becomes able to take in the mother as a whole person, with her good and bad parts.

In Klein's analysis, the role plaid by feeding in the development of the subject cannot be easily dismissed. Worried that their sadistic impulses might destroy the objects of their drive, and afraid of retaliation from the objects that have been attacked in phantasy, infants move to different, more external objects that relate symbolically to the ones left behind. In Klein's theory, the transfer of desires and anxieties from object to object, training infants to substitution and representation, also introduces them into the symbolic and semiotic dimension, which constitutes the basis for language and learning. If we interpret aggressive impulses as incorporation of knowledge, it becomes clear that our hunger, and our desire for ingestion, push us along the path of symbol formation, socialization, and culture.

Nevertheless, to be part of culture and of society, growing infants must learn to repress their destructive, ingestion-based drives, which, nevertheless, in adult life, will constitute the core for all desires for control and power, perceived as potentially dangerous for collective life. For these reasons they must be transformed and expressed – sublimated, in psychoanalytical language – in acceptable and constructive forms. But they keep on exerting a deep influence on the way we deal with reality as adults.

The permanence of the anxieties, drives, and fear connected with the ambivalent relationship to the mother's breast (or any source of nourishment) would explain why we identify not only with the victims of vampires, but also with the monsters themselves: although we have repressed our infant memories, we might still subconsciously maintain some cannibalistic instincts (Copjec 1991: 34). The recurrence of these monster-like figures in pop culture can only be explained as an embodiment of the drives connected to our daily and necessary feeding experiences, which ostensibly remain relevant throughout our adult life, even though psychoanalysis seems to focus on them only during the first phases of life. We should speak not of transitory phases that once finished are gone forever, but rather of long-lasting attitudes and approaches towards the external world.

Hunger as Void

The relative lack of interest of psychoanalysis in the role of eating and food in adult life continued also with the French analyst and theorist Jacques Lacan, who, however, as will see in Chapter 4, dedicated much attention to body images. In the later portions of his career, Lacan interpreted children's desire for the absolute fulfillment of their own necessities as an impossible symbiotic fantasy centered on total fusion with the mother, a bodily *jouissance* (absolute enjoyment) that constitutes the ultimate experience of the Real, in Lacan's theory a dimension that cannot be talked about and categorized, beyond symbolic culture and even imagination. However, this bliss can never be achieved because it actually never existed, creating the constitutive lack and longing that lie at the core of human beings and their desires. From the moment when children learn to verbalize their needs by acceding to the symbolic realm of culture and language, the demands addressed to mothers are more a plea for recognition and unconditional love than an actual request for them to meet a given necessity. Whatever the response, children can never be absolutely certain of their mother's love. As a consequence, what is left of the demand after the specific needs have been satisfied emerges as desire, which actually expresses the wish for the fantastized total unity with the mother. For Lacan, human subjects are centered on this fundamental gap, a void that he called *béance* and that explains their deepest motivations and wants. It is as if a bottomless hunger was placed at the core of what we are: whatever we acquire, ingest, and consume could never fulfill it. We face again the insatiable voraciousness of vampires, their unspeakable desire, and their existence beyond social or cultural boundaries.

Jacques Lacan also examined infants' destructive, cannibalistic drives. Investigating young children's behavior, he pointed to their "motor impotence and nursling dependence," determined by a "veritable specific prematurity of birth" (Lacan 2002: 4, 6). The organic inadequacy and lack of bodily integrity frustrate children, who, as we will see in Chapter 4, try to find the completeness and wholeness they need in their own images reflected in mirrors. According to Lacan, the infants' fragmentary body experience is manifested in later life in sadomasochistic fantasies and dreams centered on body fragmentation (*corps morcelé*). This fantasy is also connected with and maybe produced by the anxiety caused by the infants' own aggressive impulses towards the mother's breast, from which they fear retaliation in the form of devouring. Lacan finds the origin of aggressive tendencies in the frustration deriving from the disturbing realization of the gap between the children's lived experience of the fragmented body and their narcissistic identifications. These tendencies build on an already present fantasy aggression towards the bad breast and the ensuing fears of retaliation. In "Aggressiveness in Psychoanalysis" (1948), Lacan contended that this tendency might find its roots precisely in "the images of castration, emasculation, mutilation, dismemberment, dislocation, evisceration, devouring, and bursting open of the body, in short, the imagoes that I have grouped together under the heading 'imagoes of the fragmented body'" (Lacan 2002: 13). Nevertheless, the interest in the ambivalence towards eating and being eaten that Lacan tackled in his early writings almost disappears in his later works, where he shifted his increasingly abstract analysis to fantasies and drives. He concentrated on sexuality, fetishes, the gaze, even on the voice, leaving aside good, plain hunger.

Despite the fact that in the work of some of the most influential psychologists and psychiatrists the interest in these themes is often limited to the earliest phases of human development, we are led to admit that hunger and more generally desire for consumption do play an important role in our adult life. Sometimes they can become so intense that they make us uncomfortable. From childhood, we are taught various forms of self-control, aimed at easing our life in families, communities, and society. Unbridled desire is frowned upon, if not condemned. Only children, at times, are able to get away with it; after all, they are considered adults in training. For this reason, pop culture has often used young characters to poke fun at the defects and vices of adults. The movie *Willy Wonka and the Chocolate Factory* (1971) and its recent remake by the visionary filmmaker Tim Burton, *Charlie and the Chocolate Factory* (2005), both based on the book *Charlie and the Chocolate Factory* written in 1964 by British author Roald Dahl, are in different ways a gentle critique of excessive consumption. All the characters embody one form or another of limitless, stupid greed that inevitably leads to self-destruction, even if imaginary. At the same time, though, they offer an interesting insight into the voraciousness and the drives that lurk in all of us; that is probably the reason for the success of the movie with both young viewers and adults. Through the various characters, we indulge vicariously in our vices, knowing that even the worst punishment is not for real. All of the winners of the famous Golden Ticket granting entrance to the mysterious chocolate factory, together with their chaperones, are clearly blown away when they access the core of Wonka's reign: the room with the chocolate river, where everything is edible. At one moment or another, all of them give in to their curiosities and cravings, even little good Charlie. For our discussion, Augustus Gloop is the most interesting among the children who are invited to visit the fabled factory. In the 1971 movie he is represented as a hefty German boy; we see him for the first time when he is interviewed in a traditional *Stube*-style restaurant together with his parents, all of them overweight and stuffing their face with sausages and other meats. In both movies he ends up falling into the chocolate river and disappearing into the pipes of the factory. The substance he was trying to ingest so greedily metaphorically devours him, while the Oompa Loompas, mysterious little creatures working for Wonka, offer a moral commentary on the events, in a spirit not too distant from Dante's while he travels through the different levels of Hell in the *Divine Comedy*. After all, the Florentine poet also dedicated a special position to the gluttonous, in Cantica VI: a smelly place where they are hit by an endless rain of dirty water, snow, and hail. The whole *Divine Comedy* works according to the logic of the *contrappasso*, or retaliation: each category of sinners is punished by a torture that is closely connected with their sin, often its contrary. The same rules work in Wonka's Chocolate Factory.

Sometimes pop culture characters are not punished for their greed: this is the case for the satirical cartoon series *South Park* created by Matt Stone and Trey Parker, with its cohort of excessive, vulgar, and politically incorrect characters. Eric Cartman, a child overfed by his single mother, who tries to overcompensate for the absence of a father and her quite unruly sexual drive (in one episode she appears on the cover of *Crack Whore* magazine), perfectly represents the bottomless voraciousness of the infant. Although capable of articulating his desire in words, Cartman is led by a bottomless hunger, and more generally a drive towards all sorts of consumption, that cannot be controlled and does not abide by laws of propriety or even simple humanity. In episode 2 of the first season, "Weight Gain 4000," Cartman has to appear on TV because he has cheated his way into winning a national "Save our Fragile Planet" writing context. Aware of his poor shape he decides to bulk up, lured into using a product, Weight Gain 4000, that assures "over 4000 grams of saturated fat per serving." With the battle cry of "Beefcake," Cartman sets to consume ridiculous amounts of the substance, proud of becoming so big he cannot even get on the school bus. Finally he ends up on a TV talk show about obese people; still all he can see and appreciate is that he can consume and grow without limits.

In episode 8 of the first season, "Starvin' Marvin," at Thanksgiving Cartman and his friends see a TV commercial for distance adoptions: $5 a month to sponsor a child in Ethiopia, and a sports watch for those who call to start the adoption paying by credit card. By mistake, instead of the watch, they receive a child, quickly named Starvin' Marvin. The little Ethiopian gets a crash course in consumerism. He is taken to an all-you-can-eat buffet, where Cartman manages to eat all his food. In the meanwhile, a mad scientist creates a genetically modified breed of Thanksgiving Turkey that reproduces very fast and attacks the citizens of South Park. Could there be a more direct expression of the fear of being ingested by the objects of our hunger? Also Cartman is punished by retaliation: Starvin' Marvin succeeds in sending him to Ethiopia in his place. The little fat white boy finds himself among starving people, until Marvin gets back to Ethiopia, bringing all the killer turkeys, which in the meanwhile have been killed.

The dread of being devoured often surfaces in the show. In episode 2 of the second season, "Cartman's Mom is Still a Dirty Slut," the citizens of South Park become anthropophagic when they get stuck in a snowstorm. The absurd but significant twist is that they begin drawing straws to decide who will be sacrificed for the others' survival just four hours into the storm, after a very abundant breakfast and with plenty of food still around. By the end of the storm, they have eaten three people, and they decide to bring the leftovers home in doggie bags. *South Park* makes us laugh, but also makes us squirm in our seats. In its absurd irony it confronts us with questions about and insights into ourselves that we would rather not face. In some way, comedy accomplishes the same function as scary stories. Both operate as imaginary representations and collective discharges of subconscious elements that are culturally perceived as unclean, if not dangerous.

The Famished Undead

Vampires, zombies, and other devouring creatures, including cannibals, have been around for a long time in Western culture. There are different theories about the origin of the word "vampire" itself. It could come from the Turkish *uber*, witch, and its Slavic derivatives *upior* and *upir*, or from the Greek verbal root *pi*, meaning "to drink." It seems that the expression "vampire" itself appeared for the first time at the end of the seventeenth century in France, and became more common in the eighteenth century, with *Dissertations sur les Apparitions et sur les Revenants et les Vampires*, published by Dom Calmet in 1746 (Dundes 1998: 4–5). It became a common word in the rest of Europe more or less in the same period, although it was not used in Eastern Europe, where the superstitions regarding vampires were actually common and where these monsters were rather called *strigoi*, *moroii*, or *varcolaci* (Klaniczay 1990). Vampires already showed traits that would later appear also in Western pop culture: they were considered as a sort of reanimated corpses, which could only be defeated by totally destroying, cutting, and burning their bodies. They can take "power" away from people, and in particular milk from nursing mothers (an interesting reference to the breast). In other legends they suck human blood. Perhaps surprisingly, there is no actual reference to the fact that a fifteenth-century prince from Romania, the Voivode Dracul, a sworn enemy of the Turkish invaders, whom he massacred by the hundreds, was a vampire.

At this point, we cannot avoid a historical question with heavy social and political undertones: why does a stable kernel, which we have demonstrated reveals close connections with the psychological development of human infants, appear under different forms at different times and places? The answer, which we will try to clarify in the following paragraphs, is that this constant core element of the human experience, which as adults we tend to forget about or to deny, surfaces in forms that mutate and vary in order to fit in the network of ideas, values, practices, discourses, and material realities of different cultures and societies at different moments of their historical transformation. This would explain why the uneasiness about our "cannibalistic" drives expresses itself as a humorous critique of unbridled consumerism and shameless gluttony in pieces of pop culture like *Willy Wonka* or *South Park* in America at the turn of the twenty-first century.

In the case of vampire legends, historian Gàbor Klaniczay argues that they emerged in the Austro-Hungarian empire during the seventeenth century when witchcraft became less culturally relevant, under the new mentality influenced by rationalism and scientific advances that were investigating blood (Klaniczay 1990: 168–88). The same factors might have determined the success of vampire stories in

Western Europe, later amplified by the Romantic taste for the mysterious and the horrific, often interpreted as a cultural reaction to the rationalism promoted by the Enlightenment.

Some elements that we find in vampirism within Western traditions, i.e. the undead or the returning dead and the thirst for blood, can be traced also in other traditions, like Voudoun in all its incarnations, both in the original cradle in Benin and in the Americas (Voodoo in Haiti, Condomblé in Brazil, Obia in Jamaica, Santeria in Cuba).

Voodoo sacrifices follow the classical pattern of immolation rites. The following paragraph will rely on the research of the anthropologist Alfred Métraux, which to this day is still one of the best works on the subject.

> The act of killing is always preceded by a rite which is akin both to Communion and divination. The victim can only be put to death if has first eaten some food and drunk some liquid of a sacred nature. … As soon as the animal has eaten or drunk, it becomes the property of the *loa* (voodoo divine entity, note) and partakes of his divine nature. … This participation in the sacred nature of the victim can be taken as a total identification of the people performing the sacrifice with the creature sacrificed. (Métraux 1972: 170)

Here we find again the element of ambivalence that we have recognized in many phenomena connected with ingestion and consumption: a form of identification between the eater and the eaten.

In Haiti the thirst for blood is the main trait of the so called *loups-garous* (were-wolves), female vampires who make small children die by sucking their blood.

> To suck the little victim's blood, a werewolf gets into the house in the form of a cockroach or some other insect, or slides a straw through the wattling so that it rests against the child's cheek. Opinions differ as to how vampires operate. Some say they "drain" a child gradually, others that they have only to take three drops of blood for the child to die of an illness, caused magically. (Métraux 1972: 304)

The insatiable desire for incorporation puts *loups-garous* outside the realm of humanity, to the point where they can change their shape at will.

In the case of Voodoo and similar religions, it is quite difficult to trace the development of beliefs and practices before their arrival in the New World. And after that, for centuries the only written documents we can access originated, of course, in the environment of colonial culture and practices (Bodin 1990; Burton 1997; Fernàndez Olmos and Paravisini-Gebert 2003). However, it is not unreasonable to make a case for the influence of the slave–master relationships in the development of the core concepts of Afro-Caribbean religions and in the creation of myths, ceremonies, and traditions. Food played an important role in the Voodoo cult: to each divine entity corresponded certain produce and substances, including blood

(Rigaud 1985: 91–100). We must not forget that food was precisely a sensitive point in the power relation between the white masters, who depended on the slave for the production, transformation, and even service of food, and the slaves, who often struggled to secure enough food to survive. Somehow, the white masters were not only using the food produced by the slaves, but also consuming the slaves themselves, sucking their vital energy. It is likely that this grim reality gave depth to mythical figures such as zombies and *loup-garous*, whose traits also reflected the fundamental ambivalence about devouring that we have already discussed.

This hypothesis is sustained also by historian Luise White in her work on rumors and stories about vampires in colonial East Africa.

> Vampire stories offer a better, clearer, more analytical picture of the colonial experience than other sources do. … Vampires themselves are revealing beings: a separate race of bloodsucking creatures, living among humans on fluids that they extract from human bodies; vampires mark a way in which relations of race, of bodies, and of tools of extraction can be debated, theorized, and explained. (White 2000: 307)

In East Africa stories, firemen, game rangers, and mine managers become blood-takers, using modern instruments like injections and working on behalf of the white colonizers, who crave the vital fluids of the Africans. The core element for these legends might be of Indian origin. The first word used for vampire is East Africa is in fact *mumiani*, which appeared in Swahili dictionaries in the nineteenth century. It would refer to a mummy, but also to a medicine. At about the same time, the word *momiai* was used on the west coast of India to indicate a sort of medicine based on blood. In Indian lore, this blood was often thought of as extracted through torture in hospitals, probably because these institutions were identified with the colonizers, and most people did not understand too well what was going on inside them. Indian soldiers working for the British could have brought these stories to Africa (Pels 1992). Whatever their origin might have been, the legends were absorbed in the web of the culture, the mentality, and the material realities of the specific colonial power structures, assuming new meanings that helped make sense of a different situation.

Cultured Cannibals

Many Africans believed that white colonizers were eager not only to drink their blood, but also to eat their very flesh. These kinds of stories probably began circulating when the arrival of the European explorers first, and the slave merchants after, radically changed the customs and the economic flows traditionally connected with slavery in Africa. In colonial Katanga, today's Congo, people believed that Africans were hired to capture other Africans, make them "dumb" with injections, fatten them, and them give them for white men to eat on special occasions like

Christmas (White 2000: 270). Similar legends and contemporary urban myths can be found also in other countries that have a colonial past, such as Brazil and Bolivia (Scheper-Hughes 1992; Watchel 1994).

In Western cultures, however, when we think of cannibals we tend to refer to the anthropophagic customs of barbaric or anyway savage populations. Anthropophagy has actually been present in Western collective imagination since its origin. In Homer's *Iliad*, the hero Achilles wishes he were able to unleash his fury to the point of desiring to eat his enemies, marking this act as the ultimate taboo that would set him apart from humankind, while in the *Odyssey* Ulysses faces the man-devouring Cyclops (Buchan 2001). Also Ovid, in the *Metamorphoses*, refers to this practice (Kilgour 1990: 28–45). Later on, Romans accused the Christians, and the Christians in turn accused the Jews, of consuming human flesh. Literary critics and theorists have been very sensitive to the theme of incorporation, often analyzed in terms of a scrambling of the fundamental dichotomy between inside and outside that constitutes one of the bases for the development of autonomous individuals. As philosopher Judith Butler maintained, "a movement of boundary itself appeared to be quite central to what bodies are" (J. Butler 1993: ix). All that finds itself outside the boundaries defining one's identity can be perceived as threatening. This need for a stable and contoured integrity leads individuals and social groups to push whatever they perceive as unfamiliar towards the outside, creating an external space of absolute difference, which can never be part of the subject and which at the same time defines the subject. "Abject and abjection are my safeguards. The primers of my culture," affirmed the French cultural theorist Julia Kristeva, who also noted: "Food loathing is perhaps the most elementary and most archaic form of abjection … it is not lack of cleanliness or health that causes abjection but what disturbs identity, system, order. What does not respect borders, positions, rules. The in-between, the ambiguous, the composite" (Kristeva 1982: 2–4). Individuals identify with the norms regulating their eating habits, which, together with sex, play a key role in defining taboos and pollution fears, as the British anthropologist Mary Douglas demonstrated in her studies about purity (Douglas 1969). The lack of boundaries and distinctions constitutes a pending danger for any social structure. When individuals or groups share the same desire, or, better, when they happen to desire the same thing, they erase the distinction between each other, the differences that define them as individuals and that constitute the basis of any social interaction. This negation of boundaries can lead to an explosion of violence, precipitating society into chaos, argued the French philosopher René Girard, who defined this phenomenon as a "mimetic crisis" (Girard 1979).

What I am interested in pointing out is that starting from the fifteenth century, when Columbus first met the natives in the Caribbean, anthropophagy became in the mind of many "cannibalism," a word that itself derives from the name of those populations, the Caribs. I will not get into the highly debated question of whether cannibalism actually ever existed, and if so, what its function was in the societies that adopted it. What is significant in our context is that a concept already existing in Western culture in connection with eating and ingestion, and with all the ambivalences and the psychological relevance that we have examined, was used to reinforce the boundary between civilization and savagery, as a screen for colonial violence at a historical moment when European powers were spreading their influence all over the globe.

Some political theorists see in the apparition of cannibals an expression of the European proto-capitalist appetite. After all, in *Capital*, Karl Marx compared capitalists to werewolves, vampires, and parasites living off labor (Marx 1990: 353, 367, 645). To this day, the term "cannibalization" is used in business language to incorporate a competitor's market share (Bartolovich 1998: 208). This element actually reminds us of the inner contradictions and ambivalence that we find every time we deal with ingestion:

> [Capitalism] continuously comes up against the "physical obstacle" to its own consumption, which it then must meet with ingenious methods to consume more labor power without killing off its agent. ... To the extent that proto-capitalists did feel drive toward exhaustive consumption, they were working against their own long-term interest which it took them some time to learn. The training of appetite, unsurprisingly, becomes a preoccupation of period commentators on trade, discovery and production. (Bartolovich 1998: 213, 216)

In other words, devouring always comes with the fear of destruction.

Cannibals have become a common feature in many contemporary pieces of pop culture. In 1993 a U.S. movie, *The Miracle of the Andes*, told the story of the Uruguayan Air Force Flight 571 disaster in the Andes, where the survivors ended up eating each other. In the 1970s a few Italian moviemakers originated a whole genre of low-budget cannibal B-movies that enjoyed a certain success for some years and were characterized by a tendency to pure splatter and heavy sexual undertones. Usually the main characters find themselves in a horrific situation during anthropological expeditions or quests for lost loved ones, which always take place in beautiful, lush, and uncontaminated nature. The first of these films was *Ultimo Mondo Cannibale* (Last Cannibal World, 1977) by Ruggero Deodato, followed in the same year by *Emmanuelle e gli Ultimi Cannibali* (Emmanuelle and the Last Cannibals, 1977) by Joe D'Amato and *La Montagna del Dio Cannibale* (The Cannibal God's Mountain, 1978) by Sergio Martino, starring Ursula Andress, and what is considered the masterpiece of the genre, *Cannibal Holocaust* (1980), again the work of Mr. Deodato. The genre flourished until the mid-1980s, and enjoyed a certain commercial success abroad. It is interesting that those were precisely the years when Italy was profoundly shaken by internal terrorism, both from the extreme right and from the extreme left. Assassinations, urban guerrillaa, and even major massacres made evident to all citizens a different side of politics. Just a few years earlier Marco Ferreri had filmed *La Grande Bouffe* (1973), in which four successful bourgeois characters decide to get together to kill themselves by binging, and Federico Fellini had created the movie version of the Latin writer Petronius's *Satyricon* (1969), with a memorable and excessive dinner scene where power and overeating are clearly connected.

Cannibalism appears also in comedies: the first example is probably *Sweeney Todd: The Demon Barber of Fleet Street* (1936), which then became a musical with lyrics by Stephen Sondheim and in 2007 was made into a film by Tim Burton starring Johnny Depp. In the play, Sweeney's thirst for revenge ends up in a flourishing business in pies filled with human meat. In the same spirit, we can mention the film *Delicatessen*, a 1991 black comedy written and directed by Jean-Pierre Jeunet and Marc Caro, centered on a butcher who serves to his clients the flesh of his apprentices, and *Eating Raoul*, a 1982 black comedy by Paul Bartel where a mild-mannered married couple gather the money they need to open their restaurant by advertising themselves as an S&M escort duo and killing whoever shows up for their services. In a more serious key, in 1989 Peter Greenaway directed the visually amazing *The Cook, the Thief, His Wife and Her Lover*, where in the end the thief of the title is forced to eat his wife's lover, whom he has killed. In *301/302* (2004) the Korean filmmaker Chul-soo Park depicted the love/hate relation between two women, one fixated on cooking and the other anorexic, which ends up in tragedy with the former eating the latter. The most famous pop culture cannibal both in books and on film is arguably Hannibal Lecter, played by a fantastic Anthony Hopkins in Jonathan Demme's 1991 *The Silence of the Lambs* (a role he reprised in *Hannibal*, 2001, and *Red Dragon*, 2003). The tense and charged relationship between the detective Clarice Starling (Jodie Foster) and the psychiatrist-turned-anthropophagist who helps her to capture other criminals delves deep into all the complexity related to ingestion of symbolic – and at times physical – otherness.

Hungry Powers

The recurring fear of being transformed into food and the dread about one's own devouring instincts and the taboo placed on anthropophagy have been considered as the origin of table manners.

> Table manners are social agreements; they are devised precisely because violence could so easily erupt at dinner. Eating is aggressive by nature, and the implements required for it could quickly become weapons; table manners are, most basically, a system of taboos designed to ensure that violence remains out of the question. (Visser 1992: xii)

In *Totem and Taboo*, Freud imagines that the beginning of society was the murder of the original father by his sons and their shared consumption of his flesh.

> One day the expelled brothers joined forces, slew and ate the father, and thus put an end to the father's horde. ... Now they accomplish their identification with him by devouring him and each acquired a part of his strength. The totem feast, which is perhaps mankind's first celebration, would be the repetition and commemoration of this memorable, criminal act with which so many things began, social organization, moral restrictions, and religion. (Freud 1998: 122)

Meals connect those who share them, confirming their identities as individuals and as social groups, all while excluding those who do not participate in them. As the German political writer Hannah Arendt wrote, "to live together in the world means essentially that a world of things is between those who have it in common, as a table is located between those who sit around it; the world, like every in-between, relates and separates at the same time" (Arendt 1958: 48). The political relevance of communal eating emerges in the work of many political scientists. The ambivalent fears and desires connected to it, as we have already seen, are not culturally acceptable, since they constitute a negation of culture itself as social interaction and negotiation. Yet they play a fundamental role in the constitution of power, as the Nobel Prize recipient Elias Canetti poignantly exposed it. In a section aptly called "The Entrails of Power" from his masterpiece *Crowds and Power*, Canetti argues that teeth are "the very first manifestation of order," "the most striking natural instrument of power" (Canetti 1984: 207). More precisely, smoothness and order, which allow teeth to fulfill their task, and their shape reminscent of a prison, have become attributes of power. Indeed, for Canetti, power is a form of digestion, often sucking all substances from the subjects it supposedly represents. As is the case with the body, if this process of ingestion and digestion is interrupted, the result is death, the dissolution of power. It is not by chance that in the past the king or anybody holding any kind of power had to show their authority by an unusual capacity of consumption, which was often visible in full bodies and huge bellies.

> It may be useful to have a look at eating in general, independent of the eater's position in the social scale. A certain esteem for each other is clearly evident in all who eat together. This is already expressed by the fact of their sharing. ... But the touch of solemnity in their attitude cannot be explained by this alone; their mutual esteem also means that they will not eat each other. ... People eat together, bare their teeth and eat and, even at this critical moment, feel no desire to eat each other. (Canetti 1984: 220–1)

Now things have changed, and power tries to disguise itself in slim and toned bodies that are submitted to all kinds of stress to display eternal youth and vigor. Obesity and lack of physical fitness are considered traits of the lower classes, unable to control their impulses and to adopt a good diet. However, the implicit danger lurking in this kind of digestive power is still cannibalism, the fear of being destroyed and consumed by those who are stronger: a fear that is the direct reflection of our own drives aimed at ingesting the world to bring it under control within ourselves.

–3–

Tasty Utopias
Food and Politics in Science Fiction Novels

The alien is always constructed of the familiar.

Delany 1985: 143

The Challenges of Science Fiction

As we noticed when talking about cannibals and vampires, the desire for excessive eating and ingestion is often overlooked or even repressed by culture and society, only to re-emerge in imaginary creatures, legends, and myths. It is almost as if we were scared of facing our own unruly appetites, so we project them outside onto evil characters that deserve to be despised, fought, and destroyed. For these reason, fictional monsters can also come to represent the dynamics of power at both the personal and the social levels, stimulating further – and often involuntary – reflections about the mechanics of dominance and authority.

The terror of being cannibalized and the fear of menacing and mysterious powers, whose actions cannot be fully understood and foreseen, emerge also in science fiction. Novels, movies, and comic books that focus on alternative realities and possible futures have often been considered the realm of usually young, white males. Yet, this genre is increasingly getting recognition also by wider audiences, and even some movie and literary critics are not ashamed to voice a certain appreciation. In these works, imagination takes the lead, creating fictional worlds that, nevertheless, tell us a lot about the actual realities we inhabit.

The Man in the High Castle (1962) by Philip K. Dick provides an excellent example. The whole novel is set a hypothetical present, where the U.S. and its Allies have lost World War II. Only the central states of the former U.S. remain free. The Western states constitute a puppet country under Japanese influence, while the Eastern part is controlled by the Nazis, who are still hunting for Jews, have exterminated all black people from Africa, and have dried the Mediterranean Sea to get more arable land. Slavery is legal again.

Reality is simply described as "terribly, terribly disruptive" (Dick 1992: 258). The Western world seems to have lost its bearings: people have to choose between getting some sort of perspective or "perhaps retreat into the shadows of mental illness, avert one's gaze forever" (Dick 1992: 201). In the territories under Japanese control, many people resort to the Yi Jing (I Ching), the ancient Chinese divinatory book, in an attempt at making sense of their daily experience. The oracle is consulted in order to obtain precise answers about the future, about choices to make, or just to appease fear and confusion and to come to terms with the irruption of chaos.

In this state of affairs, the Germans, the agents who constantly threaten total destruction in the name of a better, more ordered, and more logical reality, are described as monsters through the use of images with which we are already familiar. Their ubiquitous power is perceived as the "ancient gigantic cannibal near-man flourishing now, ruling the world once more" (Dick 1992: 12). It is precisely a German, Wegener, a double agent who is trying to warn the Japanese about the plans of the Reich, who introduces the specter of cannibalism in the narration. When he reflects on the internecine struggles within the Nazis, Wegener describes them as "eating each other."

> They want to be the agents, not the victims, of history. They identify with God's power and believe they are Godlike. This is their basic madness. They are overcome by some archetype; their egos have expanded psychotically so that they cannot tell where they begin and the godhead leaves off. It is not hubris, not pride; it is inflation of the ego to its ultimate – confusion between him who worships and that which is worshipped. Man has not eaten God; God has eaten man. (Dick 1992: 41)

In a very immediate way, ingestion conveys the political chaos in more physical and emotional terms. In fact, one of the key scenes in the novel takes place at a dinner table. Paul Kasoura, an upcoming young Japanese executive, and his beautiful wife Betty invite Robert Childan, an antique dealer, to dinner. The meal becomes an occasion for a subdued but tense clash of cultures. Planning to follow what she supposes to be the authentic American customs, Betty decides to go for T-bone steak, baked potato with a sauce of sour cream and chives, and a salad with artichokes, avocados, and a blue cheese dressing. As hors d'oeuvres, she serves cheese on small crackers. Before dinner, Childan was actually afraid they would present him with "a Japanese meal, the dishes of mixed greens and meats of which he had eaten so much since the war. And the unending sea foods. He had gotten so that he could no longer abide shrimp or any other shellfish" (Dick 1992: 111)

The harmony, the proportion, the balance, and the peacefulness emanating from the couple fascinate Childan. Japanese culture seems to be particularly at ease with symbols, and constitutes a powerful opposition to the chaos heralded by the Germans. When Childan and Paul Kasoura start politely arguing about politics, tension slowly builds up. It turns out that the Kasouras, nostalgically into jazz and all kinds of Americana, are far more interested in the past of the U.S. than is Childan himself, who is all wrapped up in his admiration for the Nazis. Childan reveals his racist feelings towards black, Slavic, and Jewish people. Reflecting on his dinner with the Kasouras, he muses:

Face facts. I'm trying to pretend that these Japanese and I are alike. But observe: even when I burst out as to my gratification that they won the war, that my nation lost – there's still no common ground. What words mean to me is sharp contrast vis-à-vis them. Their brain is different. Soul likewise. Witness them drinking from English bone china cups, eating with US silver, listening to Negro style of music. It's all on the surface. Advantage of wealth and power makes this available to them, but it's ersatz as the day is long. Even the Yi Jing, which they've forced down our throats; it's Chinese. Borrowed from way back when. Whom are they fooling? Themselves? Pilfer customs right and left, wear, eat, talk, walk, as for instance consuming with gusto baked potatoes served with sour cream and chives, old-fashioned American dish added to their haul. But nobody is fooled, I can tell you. (Dick 1992: 143)

Childan concludes that his hosts are not exactly human, and he decides not to try to impress them any longer, or to go along with their political ideas, even if that means to let chill fall on the meal. The event that had been planned to favor sharing and exchange reveals instead the actual distance between two cultures. In his uncompromising hate, Childan realizes that food can also be used to fabricate artificial identities and to assume positions that are far from transparent. At the time of the publication of the novel, in the early 1960s, the echoes of the Cold War and the fear of the Yellow Peril certainly enhanced the emotional impact of the narration.

The table – and eating in general – becomes an arena where cultural, social, and political struggles find visible expression. After all, what we manage to put on the table and how we do it reflect economic and political relations, as well as the dominance of technology and science.

Food has played a relevant – even if sometimes almost invisible – role in many sci-fi works. I believe this connection is revealing. Food is an important element in any society, determining many aspects of production, distribution and consumption, and providing fundamental institutions and customs. It is virtually impossible to isolate food from the social, economic, and political structures of a human group. The act of eating, located between the biological and the symbolic, allows sci-fi authors to analyze a large spectrum of phenomena, often with a certain comic impishness. Imagination is a fundamental dimension of the style and the content of science fiction, encompassing all aspects of human life.

Ingestion and consumption turn into titillating subjects for science fiction, a genre that, by imagining alternatives to present realities, constitutes an intrinsic critique of the status quo. More or less gently, it prods its audience to face the fact that the world in which they live is neither natural nor absolute. This approach is not unique to sci-fi: after all, hypotheses and projections about the future are a common ingredient of politics. Candidates up for election try to entice voters by offering themselves as possible substitutes to the political establishments in power. To achieve their goals, they often refer to images and descriptions of the upcoming time when the measures and reforms they propose are implemented. Political propaganda produces projections about the future, but to a certain extent so do activists, administrative bodies, corporations, urban planners, and even scientists and scholars. Yet, the imaginative prodding we get from science fiction is quite different, as historian Warren Belasco aptly points out in his book *Meals to Come: a History of the Future of Food*:

> Whereas think tank forecasters have had considerable difficulty conceptualizing beyond their own establishment values, paradigms, and experiences, speculative-fiction writers have freely allowed for radical discontinuities, wild cards, surprise turns, near misses, lucky breaks, unexpected decisions, and even chaos when they create futuristic scenarios. … Speculative stories have also given voice to those who are not well represented by mainstream policy analysis – especially radical environmentalists, socialists, and feminists. (Belasco 2006: xi)

Since science fiction reminds us that the world we inhabit could have been different, and could still be different, movies, comics, and books succeed in evoking realities that are at the same time foreign and fascinating. If the authors' goal is to bring the audience to temporarily suspend their disbelief, they have to create worlds that are credible enough to allow a certain sense of familiarity. Although discomfort can actually facilitate reflection, a sense of complete estrangement would be counterproductive, alienating the attention and the emotional involvement of the audience. To achieve these effects, sci-fi has employed food and eating both at the forefront of the narration and as secondary subplots. By doing so, this genre helps us to achieve a better understanding of the relevance of food for the stability of political and social structures.

At all times and places, human societies have constantly needed socially sanctioned forms of escape from reality, spaces and moment of distraction that nevertheless can also function as forms of critique of the status quo. As literary critic Carl Freedman has noticed, science fiction tends to be self-reflective; it doesn't consider its structures, its narrative mechanisms, and its tenets as unproblematic. Freedman, acknowledging his cultural debt towards Darko Suvin, the literary critic who first clearly stated that science fiction is a genre of cognitive estrangement and stimulation, suggests "the science-fictional world is not only one different in time or place from our own, but one whose chief interest is precisely the difference that such difference makes. It is also a world whose difference is concretized within a cognitive continuum" (Freedman 2000, 43; Suvin 1979). In novels, comic books, and movies, the background of the plot is never neutral. Since it takes time to understand and to get used to the unfamiliar elements and the overall environment, they stimulate readers and viewers to reflect on the functioning, the values, and the historical and social development of the fictional reality, often urging them to make comparisons between the world they know and the imaginary world. The difference between the two is likely to elicit further thinking; in this sense science fiction can become a true critique of the present at all levels, provoking modern audiences to question received ideas about reality, identity, race, and culture.

Depending on different historical moments, various cultural environments, and personal vicissitudes of the authors, the scenarios offered in science fiction can be either utopian or dystopian: they imagine the best and worse that could happen to contemporary societies, pointing out the elements in our present that could become future dreams or nightmares.

As we have already mentioned, food is prominently featured in sci-fi literature, often in connection with changes and evolutions in science and technology. One of the recurring menaces that lurch in many dystopian visions is the emergence of absolute and cruel powers, capable of literally sucking the life out of our bodies. As in the case of cannibals and vampires, the possibility that humanity itself is transformed into food constitutes the underlying theme of many narratives. The *Matrix* trilogy can arguably be considered one of the most renowned and most visually intense projections of this kind of dim future. In the first episode of the series, viewers are presented an unmistakable image of the machines keeping humans in suspended animation, attached to pipes and cables to create energy they can feed upon, with their minds living in a virtual world where humans can picture themselves living free and fulfilling lives.

The theme is far from being new. Already in the 1973 movie *Soylent Green*, inspired by the 1966 novel by Harry Harrison *Make Room! Make Room!*, humans are transformed into food and fed to other human beings in a fake attempt to fight scarcity and the consequences of overpopulation (Forster 2004). The reality is much scarier: a small group of rich and powerful citizens have secured the monopoly of the scarce fresh ingredients, and maintain their privilege by force and shrewdness. The lower classes are debased to the level of produce (Belasco 2006: 134).

A similar premise constitutes the backbone of the *Blade* movie trilogy, starring Wesley Snipes as the title character, and based on a Marvel Comics series created in 1973 by Marv Wolfman and Gene Colan. The movies walk the fine and blurry line between sci-fi and horror, but the futuristic design, the high-tech weapons, and even the technology-driven villains seem to point toward the former genre. Blade is a "day walker," a vampire who can live in the light and fights against other vampires who have created a parallel and secret culture with ancient traditions, which survives by preying on humankind. In the first movie of the series, released in 1998, Blade fights against the educated vampire Frost, who seeks to transform humanity into living cattle. One of the deleted scenes (available on the DVD version of the movie) shows human bodies kept alive just to produce blood. The vampire supreme council, which is supposed to be the political body of the monstrous creatures, rejects this use of human beings, sticking to their secretive lifestyle and refusing to transform their killing into an organized, industrial activity. To overcome the ancient ways of the elders, Frost tries to bring into life an unbeatable monster, thirsty and without limits, that can only be freed by the incantations kept in the ancient texts of the vampires. Through the literate Frost, who can decipher ancient documents whose meaning has got lost in time, the sophisticated vampire culture acknowledges its own limits and brings about its own destruction, surrendering to the devastating, famished drive that actually constitutes its foundation despite its attempts at denying it.

In the third movie of the series, *Blade Trinity* (2004), the vampires actually manage to create a blood factory with the help of conniving human authorities. Blade uncovers the illegal operation in a huge hangar, where a human scientist controls a complex high-tech system that keeps humans in suspended animation inside transparent pouches (not unlike the ones used for IV in hospitals) so that they can produce blood that is drained from them and packaged.

In these movies, the voracious and limitless consumption drive that haunts us is embodied no longer in single monstrous creatures, but in complex systems that rely on technology. Unlike horror, science fiction as a genre does not necessarily linger on gore to scare, but rather it insists on other elements that allow viewers and readers to think about wider issues.

Alimentary Havoc

What would happen if society as we know it collapsed? What if all our worst fears about our future came true? Science fiction as a genre has often tried to answer these questions with many interesting works that deal with the dysfunctional realities that could be the result of humankind's foolishness and lack of vision. Under those conditions, food offers authors the possibility to convey ideas, emotions, and even to elicit gut reactions to the events narrated, in a very direct way. Eating, hunger, and desire are familiar experiences to all audiences, and very easy to relate to. In the construction of the fictional reality, they help the audience to suspend disbelief and be sucked into the plot.

Author George Orwell was apparently very aware of these dynamics when he created one of the most famous examples of dystopian science fiction, the classic *Nineteen Eighty-Four* (published in 1949), where eating plays a central role in the plot. The world is divided into three superpowers, Oceania, Eurasia, and East Asia, all founded basically on the same totalitarian ideology under different names. The three mega-nations wage constant war against each other, in order to consume the production surplus generated by extreme forms of capitalism. To achieve its goals, the governments operate to instill hate for the enemy in their citizens and to control their minds by constant monitoring through two-ways screens, while employing the most effective and chilling forms of propaganda.

The main character, Winston Smith, works in Oceania's Ministry of Truth, the organism in charge of erasing any element of the past that could be detrimental to the regime, and of rewriting history according to the newest dictates of the Party. In the effort to overcome its historical enemies, Oceania has created a food rationing system that is, of course, not applied to the highest spheres of the party, but only to its lower echelons and to the "proles," the workers outside the Party. Nevertheless, Winston just cannot accept the fact that the world has always been like this.

… Winston had taken up his spoon and was dabbling in the pale-coloured gravy that dribbled across the table, drawing a long streak of it out into a pattern. He meditated resentfully on the physical texture of life. Had it always been like this? Had food always tasted like this? He looked around the canteen. A low-ceilinged, crowded room, its walls grimy from the contact of innumerable bodies; battered metal tables and chairs, placed so close together that you sat with elbows touching; bent spoons, dented trays, coarse white mugs; all surfaces greasy, grime in every crack; and a sourish, composite smell of bad gin and bad coffee and metallic stew and dirty clothes. Always in your stomach and in your skin there was a sort of protest, a feeling that you had been cheated of something that you had a right to. It was true that he had no memories of anything greatly different. … Why should one feel it to be intolerable unless one had some kind of ancestral memory that things had once been different? (Orwell 1983: 52)

Winston's sensory and emotional memories, elicited by taste and food, are stronger than any propaganda; they work like a compass directing him towards a past of which he has no clear rational recollection. When he meets Julia, a member of the Junior Anti-Sex league (of course, sex is banned since it is considered a dangerous distraction from the ideological goals set by the party), one of their first secret dates takes place in the countryside. The environment in itself provides unexpected stimulations to Winston's numbed senses, but Julia manages to bring back startling memories

Then, as though touching her waist had reminded her of something, she felt in the pocket of her overalls and produced a small slab of chocolate. She broke it in half and gave one of the pieces to Winston. Even before she had taken it he knew by the smell that it was very unusual chocolate. It was dark and shiny, and was wrapped in silver paper. Chocolate normally was dull-brown crumbly stuff that tasted, as nearly as one could describe it, like the smoke of a rubbish fire. But at some time or another he had tasted chocolate like the piece she had given him. The first whiff of its scent had stirred up some memory which he could not pin down, but which was powerful and troubling. (Orwell 1983: 101)

With its taste and scents, chocolate, a material element, ignites a process that will lead to a closer relationship between the two characters, expressed by the growing need to share physical intimacy and, of course, real food. Julia and Winston end up renting a room in a poor neighborhood of London, hoping to stay away from the oppressive control of the government. Much of their time together is spent eating and having sex, two activities supposedly out of political control in the "proles" world.

She fell on her knees, threw open the bag, and tumbled out some spanners and a screwdriver that filled the top part of it. Underneath were a number of neat paper packets. The first packet that she passed to Winston had a strange and yet vaguely familiar feeling. It was filled with some kind of heavy, sand-like stuff which yielded wherever you touched it.

"It isn't sugar?" he said.

"Real sugar. Not saccharine, sugar. And here's a loaf of bread – proper white bread, not our bloody stuff – and a little pot of jam. And here's a tin of milk – but look! This is the one I'm really proud of. I had to wrap a bit of sacking round it, because –"

But she did not need to tell him why she had wrapped it up. The smell was already filling the room, a rich hot smell which seemed like an emanation from his early childhood, but which one did occasionally meet with even now, blowing down a passage-way before a door slammed, or diffusing itself mysteriously in a crowded street, sniffed for an instant then lost again.

"It's coffee," he murmured, "real coffee."

"It's Inner Party coffee. There's a whole kilo here," she said. . . .

Julia got out of bed, pulled on her overalls, and made the coffee. The smell that rose from the saucepan was so powerful and exciting that they shut the window lest anybody outside should notice it and become inquisitive. What was even better than the taste of the coffee was the silky texture given to it by the sugar, a thing Winston had almost forgotten after years of saccharine. (Orwell 1983: 117, 120)

Eventually Winston succeeds in patching together his forgotten past: his memories about chocolate turn out to be connected with his childhood, when his mother brought back a piece of the sweet substance for him and his sister. He had snatched all the chocolate from their hands and run away. When he returned back home, they had disappeared. Unfortunately the repossession of Winston's past does not save him from being discovered by the omnipresent Big Brother in the end.

Throughout the novel, food vividly conveys the bleakness and the oppressiveness of a fictional political system that Orwell had modeled on the horrors of Nazi Germany and the Stalinist USSR, while stressing that only individuals, with their past and memories, with their lived bodies, with their emotions and sensations, are able to resist to totalitarianism.

The underlying theme of the contrast between market-oriented economies and centrally planned ones is translated into different systems of food production, distribution, and consumption, easier to grasp for his audience than any complex political or scientific explanation.

A similar scenario constitutes the background for the adventures of John Spartan, played by Sylvester Stallone, in the 1993 movie *Demolition Man*. Following a destructive social upheaval, order is restored in San Angeles (an urban agglomerate stretching over the whole of California) by Dr. Cocteau, who has established a squeaky-clean and curse-free, but ultimately boring, society. The theme is not at all new: variants of what Warren Belasco defines as "soft" dystopias, where freedom and personal initiative have been bartered with order and security, have populated sci-fi since its heydays, starting from H.G. Wells's 1899 novel *When the Sleeper Wakes* (Belasco 2006, 99, 121). In Stallone's movie, all restaurants have become

Taco Bell, serving only meatless and saltless dishes by law, to protect the citizens' health. Spartan, thawed from a Cryo-Prison where he has spent many years frozen in a block of ice, wakes up in an apparently safe but soulless future. The appearance of peace is shattered when Spartan finds out about a whole parallel society of free men who live underground, dealing with food scarcity and harsh conditions. Spartan finds himself totally at ease underground, in a world more similar to his old one. When he sees a stall where a Latino woman who can hardly speak English is selling hamburgers, he gladly orders one and bites into it, relishing the taste; even the discovery that the meat is actually from rats does not faze him too much. Eventually he manages to denounce Dr. Cocteau's totalitarian plans and to bring freedom back, including the option to eat according to one's desires. In *Demolition Man*'s dystopia, safe and nutritionally balanced but tasteless dishes cannot compare with the messy, smelly but tastier meals of the past. Food preferences and availability become symbols for the fight against the control from political authorities over one's personal choices, an issue that is acquiring urgency in U.S. public debate, especially when it comes to obesity, the presence of trans-fats in food, and the sale of sugar-laden carbonated drinks and other unhealthy snacks in schools.

The destiny of humankind after major global mayhem is also the premise of Stephen King's 1978 novel *The Stand*, a chilling but wildly successful bestseller, despite its massive size. A virus genetically engineered by the Army escapes into the open, wiping out most of humankind. A few survivors, genetically immune to the disease, have to find ways to rebuild their lives. Once again, food plays a major role in keeping the survivors sane, by providing memories on which individuals can anchor their identity, and by offering occasions of shared enjoyment with others, a first step towards rebuilding new communities. As in many of King's narratives, it is everyday dishes, common items, and even junk food that take the center stage. Normality is described in terms of what consumers can usually find in the aisles of any American supermarket.

Octavia Butler's most famous novel, the *Parable of the Sower* (1993), focuses on similar themes but from a totally different point of view. This African American woman's work is far from what would usually be considered pulp science fiction. Her style and the topics she tackled actually made her a very respected figure on the international literary scene.

In her novel, there is no need for a virus to cause havoc: it is society that collapses on itself because of greed and social unrest. America has broken down into almost independent gated communities under constant siege from those less fortunate, trying to get their share of wealth and, of course, food. The story is narrated by Lauren Olamina, a young woman who, born of a drug-damaged mother, suffers from "organic delusional syndrome," which makes her feel what she sees others are feeling or what she believes they feel. Nothing can be worse when so much suffering is around. The families in the compound where she lives try to fight the scarcity of food by growing fruit and vegetables. It is a difficult task for suburbanites, used to buying products from supermarkets: they need to learn from scratch what can be grown in orchards or backyards, and the fruit of their labor is under constant threat from thieves and hungry marauders. Lauren's father, a preacher in the community, even teaches people how to use acorns to make bread, overcoming their initial disgust. With the political body crumbling down, extreme consumerism and the free market show their ugly side, hitting the weakest portions of society while causing scarcity and, later, hunger.

As the price of food gets higher and higher, Lauren assembles a survival pack that she hides not to frighten the others. She gives a precise list of what she keeps in the survival pack: besides a canteen and a plastic bottle where she always keep fresh water, "a couple of spoons and forks, a can opener, my pocket knife, packets of acorn flour, dried fruit, roasted nuts and edible seeds, dried milk, a little sugar and salt ... a lot of plantable raw seed" (O. Butler 1993: 71). Food is the only hope for survival and seeds are the promise of future crops.

When Lauren's community is finally invaded, the young girl is as equally affected by the sight of the destroyed crops as by the dead people. She starts traveling, facing the dangers of a land without rules and principles, where all that counts is survival and, consequently, securing the next meal. The persistent focus on the need to eat while on the road somehow reminds us of the "Okies" in John Steinbeck's 1939 novel *Grapes of Wrath*, except that this time, in an interesting reversal, it is the "California trash" who try to sneak into a promised land, namely Canada. Furthermore, while in Steinbeck's novel the poor and the humble maintain their dignity and help each other whenever they can, out of solidarity, in Butler's dim future the social fabric is totally frayed, everybody against everybody: "Children cried, played, squatted, did everything except eat. Almost no one ate while walking. I saw a couple of people drink from canteens. They took quick, furtive gulps, as though they were doing something shameful – or something dangerous" (O. Butler 1993: 158). Water also becomes increasingly more difficult to get, because of the danger of poisoning from chemical residue like pesticide and fuel. Many travelers react to the lack of food by reverting to a state of semi-cannibalism, without killing other humans to eat them but limiting themselves to take advantage of "road kills."

Chaos seems perfectly at home in science fiction, especially when different cultural systems clash against each other. Food and sex embody these contrasts, revealing at the same time the constructed and unstable nature of other social classifications such as race and gender.

These themes assume a pivotal role in a novel by Samuel R. Delany, *Dahlgreen* (1975), where the close ties between desire, sex, the body, culture, and politics are revealed in a language and a style that in themselves defy all our preconceptions and our ideas about what science fiction novels should be and read like.

In the novel, nothing seems to make actual sense. The Kidd, the main character, appears out of nowhere, and it never becomes clear where he comes from, or where he is going. Neither do we get to know where the city of Bellona, the background of the novel, is located, in what point in time, nor the rules that regulate it. The narration itself is not linear; at times we have the disturbing feeling that the plot is missing crucial elements and that the author is not revealing important facts. Delany uninterruptedly neutralizes our attempts at making sense of the strange and estranging reality.

Dahlgren is different from other apocalyptic novels, such as the *Parable of the Sower* by Octavia E. Butler or *The Stand* by Stephen King. Both Butler and King construct narratives of migration from a catastrophe caused by human failure (a lethal virus, social unrest caused by the excesses of capitalism). The destination is a different land, where a new society will be rebuilt. On the other hand, Samuel R. Delany creates a reality without a tomorrow and a yesterday, without any goals. Bellona is a metaphor for what cannot be made sense of, for what continues to undermine every attempt to restore a damaged or threatened cultural system. It would seem that Bellona is the only place on Earth where strange events happen, even in Nature (or in what is usually considered natural). The city is shrouded in a perennial fog that dissipates only to allow the view of the most disturbing natural phenomena such as a second moon, or a falling sun. These elements would not be disruptive in a context where it is clear that the reality the author constructs is supposed to have two moons or a falling sun, as happens in other science fiction novels. Instead, Delany succeeds in giving us the impression that the reality of Bellona is our own reality, and that the action unravels in the here and the now of planet Earth. The estrangement is thus even more intense.

In Bellona, money has lost its value, and society as we know it no longer exists. Against this confusing background, food and eating habits are used to bring back a certain order into chaos, even if every group in the disintegrating social fabric seems to develop different ideas about it. Provisions are plentiful, at least at the beginning of the novel, since many people have abandoned the city. Shops are there to be emptied and groceries can be found in cellars and pantries in empty houses. In the only bar left, drinks are given for free. Food constitutes, together with sex, a key element of social behavior, a mirror for habits and culture. People try to make sense of their lives in creative ways, and their different arrangements are evident in the way they consume food. The Richards, a typical bourgeois family (with an edge, as the frequent screams heard from their apartment suggest), are stubbornly clinging to their old polite manners. Their dinners still follow the rituals of the past. Ms. Richards declares to the Kidd:

> Do you know how I thought of this moving? As a space, a gap, a crack in which some terrible thing might get in and destroy it, us, my home. You have to take it apart, then put it back together. I really felt as though some dirt, or filth, or horrible rot might get in while it was being reassembled and start a terrible decay. ... I know about eating, sleeping, how it must be done if people are going to be comfortable. I have to have a place where I can cook the foods I want; a place that looks the way I want it to look: a place that can be a real home. (Delany 1996: 227)

Some obscure rotting agent that can seep through any crevice threatens the reassuring order of domesticity, including its material aspect of cooking and eating. Reality and culture are about to burst at the seams, letting chaos penetrate and destroy, cannibalize the unstable and always reconstructed balance of society.

To avoid this, Ms. Richards tries to re-create dishes she knows with whatever ingredient she can find, elaborating original, though often disgusting, interpretations of old recipes. Whipped cream takes greenish hues; different kinds of condensed soups are mixed together. All kinds of mismatched china and silver are displayed on the tablecloth, while conversations seem to be particularly intent at avoiding any reference to the not-so-appealing reality outside their apartment.

On the other hand, in order to avoid total lack of sense, other survivors adopt a flower-power hippie-like lifestyle, roaming free in the park and keeping busy with social projects, such as digging latrines or building looms, share food within the community and with others, even with the Scorpions, a gang of rough, oddly clad youngsters. These punks *ante litteram* live in packs, embodying the very spirit of Bellona, its lack of rules, and its intrinsic disorder. They consume food in the most inordinate, uncouth manner.

> The Scorpion took the fork in his fist, swept through the mixture, spilling some, and, fork still in his mouth, chewed, with grains about his lips. Still chewing, he grinned. "Hey, that's okay." (Delany 1996: 184)

> "Baby!" Dragon lady bellowed; her shoulder shook; nobody stopped doing anything. "Adam!" She flung the words up like grenades. "Bring some more food out for 'em!" "Here you go!" Baby, still naked, pushed between the people at the door, leaning (dangerously) with steaming plates. "This is yours." Kid ignored the dirty thumb denting what must have been a hash of canned vegetables (he pulled the fork out of where it had been buried: corn, peas, okra fell off) and (he tasted the first mouthful) meat. (Spam?) (Delany 1996: 444)

Yet, in the general confusion that reigns over Bellona, where all the boundaries of sex, gender, race and class are blurred, even the Scorpions need some sort of goal. They organize the "runs," when they depredate some shops, looking for anything that can be interesting or enticing, almost trying to melt pleasurably in the chaos that enshrouds everything.

With time, though, food grows scarcer, revealing the impossibility of boundless enjoyment. People start to battle over food, but the announced and always impending final shock never arrives. Rather, reality in Bellona seems to collapse slowly, crumbling down to its primordial elements. The novel ends as abruptly as it starts, with the Kidd leaving Bellona without any clear destination.

Power and the Body

The evident relationship between social structures and the production, distribution, and consumption of food has constituted an ongoing theme in science fiction, revealing intimate and less obvious connections between individual bodies and eating that allow us to understand a different side of the political.

We cannot forget that certain aspects of culture are first and foremost experienced through the body. The way we walk, sit, and move, even our proximity to one another, are not random but follow clear – if unwritten – rules, as anybody who has been uncomfortable around somebody acting differently knows well. These bodily expressions are codified and regulated like any other feature within social and cultural life. They are signs within systems of communication, providing us with plenty of information about others. Eating and drinking habits are also far from being arbitrary: they fall under the category of those "techniques of the body" that the French anthropologist and sociologist Marcel Mauss had already outlined in 1935. Mauss defined them as "the ways in which from society to society men know how to use their bodies" (Mauss 1973: 70). These techniques are not innate, since children need to learn them slowly and sometimes painfully by imitating adults and by being taught. The correct behavior at the table during meals, the control of bodily functions, even the gestures related to eating, would all be the result of three converging factors: biological constraints and needs, psychological elements such as personal idiosyncrasies and styles, and the social environment, which exerts its influence through training, education, status, prestige, fashion, and – we could add today – the media. Parents are well aware of the influence that TV and video games have on the development and the behavior of their children, their food choices, their likes and dislikes. Mauss concluded that "there is perhaps no 'natural' way for the adult. ... Let us go further: one of the reasons why these series [of actions] may more easily be assembled in the individual is precisely because they are assembled by and for social authority" (Mauss 1973: 74; 85) We can recognize in Mauss's reflection the seed of the concept of *habitus*, which the French sociologist French Bourdieu introduced later on to explain personal and cultural preferences and taste. Bourdieu described *habitus* as

> both the generative principle of objective classifiable judgments and the systems of classification (*principium divisionis*) of these practices. It is in the relationship between the two capacities that define the *habitus*, the capacity to produce classifiable practices and works, and the capacity to differentiate and appreciate these practices and products (taste), that the represented social world, i.e., the space of life-styles, is constituted. (Bourdieu 1984: 170)

In other words, our habits, practices, and ideas about what we do and how we act are a tool to give meaning and regulate the otherwise messy activities of the body, and at the same time constitute prescriptions and standards that tell us what actions and behaviors are acceptable, and what kind of persons embody them.

Both Mauss and Bourdieu, among others, acknowledged the cultural, social, and political implications of food, which are crucial both at the individual level of personal identitifications and at the aggregate level of families, communities of all size, and even nations. At any rate, the body is far from being "natural." Instead, the ways it is conceived, it develops, it is controlled and disciplined, identified and interpreted, are inherently political. Anthropologist Arjun Appadurai has observed:

> The body calls for disciplines that are repetitious, or at least periodic. This is not because the body is everywhere the same biological fact and thus demands the same disciplines. On the contrary, because the body is an intimate arena for the practices of reproduction, it is an ideal site for the inscription of social disciplines, disciplines that can be widely varied. ... The techniques of the body, however peculiar, innovative, and antisocial, need to become social disciplines, parts of some *habitus*, free of artifice or external coercion, in order to take their full power. (Appadurai 1996: 67)

Who decides what are the correct "techniques of the body"? Who holds the power to determine what is the correct manner to sit at the table or the comfortable distance between two people when they talk?

Just as sex and gender have been widely used as arenas for political struggles aimed at controlling the individual, also food can constitute a vehicle to influence or even manage bodies in their most intimate dimensions.

What is the source of this authority? For the purpose at hand, it may be effective to consider power as diffused and ubiquitous, not necessarily connected with specific institutions. The French philosopher and historian Michel Foucault has given a very fitting definition of power.

> Power must be understood in the first instance as a multiplicity of force relations ... as the process which, through ceaseless struggles and confrontations, transforms, strengthens or reverses them: as the support which these force relations find in one another, thus forming a chain or a system, or on the contrary, the disjunction and contradictions which isolate them from one another; and lastly, as the strategies in which they take effect, whose general design or institutional crystallization is embodied in the state apparatus, in the formulations of the law, in the various social hegemonies. (Foucault 1990: 93)

Power and the principles it promotes are not always imposed on the subject from the outside, but are materialized through norms and regulations in the body itself. Although we perceive our body as natural – we are actually *taught* to perceive it as such – it would be naïve to assume that these crucial elements of the embodied experience are irrelevant for any power agency (as diffused as it can be). Power needs to be reinforced with legitimacy, so that its subjects voluntarily adhere to its dictates and rules. The only way to do this is to employ the narratives, prescriptions, objects, and practices, including the "techniques of the body," that facilitate the transmission and diffusion of symbols and ideas in the public space of communicative and material exchanges. The way we think of and experience our physical needs, the way we choose, store, prepare, cook, ingest, digest, and excrete food, are far from being neutral or natural. These elements all share an ideological function, in the sense that they tend to propose, legitimize, and strengthen specific values and goals for society at large. They also reinforce the ideals of order and rationality that still constitute the core of most political orders, hiding the core elements of violence and disorder that in different degrees underlie any social structure.

These subtle forms of control are usually excluded from the public discourse to create the illusion of the neutrality and naturalness of a body that, instead, constitutes the battlefield for cultural, social, and political struggles.

Dissolving the Body

Since its beginnings as a genre, science fiction has paid attention to the subtle influences that politics and society exert on our bodies. As a matter of fact, novels, comic books and movies have often illustrated transformations caused or induced in our bodies by technology, environmental catastrophes, and genetic mutations. Stan Lee and his collaborators at Marvel Comics have created a plethora of superheroes who are a visible expression of physical mutability and instability, and who have recently acquired a second life thanks to an apparently never-ending series of blockbuster movies. Following exposure to cosmic rays in outer space, Mr. Fantastic and the Thing of the Fantastic 4 have seen their bodies changed, respectively, into elastic matter and a rocky mass. Similarly, the Hulk was born from exposure to Gamma rays during a scientific experiment. The X-Men are a group of powerful mutants, some sporting visible body changes: the Ice Man can turn into ice, the Angel, as the name suggests, has wings, while Wolverine has his skeleton implanted with adamantium, an extremely hard metal, and can threaten his enemies with retractable claws grafted onto his hands. In an everyday reality where plastic surgery, tattoos, piercing, and other kind of body changes have become a common occurrence, the fictional character of the sci-fi cyborg, part human being and part machine, does not seem so far-fetched as it was when it first became popular in pop culture in the 1980s. After all, contemporary medicine actually manages to substitute whole parts, if necessary. The second placement in a 400-meter competition in July 2007 at the Golden Gala in Rome of 21-year-old Australian Oscar Pistorius, racing on carbon fiber blades attached below his knees, had a huge impact all around the world.

One way to make bodies change is, of course, by eating. Consumers are often acutely aware of the dangers connected with ingestion: growing fears of allergies, intoxication, poisoning, or even cancer all play a huge role in the acceptance of processed items and of ingredients containing genetically modified organisms. Various food scares (the avian flu, E. Coli and "mad cow disease," just to mention a few) have left deep scars in the collective imagination of the West. The consequences of technology on what we eat, and indirectly on our bodies, are quite intuitive: whoever controls food has a solid clutch on our physical existence.

Science fiction has always been sensitive to these themes. We already find them in the short 1904 novel by H.G. Wells, *The Food of the Gods*. The plot revolves around the invention of a substance, officially called Herakleophorbia (food of Hercules), but usually referred to as Boomfood, which accelerates the growth process of all living beings. The novel is a comical, almost grotesque, but in the end tragic reflection about the impact of science and politics on food.

The substance, which initially is supposed to be tested only on chickens, is inadvertently diffused in the environment, so that soon huge hens and ferocious giant rats plague a small village in the English countryside. Eventually the Boomfood is given to children, creating a generation of giants. The locals try to defend themselves while pretending that everything is normal, unable to admit that reality as they know it is being devastated. A whole nation tries to convince itself that there is no mutation in the essential order of things, that they are just witnessing mere accidental glitches of reality, to the point that they start considering bigness as a natural phenomenon, almost forgetting how things were before.

The Boomfood is a metaphor for the inevitable transformations brought about by technology. Wells seems to suggest that there is no such thing as Nature as a place of balance and order, that the "naturalness" of food itself is just a cultural construction. What we usually consider as "natural reality" is just one possibility, defining itself against the background of ever-impending chaos. The invention of Boomfood would not be bad in itself, but it becomes dangerous when it is mismanaged by men excessively taken with personal interests or political goals.

> The Food had been at first for the great mass of mankind a distant marvel, and now it was coming home to every threshold and threatening, pressing against and distorting the whole order of life. It blocked this, it overturned that, it changed natural products, and by changing natural products it stopped employments and threw men out of work by the hundred thousand; it swept over boundaries and turned the world of trade into a world of cataclysm; no wonder mankind hated it. (Wells undated: 146)

Although writing at the beginning of the twentieth century, Wells describes here a very contemporary situation. Nowadays many consumers try to get better control on what they eat and the politics that surround it, but at the same time many others refuse to even think about what their food actually is and about the consequences of scientific research on their eating habits and their bodies. Rather, they prefer to stick to the almost virtual reality of the comforting images constructed and offered by tradition, family culture, and the marketing department of food corporations working to sell their products.

Isaac Asimov, one of the undisputed masters of science fiction, tackled the theme of the body and food in *The Gods Themselves*, published in 1972. In a parallel universe, which is exchanging energy with our world through a positronic pump, living beings belong to two categories: the Hard Ones and the Soft Ones. In turn, the Soft Ones come in three kinds: the Rationals, the Emotionals, and the Parentals. The three subspecies are morphologically and functionally distinct, but totally complementary, to the point that they live in Triads. The Emotionals, female, are ethereal, can expand and become thinner, and nourish themselves by absorbing energy directly from the sun on the surface of their planet. Here they roam in herds, getting flat to expose as much body surface as possible to the satisfying rays. The Rationals, males, trained by the Hard Ones to think, learn, and study, are the thickest of all the Soft Ones. "Their thick substance absorbed food so rapidly, they were satisfied with a simple walk in the sun, while Emotionals basked for hours at a time, curling and thinning as though deliberately to lengthen the task" (Asimov 1984: 82). The Parentals, males, give birth and take care of the offspring, who are conceived in a mysterious but extremely pleasurable melting process where the three components of the Triad lose conscience and fuse into each other.

Later on in the narration, it becomes clear that, during the melting, Triads temporarily constitutes Hard Ones, and after generating three offsprings they turn into Hard Ones for good. The enjoyable fusion becomes possible only if the three components get all the food they need to melt. In this context, individuals rooted in rigid singularities are unable to reach the state of fertile bliss. In the fictional life of the Soft Ones, the elements that are usually considered as components of human nature (rationality, emotions, motivations) are split into multiple bodily incarnations. Also the usual sexual arrangements are subverted: the Parentals, who generate offspring, are male. Asimov seems to point to the intrinsic instability and lack of unity of human nature as we know it.

In the novel, the most interesting reflections concerning food come from Dua, one of the Emotionals, who throughout the narrative shows ambivalent feelings about nutrition and her body, almost echoing the fears and convictions of an anorexic. She knows that by accepting food she would be more open to melting, but she also feels that by so doing she would lose her individuality and give up control over herself. She has heard about experiments aimed at making the food/energy better, but she is extremely suspicious: "Would they improve it? Would they make it taste better? Even delicious? And would she have to eat it then and fill herself with it till the full sensation gave her an almost uncontrollable desire to melt? She feared that self-generating desire" (Asimov 1984: 96).

Finally the Parental in her Triad, stubbornly determined to generate another offspring, succeeds in having her absorb the energy coming from the parallel universe through the positronic pump. In the act of incorporating elements from a remote world, the Emotional Dua becomes aware of the limits of her own world, of its destructiveness and cruelty. As a matter of fact, the Hard Ones are actually taking energy from the parallel universe, perfectly knowing that this eventually will lead to its total destruction. Dua is willing to destroy her whole reality to save the parallel one, and she expresses her rage in terms of her relationship to food.

> Why should she care about cold, she thought, when she had been fattened in order that she might do her duty – fattened, mind and body? After that, cold and starvation were almost her friends. ... She was conscious of hunger, continuously, all the more so since it seemed to tire her to remain in the rock. It was as though she were being punished for all the long time in which she haunted the Sunset and ate so skimpily. (Asimov 1984: 148, 161)

Interestingly, the Hard Ones seem not to be concerned with food or reproduction. Detached from the lower strata of the bodily experience, in the metaphorical and physical hardness of their unity, in their solid and unbreakable subjectivity, they do not have any second thoughts about destroying a whole universe. Identity politics, with their tendency to transform particular claims into absolutes, seem bound to annihilation.

In Asimov's novel, the openness of the body and its indefiniteness, sex, and ingestion are not subtly ironic, but acquire an eerie, haunting aftertaste, revealing the inconsistency of regulated identities and, as a consequence, the relativity of any society based on those premises. The novel makes clear that the physical structure of a subject, far from being natural, is one with his or her cultural and social arrangements. Therefore, it is politically relevant.

The Liberating Grotesque

> ... to consecrate inventive freedom, to permit the combination of a variety of different elements and their rapprochement, to liberate from the prevailing point of view of the world, from conventions and established truths, from clichés, from all that is humdrum and universally accepted ... to realize the relative nature of all that exists, and to enter a completely new order of things. (Bakhtin 1984: 34)

Does not this description perfectly fit with what science fiction is, or should be at its best? Yet, the quote is not taken from a critical appraisal about this genre, but from the Russian literary critic Mikhail Bakhtin's essay about the French Renaissance author Rabelais and so-called "grotesque realism." The argument Bakhtin makes is that through laughter, the dimension of the grotesque reminds readers of their bodily dimension, of their flesh, of what are usually considered the less noble aspects of humanity: the belly, the reproductive organs, defecation, copulation, and birth. According to Bakhtin, the grotesque plays an important role in the re-evaluation of the flesh against asceticism and the refinement of habits that has shaped Western culture from the end of the Middle ages. The body, food, and sex, ridiculed and for this very reason liberating, provoke readers to reflect the artificiality of cultural boundaries, questioning the rigidity of political and social structures that are ultimately founded on this material dimension.

According to Bakhtin, the grotesque body is not a closed unit, isolated from the rest of the world. It changes and grows, always transgressing its own boundaries. It incorporates the external world in the act of nourishment (Bakhtin 1984: 26). This unstable body becomes the occasion for the comical.

I believe this is a key element to an understanding of certain comic or ironic undertones in science fiction. The body, human or alien, that becomes the object of ridicule is a body that refuses all the "natural" categories we usually attribute to it. Every element is not just a given, immutable, fixed characteristic, but it is sucked into a dialectic where everything is plausible, where innumerable possibilities for body structures and functions are available. The human body is revealed as cultural sediment, a product of history, society, and politics, of practices, images, and even language. Just as in the pre-modern grotesque described by Bakhtin, in sci-fi the body is open to a mysterious and potentially frightening universe. In this context, food, in its intimate and constitutive connections with the body, becomes a perfect metaphor for all these elements. We can devour and be devoured, as Melanie Klein reminded us. Food becomes the symbolical substitute for different cultural systems that collide or at least interact in science fiction narrations, showing their intrinsic relativity and arbitrariness. The body itself becomes relative and arbitrary, in its encounters with other bodies and alien organisms, in environments where there is not necessarily a hierarchy among living beings. The political implications against any hegemonic claim to order and universality are enormous.

Science fiction shows all its potential for the comical and its critical power in the novel *Memoir of a Starship Cook* (2000) by the contemporary Italian author Massimo Mongai. The main character is Rudy "Basil" Turturro, a young Terrestrial cook who decides to explore the universe as a chef in a starship. All his adventures revolve, of course, around food. Mongai often resorts to irony and goofy farce, even if the themes he deals with are totally serious. In his comical novel, the flesh is never hidden or downplayed, but it rather becomes the field where the political expresses its most intimate and physical dimension.

In the novel, earth has solved all problems of hunger and undernourishment by developing an agriculture based on soy and seaweed, eliminating pollution. Organically grown foods are available only to the richest, because of their flabbergasting costs. The consequence is that humanity has lost its taste for eating. "People don't eat any longer, they just nourish themselves. . . . It is very sad that there are few human beings left who wonder if it was worth it to save the species, if this was the price to be paid" (Mongai 2000: 16, 21)

In Chef Turturro's world, humankind has developed interplanetary ties by joining the so-called Agora, a loose-knit commercial organization that connects most of the sentient beings of the known universe. This arrangement, of course, provokes new problems, compelling humans to face their fears about aliens. The solution is a pro-alien vaccination, a psychological and behavioral immunization that is administered together with hypnotic conditioning and some chemical substances. The aim is to avoid any a priori rejection of the aliens. This dread is not only a human trait, but also very common in the whole universe.

> [M]asses of sentient beings were unable to fight the fear of the different. The solution is not fighting this fear. It is better to accept it, to tolerate it, to guarantee the right to fear, together with the imposition of the duty of tolerance, or at least of laws that prevent all intolerance that limits the others' rights. It is important to tell everybody: if you are afraid, don't worry; your right to fear is untouchable. Personally I believe that this fear, in the end, is only the fear of being eaten. (Mongai 2000: 134)

In the temporary social arrangements of the starship, different species interact against the void background of outer space, unleashing the primal fear of being devoured, ingested, both metaphorically and materially. The theme is a classic of science fiction: we can mention Ridley Scott's movie *Alien* (1979), which represents humans not only as food for extraterrestrial monsters, but also as incubators for their offspring, and John Carpenter's *Ghosts of Mars* (2001), where alien presences on Mars take possession of human colonizers, pushing them to kill and eat each other.

Also in Chef Turturro's vessel, an impending catastrophe constantly threatens to destroy the clearly fragile equilibrium: it is the so-called "xenoclautrophobic crisis," when everybody suddenly realizes that the other alien species on board can present a real and present danger, and terror escalates to self-destruction. Different episodes of cannibalism haunt the narration, causing temporary crises when the passengers of the ship are reminded of the fact that, after all, they all can become food for another species. Interestingly enough, these cannibalistic acts are always somehow connected with sex and reproduction. One huge beetle-like female creature devours her spouse after copulating; a diplomat almost lets himself be eaten by his own people to let them reach the sexual excitement necessary to reproduce. As Chef Turturro affirms, "Mother Nature does not exist ... In the best hypothesis, nature is an indifferent stepmother. In the worst, it is only an enormous, immense, interplanetary restaurant ... Believe me: nature is a restaurant where everybody is sitting at a table and on the menu at the same time" (Mongai 2000: 149).

In Mongai's novel, the fear of devouring and being devoured, implying the fragility of body boundaries and individualities, pervades the whole plot. The presence of alien creatures, with different functionalities and needs, underlines the relativity of what we consider natural and normal.

Race and its political and social ramifications often come to the forefront in science fiction, in extreme but effective ways. *Stars in My Pocket like Grains of Sand* (1985), one of the most engaging novels by Samuel R. Delany, develops this theme in an original and unpredictable story-line, where gender and sexuality also add several layers to the plot. The main character, Marq Dyeth, is an Industrial Diplomat, a sort of interstellar envoy whose main task is to arrange commercial exchanges between different worlds. His task requires a very developed capacity to mediate between alien cultures. When we first meet Marq, he is doing business with a large and blue sentient being, "who tended to come apart into jellylike pieces only to flow together about the translator pole." The creature is trying to make small talk and to be polite:

> If you're hungry, I'd be highly complimented if you'd eat some of me. Indeed, if there's any of you you can spare: body, hair, nail pairings, excrement, dried skin ...? Really, our two chemistries are very similar, notoriously complementary. One speculates that it's the basis for the stable peace that endures between our races throughout the lowlands of this world. (Delany 1985: 69).

Cannibalism becomes a sort of gift exchange between races. Interestingly, this invitation to ritual ingestion is uttered by a being that does not have a defined and fixed body, but an always recomposing matter that changes hues of blue to express different emotional states. Once again, unstable bodies become a material metaphor for the intrinsic inconsistencies of cultures and identifications. As a consequence, on Velm, Marq Dyeth's planet, no flesh is consumed if not cloned and artificial. Marq Dyeth recalls with horror when on another world he happened to chew on a bone, a piece of animal meat. Nevertheless, one of Marq's relatives does not hesitate to collect cellular material from a visiting guest in order to produce meat from him, adding: "We will savor the complexities of your flesh for years to come, and it will lend its subtleties to myriad complex meals" (Delany 1985: 303).

Velm is inhabited by two kinds of sentient beings: the humans and the evelmi, dragons with wings, scales, and multiple tongues used to express and taste different things, "the taints and feints that humans could communicate through body odor alone if our olfactory systems had not fallen by the evolutionary wayside" (Delany 1985: 120). We are informed that "evelmi have twelve basic tastes and no nasal-based olfactory sense – though they can detect, with some tongues, even a molecule or two lingering in the air" (Delany 1985: 310). Eating is for the evelmi a legitimate means of intellectual and emotional knowledge, so that their multiple tongues become heuristic tools.

> She leaped against me ... small tongues playing in my mouth. I opened wide, so she could be sure to taste me properly. ... While with her nether tongue, the one below the three she was tasting my mouth with, she was saying in that slow-motion basso: "Marq, you're back! Where have you been? What did you see? Tell us how many stars you've swallowed since I last saw you? How many worlds have you chewed up and spit out?" (Delany 1985: 187)

For the evelmi, taste is a relevant part of communication: as a customary greeting, an evelmi friend of Marq's, Santine, offers him several stones to lick (Delany 1985: 108). Furthermore, the members of the same family, which is not biological but based on adoption, including both humans and evelmi, drink from each other's tongues, lick each other's mouths, and so on. These unusual acts of familiarity between different beings hint also at the fact that the two species are capable of receiving sexual pleasure from each other, an eventuality that is not accepted in other parts of the planet Velm, where humans and evelmi are constantly at war. Since eating is a fundamental social activity, charged with emotional and intellectual connotations, it is performed in highly codified fashion, which includes hands, implements, communal and individual feeding. In a key sequence, a ritual battle is waged during an official dinner between Marq's family, the Dyeths, and another clan, the Thants. While the Dyeths support the "Sign," a sort of political organization that promotes non-identitarian socialization, where difference is celebrated at all levels, the Thants have shifted to the Family, favorable to a rigid and uniform cultural stability. During the dinner, while the Dyeths engage themselves in complicated rituals that include also mutual feeding, the Thants refuse to accept food and even to acknowledge their presence. They keep on stigmatizing in loud monologues the supposed corruption of the Dyeths, referring to their alleged sexual perversions and avoiding engagement in symbolic exchange with them. Food and dining become arenas for the clash between identitarian and non-identitarian politics. As a matter of fact, the metaphorical connection between eating and politics is frequent in the novel.

> Several centuries ago, a northern tribe developed a ceramic cooker, essentially a large clay pot, called a kollec. ... You put water (or sometimes oil) in the kollec's bottom, and on top of that you put a complicated seven-layer shelf with various perforations for rising steam, various ducts to conduct juices down from one layer to bypass another and shower over another still lower. Food on the different shelves cooks at different rates. Juices percolate to form a general gravy at the bottom. Individual essences are collected in draining cups at shelf edges on their respective levels. Elaborate meals can be prepared with a single kollec, and in a number of northern cities humans have all but taken it over for their own foods – omitting the inedible flavored stones and unchewable barks that still make up a large part of Velmian cookery but that we humans in the south are learning to appreciate if not actually enjoy. (Delany 1985: 290)

The ceramic cooker becomes the image of the whole of society. For the people of Velm, society and its political life cannot be separated from their material basis and food, which, like a pot, is not "natural" but man-made, an effect of culture and performance. Even so, in the throngs of desire for his lover, Marq Dyeth exclaims: "Metaphors of taste are so inadequate to describe what in reality is an appetite!" (Delany 1985: 339). The act of eating has always something that cannot be fully expressed.

In the novel, food expresses all its political values: the sharing of eating, desire, and sex with alien beings requires a complete rethinking of one's subject position and individuality. One's role in society and one's relationship with otherness cannot be but deeply influenced. The reader is implicitly invited to embark on the same path, which implies a revision of ideas and practices concerning body, sex, gender, and race.

Food, the body, and its arrangements, considered to be as cultural and as arbitrary as language and customs, reveal the political negotiations and the power struggles that generate them. These tensions become even more powerful when they influence our daily activities and our relationship with our own bodies and our images. What we think of our bodies, the way we perceive and experience them, are also deeply determined by the society and the culture we inhabit. Even our desires might be less personal and autonomous than we think. Food becomes a tool, and sometimes even a weapon, in the struggle waged to respond to the expectations and the ideals proposed to us through pop culture in its various expressions.

It is time to move from the imaginative universes of science fiction to a more mundane and apparently unrelated activity: dieting.

–4–

Quilting the Empty Body
Food and Dieting

She was very beautiful, but so proud and haughty that she could not bear to be surpassed in beauty by anyone. She possessed a wonderful mirror which could answer her when she stood before it and said –

"Mirror, mirror upon the wall, Who is the fairest of all?"

The mirror answered –

"Thou, O Queen, art the fairest of all,"

and the Queen was contented, because she knew the mirror could speak nothing but the truth.

Grimm and Grimm 1898: 9

Reflections and Visions

How many times do we look in a mirror? Every day, when we get up, we often catch ourselves staring at the sleepy-eyed face that we recognize as our own, with a mix of curiosity, boredom, and matter-of-factness that confirms to us the sometimes dubious fact that we do exist. We look awry at our reflection in the hallway mirror while rushing to work. We peek at ourselves as we walk past a shop window. We may even sneak a glance at ourselves while sipping a drink in our favorite bar, often wondering how we came to have such a dismayed demeanor.

Our reflection is a constant – though not always welcome – presence throughout our lives. We all remember the endless time spent in front of mirrors while growing up, during those awkward teen years, trying to figure out the right look to be hip, and at a total loss as to why our parents did not make us cool enough.

Mirrors often continue to haunt us as adults. After all, who is totally comfortable, at all times, with his or her reflection? Too frequently, it does not exactly match what the world around us promotes as acceptable or preferable. It is not only a question of clothes, hairstyles, or accessories. Our body itself frequently bothers us, to the point where we end up perceiving it as some external burden imposed on our real self, that inner self that does not succeed in shining through the obtrusive flesh.

This is what dieting is all about. It is about trying to get rid of the uncomfortable cocoon that constricts us, depriving us of what we feel we deserve as human beings. It is about bringing out the image of us that we know people around us will appreciate. It is about reconciling our outer image with the inner image that we perceive as the authentic self we identify with when we think of who we are.

We try our best to feel in control of our outer image. Actually, enjoying total mastery over the body and its appearance often constitutes a powerful fantasy that influences the way we manage and organize our daily activities. With health as our primary goal, but often with fitness and good looks as a secondary but not so irrelevant objective, we strive to eat correctly, to exercise, and overall to maintain a wholesome and active lifestyle. An important wellness industry has developed in most Western countries, from beauty farms to massage parlors, from colonics to diet gurus. The image-obsessed media intensify the relevance of these themes, with shows, TV news, books, magazines, and, more recently, even podcasts.

Pop culture bombards us with a barrage of health tips, slimming products, food supplements, and, above all, diet regimes that promise fast and painless loss of weight, long-term wellbeing, and a boost in self-esteem. Despite variations in food choices, basic tenets, and general approach, diets very often offer similar, simple, and easy-to-follow solutions that we are required to adhere to with a true act of faith. The fact that we do not fully understand the principles and the implications actually eases our sense of insecurity, freeing us from the disturbing necessity of understanding complex scientific explanations and, above all, of making independent choices. According to the French psychoanalyst Gisèle Harrus-Révidi, diets can be considered as modern substitutes of the religious and cultural taboos of the past. No transcendental being tells us any longer what is right and what is wrong, assuring us of our salvation if we follow the rules. Contemporary narcissism, focusing on the body in the attempt to make it absolute and somehow immortal, shifts its allegiance from otherwordly powers to more mundane authorities. Nevertheless, the fundamental mechanism remains the same: the need to obey prescriptions that – with a leap of faith – we believe will save us, or rather will save our bodies (Harrus-Révidi 1994).

Attention towards the body and the embodied self is growing not only among scholars and scientists but also in the media and popular culture. American hit TV shows such as *Extreme Makeover*, *Celebrity Fit Club*, or *The Biggest Loser* actually focus on the change of body images through plastic surgery, dieting, and extreme exercising. Other shows like *America's Next Top Model* or *Man Hunt* pursue ideals of beauty and success that actually represent commonly shared fantasies. The high ratings for these shows are a clear indication that those fantasies have a deeper and larger impact than we all would care to admit.

Imaginary Bodies

Self-help literature is a thriving industry, responding to the needs of audiences always looking to progress in their lives, aiming at overcoming obstacles in their quasi-constitutionally sanctioned pursuit of happiness. There is nothing wrong with it – we all strive to improve ourselves at all levels. We acknowledge that a healthy self-esteem gives us better chances in our career, in our interaction with others, and in our emotional lives. When we appreciate ourselves, we unconsciously tend to send out positive vibes that the world around us seems ready to receive and reflect back on us. Our body language changes and communicates in different ways. It does feel good.

The importance of body images and the power of identification, often based on visual elements, did not go undetected in the work of Dr. Robert C. Atkins, one of many researchers and practitioners who focused their efforts on all those who try hard to lose extra pounds, often fighting against serious obesity and other weight-related problems, in order to improve their general health. Although he never tackles the subject directly, references to body images and identification are quite frequent in his writing. His most famous book, *Dr. Atkins' New Diet Revolution*, begins with these words: "Lose weight! Increase energy! Look great! This book will show you how it's done" (Atkins 2002: 3).

We will analyze the Atkins diet as an example, since in its deep psychological mechanisms it is quite similar to the myriad diets that thrive in pop culture: the Zone diet, the South Beach diet, the Shangri-La diet, and, to some extent, programs such as Weight Watchers or Jenny Craig.

In the very first chapter of his book, Dr. Atkins actually gives us the visual picture of our future better self:

> The you in the picture I'm conjuring up is finally the weight you've always had as your goal, or fairly close. You feel great – full of energy. Your skin is glowing with health. If you've been exercising, your toned muscles show it. The you in the picture isn't worried about weight loss anymore. You no longer need to spend your time planning the stages of a new diet, constantly concerned about your eating, feeling guilty when you break promises you've made to yourself. (Atkins 2002: 5)

The mirror hovers in all diet books. Even when it is not directly mentioned, we are aware that it is the first test dieters have to face to measure their improvements, together with the scale. TV commercials for slimming products or dieting programs often offer "before and after" images. The involvement of celebrities, such as Kirstie Alley (who recently passed the torch to Valerie Bertinelli) for Jenny Craig or Sarah Ferguson, the Duchess of York, for Weight Watchers, amplify the perception that body image issues are not limited to the commoners, but also include jet setters and high society. Daytime TV mogul Oprah Winfrey has kept audiences all over the world involved in her struggle against weight. She has recently endorsed fitness guru Bob Greene's Best Life Diet, which includes a Bestlife™ stamp of approval on many food products widely available in shops and supermarkets (Greene 2006).

The Atkins diet, despite its decrease in popularity in recent years, is particularly interesting because it is often perceived as masculine, or at least man-friendly. As historian Amy Bentley has noticed, men, and especially American males, whose culture places meat in a very special and central position, feel comfortable with a regimen that actually prods them to consume rib-sticking food in large quantities (Bentley 2005).

The image the mirror reflects plays a major role in motivating dieting persons: every slight change, confirmed by the scale, gives them new reasons to hang in there and go through the ordeal. On the other hand, body images, when they do not correspond to personal or social expectations, can also provoke frustration and anger. Dr. Atkins, too, is aware of this danger, and he warns his readers about it. "You can make it the best body possible if you don't fall into the trap of demanding a perfect figure and weight loss schedule that exists only in your head" (Atkins 2002: 281). And again, "building muscle mass does not mean becoming one of those bulging body-builders. If you keep at it, you will begin to notice a gradual sculpting taking place under your skin – and I guarantee you're going to like how it looks" (Atkins 2002: 293). The message is: use the improvements in your body image to gain momentum to continue with the diet, but do not model the visual expectations with which you identify your inner self with images that are out of reach. We simply cannot attain a body type that is not ours. Rationally, we know it. Yet we are willing to incur great sacrifices to get as close as possible to the body models that we perceive as desirable.

The question is: where do these unrealistic images come from? Why do actors, models, body-builders, and celebrities become so relevant in our fantasies? And why do they have such a power over us? Who decides what body images are the right, successful, and positive ones? How does mainstream culture adopt these images? Or, rather, does mainstream culture create them? Why do these external and abstract images have such a strong clutch on our emotional wellbeing? In general, why are images so important to our inner lives?

To get a better understanding of these phenomena, we will refer again to the analytical tools provided by French psychoanalyst and theorist Jacques Lacan, whom we have already mentioned in Chapter 2. Starting in the 1960s, this controversial intellectual developed a totally new practical approach and theoretical framework to psychoanalysis. Very divisive and difficult to read, although groundbreaking in many ways, Lacan has left a legacy that is still exerting a powerful influence, especially in Europe, where his ideas are being applied to cultural, social, and political issues, as in the work of Ernesto Laclau, Chantal Mouffe, and Slavoj Žižek. Based on his psychoanalytical experience, Jacques Lacan developed a theory that he defined as the "mirror stage." Analyzing the dreams and recurring fixations of some patients, he realized how often fears relating to the fragmentation of the body haunted them: limbs missing or misplaced, aggressive disintegration, growing wings. From where do these anxieties come? As we mentioned in Chapter 2, Lacan found the answer in the development of infants. "The human child, at an age when he is for a short while, but for a while nevertheless, outdone by the chimpanzee in instrumental intelligence, can already recognize his own image as such in a mirror" (Lacan 2002: 3)

Since childhood, we learn to cope with the confusion about ourselves. Who are we? How do we fit in the world that surrounds us? What is our role in the family we find ourselves in? What are we supposed to do? These feelings generate constant insecurities, enhanced by the fact that, especially as infants, we do not have much control of our own bodies. We depend on others to be fed, to be cleaned, and to be protected. Children cannot walk, and many of their gestures and movements are tentative. Lacan actually considers children's condition to be the consequence of a "veritable specific prematurity at birth" that traps their body in a "motor impotence and nursing dependence" (Lacan 2002: 4–6).

According to Lacan's observations, between 6 and 18 months of age, infants are particularly taken with their own images as they see them reflected in mirrors. We all have enjoyed watching small babies playing in front of mirrors, making faces, discovering their own body and movements. Adults often join them in the games while holding them. For Lacan, this intense interest is stimulated by the fact that the images reassure babies about the control they can actually exert over their own body, perceived as uncoordinated and out of control. The reflection, on the other hand, appears complete and coordinated in its actions. The images that surround us as infants and children, easily accessible and reassuringly undivided, provide us with the first safety net from anxiety. The relief infants experience by looking at their own reflected image leads them to identify with it: the image is chosen as a preferential self, much more complete and self-sufficient than the one experienced through their own developing body. The mirror image becomes the core around which the ego is constructed, the center of that aspect of the subjective experience that Lacan labeled as "Imaginary," the dimension of identification with visual images.

This ego is nevertheless external to the self. It can be considered ideal in that it is built around what we would like to be, to respond to what the world around us considers us to be: good looking, strong, with our daddy's eyes. For this reason Lacan calls it the ideal-ego, functioning as a lighthouse in the building of a functioning individual. This first identification process is at the same time reassuring but also alienating, since the ideal-ego is somehow fictional and located outside of the bodily self. Lacan ascribes to this element the frequent ambivalence that even as adults we all experience towards images or heroes or persons we identify with. More or less consciously, we want to be like them, but at the same time we hate them because we know we cannot be like them. In the case of the Atkins diet, the ideal-ego proposed as a stimulus to lose weight is what we want to look like and feel like. The ambivalence is lurking, right there: a slim figure is a goal that also scares us, because we fear that we might not reach it.

Throughout the book, Atkins often refers to visualization to cheer his followers up. The "you in the picture" is always there to provide resiliency to the dieting and often struggling self. After the Induction phase, where Atkins neophytes are required to give up all kinds of carbohydrates without renouncing other foods like protein and fat, they are also reassured about the results: "You are probably now catching glimpses of that new person on the horizon – if not in your own mirror. That new you is thinner, happier, healthier, and more confident" (Atkins 2002: 154). "Remember my suggestion to continually visualize yourself at your goal weight. Think about how much you deserve to look and feel good, to enjoy the happiness, health and sense of well-being that will come with your weight loss" (Atkins 2002: 279)

In the Eye of the Beholder

Does this desire for a better body derive from the images themselves, or does it come from some other place? Even if the images – particularly their own reflection - provide children with protection and reassurance, they would not seem to be strong enough to exert such a great influence on the psyche. How can they become the base for the whole phenomenon of identification? Growing up, the social environment offers us all kinds of images with which we can identify, especially when it comes to our body. However, we cannot forget that preferred body standards change with history and culture. For example, the Venus by Botticelli, a female character in a painting by Rubens, Marilyn Monroe, the 1970s fashion model Twiggy, and the more contemporary Jennifer Lopez embody very different ideal of female beauty. In contemporary Western culture, some ethnicities have clear preferences for more sensual, voluptuous bodies. Context exerts a major influence on the relevance of visual elements, which, without anchorage to something stable, would not seem able to have enough strength to activate a full-blown identification process. Without some cohesive thread, body images by themselves would be so fleeting that they would probably re-create the same anxieties and fears about dismemberment and lack of bodily control that they are supposed to exorcize in the first place.

Where does the power of body images come from then? Does the identification work only at the level of the physical image or does it involve other elements? If we go back to the first imaginary identification of children with their reflected images, it is easy to realize that the relevance of those images as preferential ideals is not only motivated by their visual appeal. Other elements lead the child to identify with the reflected self. Think about how many times we have said to a child: how cute you are ... how much you look like your mother ... look at those lovely eyes ... you're such a good girl ... or well, let's hope the shape of that nose will change while growing ... you remind me so much of that bastard of your father ... what a bad girl you are! Many verbal elements interact to influence or reinforce the identification process that forms the core of the child's ego. The image of our own body is never just that: in the eyes of the surrounding beholders, and as a consequence in ours, it is the image of a boy or of a girl, of a cute or of a not-so-cute child, of a good or of a bad child, of a son or a daughter, of a brother or a sister. These images introduce us to concepts and practices (age, sex, gender, beauty, values, even desire) that make us functional members of a given society, easing us into the roles that add other layers to our personality. The ideal-ego, based on the visual elements that children perceive of themselves in the mirror, is reinforced by what Lacan calls the ego-ideal, composed of all the elements that originate in other people's projections about the children's future and personality. In this case, what counts is the perspective from which the child is viewed. The images reflected in the mirror, through the filtering gaze of family and friends, acquire meaning. The images become signs for something else. They come to stand for affection, family relationships, gender roles, and moral judgments. These cultural elements, deriving from the social, economic, kinship structure of the community that incorporates the children, become part of the identification processes that shape the development of the children's ego. Lacan defines this cultural network of meanings as the "Symbolic," the second dimension of subjectivity. The definition refers to the fact that all of its elements have meanings, they stand for something else. In this sense, they can be considered symbols. In Lacan's view, these symbols are not just juxtaposed, next to each other or piled up without any specific order: they constitute a system, where each element actually gets its meaning from its relationship with all the other elements composing the system. If food is a cultural system, then, according to Lacan, it cannot be but a part of the Symbolic. How does food specifically affect our relationship with our body images (the ideal-ego) and with the values that our culture grafts onto them (the ego-ideal)?

It is intuitive that dieting plays a relevant role. Let us go back to Mr. Atkins. We have seen how he employs body images to prod his followers to persevere in their dieting efforts. The body ideals Atkins refers to are precisely those that are culturally perceived as more acceptable and, in some cases, desirable in our contemporary Western societies: health, fitness, and slimness. The cultural and visual elements are tightly knit to ignite effective identification: by trying to achieve a specific body type the dieting persons not only satisfy their imaginary fantasies, but anchor themselves securely in the symbolic network of signs that constitute their culture. The empty material body, made only of visual elements, fills up with meaning.

We have seen how meanings in any culture constitute a system, where all the elements get their sense from their relations with all the other elements. We have ascertained that also food is a cultural system. Within food, we can consider diets as a specific subsystem, functioning according to interconnected rules and meanings. Dr. Atkins, it goes without saying, never forgets about food and eating habits, since the body constantly tells us that it needs nourishment. He clearly points out the direct connection between a negative body image and bad nutrition, considered a malfunctioning network (a cultural subsystem) of negative dietary practices, unhealthy food, and a general defeatist attitude about food. At the same time, Atkins acknowledges the fact that insufficient food intake plays against achieving healthy nutrition patterns through dieting, and, as a consequence, can keep us from achieving the desired body image. "Deprivation is no fun. Once the biological gap between hunger and fulfillment grows too large, the rebound can be amazingly rapid as well as heartbreaking and humiliating. But that's the problem of diets that restrict quantities. The Atkins program refuses to accept hunger as a way of life" (Atkins 2002: 10). "Nothing is more difficult to endure for a lifetime than being constantly hungry" (Atkins 2002: 104). "Your resistance is at its greatest when you're satiated" (Atkins 2002: 247). Hunger is perceived as an uncontrollable instinct, a bodily necessity that surfaces when we least need it. Atkins often opposes hunger to pleasure, which in his writing appears as something we have definitely more of a clutch on: "The controlled carbohydrate nutritional approach is not one of deprivation. Sheer hunger is the main reason for the failure of most weight loss efforts. A lifetime eating plan needs to be palatable, pleasant, and filling" (Atkins 2002: 19); and further down, "When doing Atkins, you'll find that your appetite has diminished, but your satisfaction from the food you eat has increased" (Atkins 2002: 44). It is not only about counteracting the physical pangs of hunger. Dr. Atkins is well aware of the psychological relevance of food and of the satisfaction we derive from it. He affirms: "I equate healthy eating with gastronomic pleasure" (Atkins 2002: 5). "This is an obvious win-win situation. It offers you the pleasure of eating and the promise of being healthier than before" (Atkins 2002: 6). Dr. Atkins refer to contentment and fulfillment several times: "Eating Atkins-style is a food lover's dream come true – luxurious, healthy, and varied" (Atkins 2002: 19) "You're doing Atkins, and naturally you begin by eating – something you've previously done with some degree of guilt. Say good-bye to all that. It's time to plow into prime ribs and that cheese omelet" (Atkins 2002: 136). Right in the first chapter of his book, Dr. Atkins states: "I'll help you adopt a permanent way of eating that lets you lose weight without counting calories, makes you feel and look better, naturally re-energizes you, keeps lost pounds off forever with a lifetime nutritional approach that includes rich, delicious foods" (Atkins 2002: 4).

It is evident that in Atkins' approach not all victuals are necessarily evil. Only some specific elements of the food system are held responsible. For this reason, we can successfully change our ways of eating, our habits, and to some extents our cultural principles about what is good and bad for us, without giving up pleasure and satisfaction. On the Atkins diet you can still enjoy "rich, delicious foods" (Atkins 2002: 5). "I encourage you to eat until you're satisfied. Just don't confuse being satisfied with being stuffed" (Atkins 2002: 138).

Quilting the Flesh

What is the relation between hunger (the biological need for food), pleasure (the psychological state deriving from satisfying desire), body images, and the culture that provides and frames them in a wider context, making them more or less desirable?

We have seen how in Lacan's theory the various elements in any system only acquire their meaning from each other and their mutual relations. However, these relations, and the role that each element plays in the system, are never stable. Meaning, Lacan would say, is slippery and mutable, the result of continuous negotiations. The signs – the elements of the system – stay the same, it is their meaning that changes. In order for any cultural system to acquire a certain stability, allowing its users to share values, ideals, language, and the practices connected to them, certain signs must emerge as dominant, becoming the pivot around which all the other cultural signs determine and adapt their meanings. As noted in the Introduction, Lacan refers to these pivotal signs as "upholstering buttons." The stuffing of a chair would go everywhere and create uncomfortable lumps if the buttons in the upholstery did not keep it in place. Likewise, meanings would shift constantly all over the place, staying undefined and confused, if some signs did not play the role of the buttons, keeping the whole system in place.

Atkins is aware that the enticing body images that he projects to cheer up his followers need to be anchored in cultural, symbolic elements to acquire consistency and relevance. The upholstery buttons in the food system he proposes are the "bad foods" that need to be avoided to reach the results we want: carbohydrates. Atkins' whole nutritional discourse revolves around them, in a neat and sensible way. "Those foods are bad for your health, bad for your energy level, bad for your mental state, bad for your figure. Bad for your career prospects, bad for your sex life, bad for your digestion, bad for your blood chemistry, bad for your heart. What I'm saying is that they are bad" (Atkins 2002: 15). Atkins frequently describes the excessive consumption of these foods, also called trigger foods (Atkins 2002: 219), as an addiction, or as an obsession, or even as enslavement (Atkins 2002: 139). When they give them up, dieters may even suffer from withdrawal symptoms, "ranging from fatigue, faintness and palpitation to headache and cold sweats" (Atkins 2002: 141), More importantly, Atkins declares: "The most dangerous food additive on the planet is sugar in all its forms" (Atkins 2002: 253) and "Sugar is a metabolic poison" (Atkins 2002: 24). Sugar should not even be allowed to enter the dieter's home, for the benefit of the whole family (Atkins 2002: 253)

Around this main tenet, Dr. Atkins develops his entire scientific theory, reorganizing the whole field of nutrition and food-related health: carbohydrates are responsible for higher levels of insulin, diabetes, and high blood pressure. The need to avoid carbs revolutionizes one's food intake patterns, one's daily routine, and one's social life. The dieters' families are required to participate in the efforts aimed at losing weight, while their friends are expected to accommodate their dietary needs. Such a profound change in culture and science reverberates also in everyday life, in practices and common interactions. At a larger social level, the interest in the Atkins diet has given birth to a different lifestyle, originating TV shows, printed media, and the production and commercialization of new products, which somehow entail the restructuring of the layout in retail stores and supermarket. Where should the new products be physically placed for the customer to recognize and buy them? In a special low-carb aisle or mixed with the same category of products even when these reflect other lifestyles? Should they be treated like ethnic products, gathered together even when they belong to different categories, to manifest the needs and interests of a specific community? Or should they be distributed in special stores only selling low-carb products?

A Leap of Faith

Atkins places carbohydrates, the "bad" elements that need to be avoided, at the center of his nutritional approach, reorganizing the dieting person's whole life and its relationship with family and society. How is this possible? This lifetime commitment to the Atkins lifestyle requires a veritable act of faith, as Atkins himself repeatedly points out. "You must have faith" (Atkins 2002: 136), he proclaims, and later: "One of the obstacles you may find in the real world is people – the very same people upon whom you normally rely for advice and support" (Atkins 2002: 252). Those who do not follow Atkins are labeled as nonbelievers (Atkins 2002: 252) or naysayers (Atkins 2002: 253).

The dedication of dieters to the Atkins plan clearly responds to a psychological need, otherwise the complete obedience and self-restraint the diet requires would not make sense. They would be too high a price to pay, if the reward were not substantial. What can this fundamental need be? Our body, since the crisis that infants solve by identifying with their own reflected image, is always the cause for puzzlement and sense of lack of control. We can try as hard as we want, but we never get to fully understand the way our bodies grow, age, gain or lose weight. Our physical reality imposes itself over and over as something that does not always makes sense, despite all our attempts at rationalizations. Our body never totally fits into the neat system of meanings that constitute our culture, into the preferential images that we are offered, into the scientific knowledge that explains our biology. There is always too much fat, one wrinkle too many, that annoying pain in the knee, the unexpected heart attack, or the anxiety we sometimes experience in front of food. "Your body has its own wisdom, so listen to it" (Atkins 2002: 227). Atkins warns us:

> Remember two things: First, your body is not a machine. Nor is it a duplicate of anyone else's body. It has its own system, its own agenda, and its own timetable. In the long,

run, it nearly always responds to sensible management by the person in charge – you. But, in the short run, your body may decide to go its own way, for its own reasons, which perhaps we don't understand. Don't get mad at it. It's a good body or it wouldn't have gotten you this far. Be patient; you can afford to outwait it. (Atkins 2002: 183)

The body is almost considered as something external, something that we cannot control, precisely when our most powerful and engaging fantasy consists of actually managing to gain control over it. The image of our slim body, which motivated us to start the diet in the first place, the experience of our body as something we can bend to our will, the received social values about beauty and attractiveness, all give way to the stubbornness of our unreasonable flesh. Our sheer physicality subverts the expected order of the world that surrounds us, or at least our projections and hopes about it. It falls under what Lacan defined as the "Real." This aspect includes all that cannot be given a rational explanation and resists symbolization, in the sense that it cannot be absorbed into the network of meanings that our culture provides for us in order to make sense of our lives. Precisely for this reason, of course, the eruption of the Real into our internal reality is frightening. It reminds us of our frailty and inconsistencies. The Symbolic and Imaginary dimensions, on the other hand, offer respite from these fears, providing stable meanings, neat ideals, and confirmed practices. But at times it is not enough. We need to feel that our priorities and the meanings we give to reality are guaranteed by some external authority, something that gives them credibility and certainty. Since we cannot make sense of reality by ourselves, we need to believe that somebody knows its secrets and is willing to bestow them on us: an authority organizing meanings so that we can make sense of them. In diets, the "scientist" holds the authority to clarify an otherwise very confusing field of knowledge. He provides and guarantees the validity of the upholstery buttons that assure stability and certainty. In the case of Atkins the main "button" is that carbs are bad. This is the organizing element that promises the return to a lost state of harmony, unity, and fullness, not only for our individual body but also for the community (Stravrakakis 1999: 52). In this case, the fantasy consists of food systems and markets that work for the wellbeing and physical health of consumers, not to sell and make money.

The presence of an external authority that validates meaning and assures good results also relieves the follower from decisions and responsibility. One is not to be blamed for desiring bad foods. "Your compulsion holds no terrors," says Dr. Atkins. "Your food compulsion isn't a character disorder, it's a chemical disorder called hyperinsulinism" (Atkins 2002: 44). "I am about to recount a horror story that might be headlined: Innocent Human is Turned Upon By Own Hormones!" (Atkins 2002: 53). "Let me explain something about cravings. … Your craving appeared, most likely, because it was triggered by a drop in your blood sugar" (Atkins 2002: 137). The uncontrollable body, the frightening Real, to use the Lacanian terminology, is tamed by those bodily functions that play by the rules. "Lipolysis is one of life's charmed gifts. It's as delightful as sex and sunshine, and it has fewer drawbacks than either of them!" (Atkins 2002: 57). So what is the dieters' role? On one side, embracing the certainty of the new lifestyle, there is no need for willpower. "Will-power is not the issue" (Atkins 2002: 54). Dieters are repeatedly reassured about the fact that they will not be required to count calories, even when they find themselves busy counting carb grams. "I had too big an appetite and too little willpower, two facts that haven't changed much," admits Dr. Atkins (Atkins 2002: 61) "Superhuman willpower is not required to do Atkins, only the wisdom to put yourself into a position where you won't need it" (Atkins 2002: 140).

On the one hand, Atkins frees overweight people from all moral accusations: "Part of the obesity epidemic we face in the United States may be due to the misconception that those of us who are overweight are simply gluttons or lazy couch potatoes" (Atkins 2002: 259). But then again they get a warning: "Remember who's boss. You are absolutely in control of what goes in your mouth at all times" (Atkins 2002: 255). "Internalize your responses to food so what used to be a struggle becomes a conscious choice, one that serves you for the rest of your life. ... Learn how to deal with temptation. ... Develop a style of eating for a lifetime" (Atkins 2002: 195). We detect a clear ambivalence: is the desire for bad food a fault of character or not? Dealing with the nightmare of carb gram counting, Atkins' voice becomes stern. "Counting grams of carbohydrate is truly your responsibility. If you don't count, you get in trouble" (Atkins 2002: 169). Also calories reappear at times, like when we deal with exercise. "It's one of the basic laws of the universe: If you use more calories than you consume, you lose weight (You sharp-eyed readers might say, 'Whoa, I thought we didn't have to worry about calories!' That's true, but it's a great way, here, to illustrate an important point)" (Atkins 2002: 287). "Another way to organize your exercise is to count the calories you burn (You know I'm not going to ask you to count the calories you consume!)" (Atkins 2002: 291)

So although willpower is not deemed a key element in the diet, a certain degree of discipline is required. The body is disciplined and normalized not only regarding its food intake, but also in its inscription in a cultural system that gives it meaning, making it part of shared cultural practices. In the case of the Atkins diet, the individual who desires to lose weight voluntarily adheres to a system of meaning that proposes a radical alternative to the common perceptions of what is good and bad for your health, asking for a leap of faith and giving easy, clear-cut, and rational principles to follow. The body and its biological processes are given new, revolutionary meanings, all while being anchored to the common and popular ideals of physical beauty and health. By choosing a new point of reference, the danger of carbohydrates, Atkins shifts all the usual meanings and relocates them to create a system that offers an alternative to all those who have lost faith in other diets and in the possibility to acquire the body they desire. Filtered through the reassuring order of science and culture, the images they want to see reflected in the mirror can finally become flesh and blood.

Feeding Masculinities

The need for a source of certainty, an authority with the power to determine what is good for us, to guarantee health and fitness, and somehow to ensure salvation for the body, has become a very strong element of contemporary pop culture. For those who are impervious to religion and spirituality, science becomes the magic element that answers all questions. It might seem a contradiction, since modern science is built on experiment, doubt, test and trial, hypotheses, and a certain degree of uncertainty. Yet, a form of unwavering faith in the mission of science and in its power to explain everything, leaving no doubts about any aspect of reality, is still lingering in the Western culture.

Pop culture has absorbed some elements of this confidence in science – also when it comes to nutrition – although often with a certain ambivalence. We are always interested in the latest discoveries and in the results of studies and research that can reveal the solution to our big and small problems related to food, diet, and fitness. The media acknowledge this interest, feeding audiences with bits and pieces that are often superficial and unrelated to each other, increasing confusion. As a consequence, nutritional information is fragmented, but at the same time each portion acquires its own life, generating urban myths and connecting in unexpected ways with other circulating information.

Science often plays an important role in providing reassurance about food choices and body images in men's fitness magazines, a pop culture phenomenon that deals with various intimate aspects of men's lives. This new breed of publications has recently exploded in many Western countries. These magazines have now abandoned the closets of gay men and the lockers of professional body-builders to be conspicuously displayed in dentists' waiting rooms or on coffee tables next to sport magazines.

The enthrallment with the body image, previously often limited to women, is now becoming a common feature in male psychology, to the point that the expression "the Adonis complex" has been created, referring to the more pathological, obsessive forms of this phenomenon (Bordo 1999; Connell 1995 and 2000; Pope et al. 2000). A scholarly literature on body images has recently developed within the frame of theories that consider masculinities as constructed in culture and sustained in all kinds institutions (the school, the gym, the army, the workplace). R.W. Connell, one of the most relevant academics in the field, writes,

> Men's bodies are addressed, defined and disciplined, and given outlets and pleasures, by the gendered order of society. Masculinities are neither programmed in our genes, nor fixed by social structure, prior to social interaction. They come into existence as people act. They are actively produced, using the resources and strategies available in a given social setting. (Connell 2000: 12)

Masculinities are not fixed or defined once and for all; they do not represent embodiments of discrete states of being. They vary in time and place, in different historical, social, and cultural environments. As practices, they sometimes articulate contradictory desires, emotions, and ideals, denying the very notion of a static and defined identity. These concurrent masculinities are not equivalent: some tend to be considered more desirable than others, even when they are not the most common, and thus become "hegemonic," a standard against which men embodying other kinds of masculinities assess their self-perception and often also their self-esteem. Body images play a fundamental role in defining what the dominant masculinity should be like. Nevertheless, men's bodies are not blank pages that become the receptacle for all kinds of power and social determinations: they are actual agents, and they interact with other aspects of the social practices determining masculinities. As Connell emphasizes,

> To understand how men's bodies are actually involved in masculinities we must abandon the conventional dichotomy between changing culture and unchanging bodies. ... Through social institutions and discourses, bodies are given social meaning. Society has a range of "body practices" which address, sort and modify bodies. These practices range from deportment and dress to sexuality, surgery and sport. (Connell 2000: 57)

The growing attention to the male body – it has been argued – is, at least partially, a result of the mainstreaming and the normalization of gay culture (Bronski 1998). Nevertheless, also in heterosexual contexts, strong male bodies have traditionally served as metaphors for sexual potency, power, productivity, domin- ance, independence, and control. Both discourses are somehow articulated in the contemporary hegemony of the muscular body type (also known as mesomorphic, as opposed to ectomorphic, slim, and endomorphic, overweight), often in connection with a phenomenon sometimes defined as "re-masculinization" (Jeffords 1989). Until a few decades ago, the aspiration for a muscular build was a prerogative of a small circle of professional and amateur body-builders, who were also involved in different forms of competition, giving to the whole scene the veneer of a sport. In time, after large sections of the gay community embraced the muscular body as desirable and prestigious, the same attitude became more and more visible, also in heterosexual – or should we now say metrosexual? – circles. A renewed attention to the body and its appearance goes well beyond the concern for its athletic potential, which was a normal element of the sport subculture, uniting all men, gay and straight, in the same awe of the bulging muscle. These phenomena explain the growing success of men's fitness magazines, which, at any rate, carefully avoid dealing with issues of sexual preference, and ban any hint of homoeroticism, which is, nevertheless, always lurking behind the glossy pages of the magazines.

The growing prestige granted to the muscular body places increasing pressure on men to take greater care of their looks (Wienke 1998). Men seem to adopt different strategies to make sense of their bodies when they do not meet the hegemonic expectations: the three predominant ways to adjust the discrepancy between the ideal and the real body have been defined as reliance, where the individual works on his body to reach the model; reformulation, where each individual adjusts his conception of hegemonic masculinity to meet his abilities; and rejection, where the individual totally refuses the hegemonic model. (Gerschick and Miller 1994). In the case of reliance, usually great amounts of energy, money, and time are invested in gaining the desired body image, often with anxious undertones that reveal a certain preoccupation with control over one's body. In this context, food plays a crucial, though often concealed, role, because diets and eating habits are interpreted as a key element in the construction of a fit body.

Buy a Better Body

Needless to say, the food and supplement industry has tapped into these trends to acquire new consumers for highly processed products that ensure growing revenues for a sector structurally plagued by intense competition (Nestle 2002: 1–30). Many of the advertising pages in men's fitness magazines often play with consumers' sense of inadequacy and their desire for emulation, proposing behaviors and values in order to increase sales. These marketing strategies rely on the same capacity for dedication and effort that are crucial in the construction of hegemonic masculinities (Wolf 1991).

The language, the metaphors, and the visual images used both in the editorial sections and in advertisements of men's fitness publications reflect the idea that working out is a serious and strenuous activity. Readers are attracted to buy the magazines by alluring covers, overflowing with strapping men, bulging muscles, and enticing titles that all reinforce the promise that through discipline and exercise, and following the advice in the magazine, readers' bodies will become stronger and more appealing, a real concentration of unbridled masculinity (Parasecoli 2005).

It goes without saying, nutrition is very important for athletes, since it can improve their performance, stamina, and endurance. However, choosing the right food at the right time can be complicated and confusing, despite the help of nutrition research. Translating grams and proteins into actual, available foods is not always easy. Eating is often viewed as refueling, and it is not uncommon for athletes to develop various forms of eating disorders (Ravaldi et al. 2003; Sudi et al. 2004). This phenomenon is even more evident when legal and illegal enhancers are employed. The use and abuse of steroids in the world of body-builders deserves special notice, both for the dangerous consequences of the substances, and for the special relation with food that these hormones entail. Although the use of anabolic steroids is illegal without a prescription, they are not too difficult to obtain. Most of the steroids are acquired through illegal importation from countries where they are sold without prescription.

They are also allegedly stolen from pharmaceutical labs. Buying steroids is not hard, as they are sold illegally as "performance enhancing" drugs in gyms, fitness clubs, and athletic competitions under the street names gym candy, pampers, weight trainers, stackers, arnolds, and juice. Athletes and body-builders can also order them by mail order. Steroids constitute an alluring shortcut for men and women who want to acquire a muscular and bulging body in a short period of time. The confidence in the results of scientific research turn absolute: very specific results are expected with the consumption of very specific substances. The connections of these results with the complex balance necessary for the human body to function are secondary, and most consumers are absolutely not interested in it. In order to obtain the desired muscle development, body-builders are forced to increase and reorganize their food intake: it is not unusual for them to consume five to ten meals a day. Many actually become obsessed with food, because their growth depends closely on the amount of food consumed. Nevertheless, most body-builders think in terms not of ingredients and dishes, but of nutritional composition, in order to calculate the right amount of protein, fat, and carbohydrates. What the food is and tastes like is not influential. Besides, before contests and shows, many body-builders calibrate their diet to make their muscles more visible: protein-rich foods become the main fare, and all efforts are made to dehydrate the body as much as possible. In many cases, artificial or processed proteins are ingested: fueling is definitely the priority, while taste is at most an afterthought.

Pills of Science

In fitness magazines, science plays a very important role not only in advertising but also in the editorial content about food and nutrition, second in importance only to the stories about fitness and muscle building. In most fitness and health magazines we find sections with nutritional recommendations. However, despite the continuous reference to science, the general discourse is far from showing a scientific approach: tips are just tips. Readers are offered bits and pieces of unrelated news about this specific nutrient or the other, without connecting them in systematic and thorough explanations. As often happens in diet and nutrition writing, editorial staff opt for clear, simple, ready-to-apply pieces of advice, avoiding any difficulty in the subject matter. In the same issue, they can advise readers to add fish oil to their diet to avoid the risk of developing both an irregular heartbeat and insulin resistance, to eat strawberry and black raspberries to reduce risks of cancer, to drink soda to help quench their appetite, milk to reduce the risk of colon cancer, wine for better breath. Readers are presented with a mass of unrelated information that seems to play with their health fears.

Though often latent and disguised, a recurrent element in the nutritional discourse of these magazines is that sweets – and appetite in general – are clearly perceived as feminine. As a matter of fact, women are sometimes described as able to keep men's desire in check, probably because they are supposed to deal constantly with their own. In the pseudo-scientific lore that colonizes many mainstream media, sweets endanger the whole effort to build a muscular, masculine body: they cannot but belong to a dimension both wanted, needed, and precisely for this reason demonized, in that it could condemn the male body to lose its hardly gained frontiers (Douglas 1969).

The relevance of gender in dieting and body images is particularly evident in the different ways male and female athletes are represented in the media, especially those focusing on fitness and sports (Higgs et al. 2003; Messner et al.1993). Despite the growing interest in women's sports, the language and the stereotypes still give primacy to men; after all, competition, physicality, and aggression are considered typical masculine traits. Even the most successful female athletes are often represented in ways that underline their attractiveness and appearance, rather than their skills on the field. As a consequence, they are frequently photographed in non-athletic settings and poses (Curry et al. 2002; Thomsen et al. 2004). If their prestige as sex-symbols can be useful to get exposure in the media, the pressure on female athletes to enhance their performances while maintaining their "babe factor" creates havoc in their eating habits, with the consequence of frequent eating disorders.

In sport and fitness media, the goal of editorial features dealing with nutritional models and attitudes is usually not to follow a balanced and prolonged diet that can ensure body fitness in the long run, but rather to obtain fast results that are immediately visible in the body.

Very often, fitness magazines, especially those geared towards male readerships, present diets that consist of a series of clear rules. The idea is to control as much as possible what goes into what you eat. The control issue is paramount: not only can you not lose fat and build muscle, but you cannot maintain your body frame if you do not keep your otherwise wild appetites in check. Control clearly does not imply cooking: most of the dishes proposed in the maintenance menu require little or no preparation. If they do, it is not mentioned. So readers are told to eat lean turkey, chicken breasts, or salmon, but no information is given about how to prepare them.

This insistence on the fact that men do not really cook, in the sense they are not supposed to dedicate time and effort to fixing meals, can be an attempt to avoid any feminine trait identified with a nurturing role. Women reaffirm their nature by performing and reinforcing their role of caregivers. They are responsible with feeding not only their own but also others' bodies, ensuring their survival but submitting them to the constant temptation of the unchecked, always-invading flesh. Cooking is one of the most identifiable of these performative traits. They are the result of the reiteration of highly regulated and ritualized practices, norms, and processes (the "techniques of the body" we discussed in Chapter 3) that respond to an ideal, a shared model, and that find their first materialization in the very body of each individual (J. Butler 1993: 1–23). A part of culture, performance and practices are not artificial and dispensable, but constitutive necessities for the existence of the individual self, being the conditions of its emergence and operation, of its boundaries and stability. They mark and reinforce its submission to rules and norms, such as the culinary ones.

In all the material we have discussed, we recognize a strong wish not only to control one's body appearance, but also to curb one's desires and appetites. A fit body becomes the material expression of one's dominion over the self. As feminist theorist Susan Bordo has pointed out, the body is identified "as animal, as appetite, as deceiver, as prison of the soul and confounder of its projects." It is always in opposition with the spiritual self and the rationality that mirror the divine (Bordo 1993: 3). Historically, Bordo argues, women have been identified with the debasing dimension of the body, chaotic and undisciplined. Men, on the other side, reflect the spirit. Their masculinity is embodied in their control over the flesh, a metaphorical equivalent of their dominion over female unchecked carnality. This contrast is inscribed in the male body as a series of clear oppositions between hard and soft, thick and thin, and, of course, fit and flabby. Food is a temptation that can make man fall, unless it is stripped down to its nutritional components, purified by the intervention of scientific rationality. Within these nutrients, the main contest is between protein, the building material for good muscle, and fat, the symbol of the uncontrollable flesh. Carbohydrates are in a middle ground: they are the fuel that allows us to work out, but they can easily fall in the realm of the enemy if they are consumed in excessive quantity. The battle is fought in every man's body, and it takes strenuous efforts. Men's fitness magazines present themselves as science-based weapons offering practical advice and helping readers to discern when food is a friend and when, more often, it is a foe.

–5–

Jam, Juice, and Strange Fruits
Edible Black Bodies

That endurance is my heritage – as a woman, and especially a black woman. I'm convinced that we black women possess a special indestructible strength that allows us to not only get down, but to get up, to get through, and to get over.

Jackson 2004

Keeping an eye on dieting, sports, and wellness trends, it is easy to realize that gender plays a huge role in determining performances, practices, and ideas about food and body images. However, it is not the only element to consider: race and ethnicity, fundamental in shaping Western cultural identities, are at least as relevant. Beginning in the fifteenth century, the colonial expansion of many Old World countries brought non-white populations to the forefront of economies, social dynamics, imagination, and shared fantasies. The worldwide abolition of slavery alongside the explosion of mass migrations and new means of transportation brought an end to colonial powers and major changes in race relations. Since its foundation, the United States has been an interesting laboratory in the definition of concepts and practices concerning race and ethnicity. In this sense, it is a great place to start looking into the connections between food, the body, and the politics of race. Furthermore, American pop culture is so pervasive worldwide that it is exporting perceptions and images that, interacting with different social and political environments at the local level, give birth to interesting cultural phenomena that deserve further investigation. We have a hilarious representation of this state of affairs in Liev Schreiber's 2005 movie *Everything is Illuminated.* In a delightful scene, a young Ukrainian man – with an adoration for Michael Jackson, Shaquille O'Neal, Kangol hats, and flashy jewelry – hears in disbelief from an American that there actually exist "gay negro accountants," that Sammy Davis, Jr. had converted to Judaism, and, above all, that the word "negro" should not be used at all.

The race-related stereotypes and the misunderstandings created, diffused, and reinforced by pop culture deserve to be examined and unpacked because of their affect on culture and collective imagination. Eating and ingestion, we will see, play a crucial role in the development of these discourses, revealing how food can turn into weapons in power relationships and the political struggles that originate in them. To begin an analysis of the complex dynamics of food and race in America, we begin, not surprisingly, with beauty salons and barbershops. After all, these are businesses whose very existence depends on the importance of body image, and on how much people are willing and able to spend on it. In fact, they seem to enjoy an enduring significance in contemporary black communities, as spaces where identities are shaped and reinforced, where culture is produced, and where free rein is given to all sorts of conversations, including many that focus on appearances and bodies. It is not unexpected that food often becomes a hot topic. In the movie *Beauty Shop* (2005), Queen Latifah plays a talented hairdresser who decides to open her own beauty salon. Some white women, loyal and wealthy clients from the shop where she last worked, patronize her new business and, inevitably, learn to interact with a culture quite foreign to them. For one of these women, Terri (Andie MacDowell), this includes the strange foods, such as collard greens and monkey bread, which Ms. Rita (Sheryl Underwood), a noisy and indiscreet black woman, tries to sell from her little cart.

Ms. Rita:	Monkey bread? It just came out of me like that.
Terri:	No, no, thank you.
Ms. Rita:	For sure? I made it fresh this morning. I got some greens, some okra, knuckles … I'm just trying to put a little fat on her. Take it with you, darling …
Terri:	No, no, I really shouldn't. You see, Steven wants me to lose a few pounds …
Hairdresser:	He would not sing that song if you had one of those J Lo/Beyoncé booties!

Since the beginning of the movie, the interaction between the two characters is framed within a series of stereotypes and body images: the white woman trying to shed some pounds, the black woman providing nourishing, although unhealthy food, some minstrelsy in Ms. Rita's imitation of the monkey, the fascination of white men for black women, and the relevance of the backside, also known as the "booty," in black culture. All the topics are tackled in the light-hearted banter that can be found in many beauty salons. Eventually, Terri finds in Ms. Rita's food a way to establish a new relationship with her own body.

Terri:	So, if you had to take a wild guess, how many grams of fat would you say are in a plate of your greens?
Ms. Rita:	Baby, my greens is all fat. Matter of fact, I found every fat you could find to put in my greens, I got fat back, salt pork, Vienna sausage, ham slices, pork chops, pork rinds, and I got bacon bits in these greens.
Terri:	Talk dirty to me!
Ms. Rita:	That's right! Say it with me! Fat is good!

By the end of the movie, these new sources of nourishment, charged with sensuality, lack of guilt, and enjoyment, will have provided the white Terri with a larger behind (which becomes a source of pride), an introduction to black pop culture, and above all a new sense of herself, to the point that she decides to leave her cheating and absent husband.

This is just one example in contemporary American black pop culture where food is closely connected to black bodies, especially female bodies, and in particular to "booty." These images are so pervasive that they are often received uncritically, especially, but not exclusively, by non-black audiences, and even considered objective or "real." However, this connection between food and the booty, often used to debase black women, is now somehow part of a re-evaluation of the black female body. This emblem for sex and passion has moved from negative connotations to positive, self-affirmative ones. The booty has emerged as a site of resistance to the shame and self-deprecation often imposed by white culture and by the "gangsta" rap lyrics that are often offensive to women while celebrating their bodies.

Booty as Food

It is difficult to pinpoint the origin of certain images and labels, but since the beginning of American pop culture we notice a recurring theme of the black body perceived and described not only as a source of food, but as an edible substance in itself. The topic is made even more intricate by a strong ambivalent element of sexual attraction and repulsion, danger and fascination. The connection between the body and nourishment is even more evident in the case of the female body, also within black pop culture itself. In the past few years, a new expression has entered American slang: *bootylicious*, literally referring to the deliciousness of the derrière. The hit song of the same name from the 2001 album *Survivor* by the R&B vocal group Destiny's Child made the word popular, also describing a woman's behind in terms of "jelly," another idiom for voluptuous flesh. Jelly is an edible matter that evokes sweetness, childhood, comfort food, and satisfaction of primal drives. Peanut butter and jelly is the quintessential treat for children and adults alike. The jelly metaphor, in which the physical consumption of food somehow mirrors the enjoyment of sexual pleasure, is not new but originates in the blues era, when we first encounter the expression in songs (a "jelly roll" would refer to sexual parts or to intercourse). The idiom was introduced to the mainstream in the 1940s by the swing song "It Must Be Jelly ('Cause Jam Don't Shake Like That)."

This is just of one many occurrences where the black female body is described in terms of food, with the derrière playing a peculiar and specific role, becoming the object of sexual desires that express themselves as physical hunger, in this loose network of meanings that include pleasure, desire, spite, pride, shame, and last but not least, nourishment (Parasecoli 2007)

Nevertheless, this kind of objectification cannot be simply dismissed as the manifestation of that same misogynistic attitude that other forms of black culture, particularly certain strains of hip hop, express in idioms such as hoe, bitch, chickenhead and such.

Before starting a more refined analysis of the food/body/booty metaphors, it is necessary to briefly address the historical dimension of the issue. It is difficult to pinpoint the genesis of certain images and concepts regarding black bodies, but it is quite likely that they originate in antebellum slave society.

Having their personhood, agency, and even identity as human beings denied, black people inevitably tended to identify with the body and the flesh. Facing scarce food and nourishment, one's flesh, and particularly abundant flesh, became a sign of resistance and self-affirmation in itself. This was especially the case for women: since they were often in charge of kitchen and breastfed white children, they played an emotional and intimate role in the lives of many of their masters.

In her study of early British colonial writing, historian Jennifer Morgan pointed out that white men, feeling both desire and repulsion, often perceived black female sexuality as dangerous and consuming, almost cannibalistic, as opposed to the white female body, which is normalized and subsumed in the patriarchal order (Morgan 1997; Schick 1999). Feminist theorist Hazel Carby has shown that rape of black women by their white masters was somehow justified by their objectification and their alleged hypersexuality (Carby 1987). The derrière particularly signifies the inherent danger of the black female body, as the story of Saartje Baartman, the Hottentot Venus, demonstrates (Hobson 2005; Holmes 2007). A South African woman brought to London in 1810, Baartman was shown at a freak show on Piccadilly Circus because of her protruding buttocks, clinically defined as "steatopygia." As Janell Hobson points out in her narration of these facts, the Venus's body was freakish precisely because it was considered beautiful in Africa, reaffirming Europe's sense of its own cultural – and biological – superiority (Hobson 2003). This superiority hid a troublesome ambivalence: if the behind was considered excessive, at the same time it exerted a powerful attraction as a symbol of hypersexuality, which made it dangerous and obscene (Willis and Williams 2002). White men who liked it could be considered either as pathologically ill, or as victims of black magic. Either way, they held no responsibility for their loss of sanity or the actions that resulted from it. Nevertheless, we know this social stigma never stopped white masters from choosing black women as lovers or sheer sexual objects. It is evident that black female sexuality, psychologically threatening as it was but somehow tamed and objectified by the dominating male gaze, did not constitute a direct threat to the general structure of power and could thus be made visible in the public arena.

Food finds itself torn in a contradiction between the desires of the body, in the form of hunger and sex, and the normalizing function of the table and of any codified cuisine. The fleshy black female epitomized this contradiction: it was the source of pleasure and desire, not only for black men but for white men as well. At the same time, that same fleshy body, which provided and prepared food in a society that tended to deny its very agency, was the bearer and guardian of order and civilization as expressed by the culture of the table. The "mammy" character, with all her abundant flesh, was often depicted as an asexual being. Food thus purifies the otherwise unruly black female body, as demonstrated many years later by the creation of the Aunt Jemima character to advertise a pancake mix. As has been pointed out, the character tended to reassure white middle-class women against the increasing difficulties of finding, and above all hiring, help in the kitchen (Deck 2001: 69–94; Witt 1999: 21–53). Mammies also played important roles in the history of American cinema, portrayed by actresses such as Louise Beavers and Hattie McDaniel (Bogle 2003).

The unruly female body re-emerged as a key cultural icon with the blues divas in the early 1920s. These women, in the words of Kalammu ya Salaam, "married big-city dreams with post-plantation realities … and spoke to the yearnings and aspirations of black women recently migrated to the city from the country" (Salaam 1997: 131). They were not passive puppets for the entertainment of the patriarchal society: they affirmed their autonomy by laughing at the respectability that animated the new African American city dwellers trying to assimilate and to be accepted. They brashly used eroticism to publicly articulate sexual desire, employing not only their voices, but also their physical persona (Davis 1998). Often hefty and fleshy, brown- or dark-skinned, they flaunted their bodies in front of eager audiences, emphasizing their voluptuous forms with provocative dresses and flashy jewelry. They brazenly embodied what has been defined "the unbound carnality of hypercorporeality" (Evans Braziel 2001: 199). Bessie Smith, outspokenly bisexual, sang in "Big Fat Mama Blues" about her fleshy body, her "meat," so powerful that every times she shakes it, "some skinny gal loses her home." In this case food is not connected to nurturing and reassurance. It does not substitute what cannot be represented, excessive female voraciousness, but rather highlights and enhances it. Even the exoticized version of the blues aesthetic that Josephine Baker offered to adoring Parisian crowds, appearing on stage dressed only in a skirt made of bananas, underlines the inherent danger in the fascination with these women.

Among the themes used in blues music, culinary themes were especially common. A desirable young girl was called a "biscuit" and a good lover was called a "biscuit roller" ("If I Had Possession over Judgement Day," by Robert Johnson, 1936). The complexion of a black person also played a role: "honey " referred to light-skinned persons, while "coffee" referred to darker ones, resulting in expressions such as "honey dripper" and "coffee grinder" as metaphors for a lover. Having sex was "grinding" (coffee in a grinder or wheat in a mill) ("Grinder Man Blues," by Memphis Slim, 1940) or "squeezing lemon" ("Dirty Mother for You," by Memphis Minnie, 1935).

The cultural power of such idioms survived the end of the golden age of the blues divas. After many years spent in hiding, the booty came potently to the fore as part of the hypermasculine and misogynistic attitude often labeled as "gangsta," which considers women as male apparel just like big cars, bling bling (a common expression for jewelry), boats, and Glocks (referring to guns). Sir Mix-a-lot's 1991 hit song "Baby Got Back" reduced the black female body to an object for enjoyment, while celebrating it precisely for the trait that most differentiated it from white standards. The lyrics bluntly affirm that, if asked, any black men would agree that an attractive woman has to "pack much back."

Never had the supposed black man's preference for large backsides been articulated so clearly. Since then, booties have been displayed with abundance in rap videos, often wrapped scantily and flaunted in the face of audiences. These images are frequently paired with symbols of conspicuous consumption, including champagne and expensive liquors, while sweet foods like honey, chocolate, and whipped cream often become tools of sexual enticement. Rap performer Nelly's 2004 video for the song "Tip Drill," where he sweeps a credit card in a woman's backside, caused an outcry in the black community (Neal 2005). At Spelman College in Atlanta, Georgia – a historically black college with an all-female student body – student protests prompted the cancellation of the artist's charity event for a bone marrow drive, scheduled for April 2, 2004, after he refused to participate in a public debate where students could question him about the video (Islam Muhammad, 2004).

The emphasis on booty in rap music, paradoxically, revels in the same images of the dangerous and hypersexed black woman created in the past by white masters who did not want to take responsibility for the children born through their sexual liaisons. The issue is complicated by the fact that hip hop songs and video, even when produced by black artists for a black audience, are ultimately financed by white capital. Even if these forms of entertainment constitute a valid way out of disadvantaged situations for black youth, they often reproduce and reinforce white stereotypes concerning black culture.

To this day, black female bodies are still able to evoke some anxiety in mainstream American culture (although not as intensely as do the bodies of black males). The Janet Jackson "wardrobe malfunction" at the 2004 Superbowl Half Time show, or the comments that Serena Williams elicited when she showed up in a tight and revealing lycra outfit at the 2004 US Open, are recent examples (Bellafante 2004).

Body Images

African American women tend to have a different take on large female bodies, and that abundant flesh is often an object of admiration. This fact seems to be widely acknowledged outside the African American community, both at the level of pop culture and in scholarly research (Jackson 1992; Kumanyika et al. 1993). In the past, being able to provide nourishment and to cook for one's family was a clear indicator of the end of any state of deprivation. Food was often the only gift some families had to give on special occasions and for family or church gatherings (Bass 2001: 219–30). Black women also relied on their abilities as cooks to start business and assert their agency in the public arena (Williams-Forson 2006). In *Fat History*, Peter Stearns notes that "religiosity could involve appeals to prayer as a basis for weight control, but it also embodied a sense that God determined what size a person should be. 'God don't make no mistake', was a common sentiment. Among blacks, large women were held to be more stable emotionally and less preoccupied with superficial issues" (Stearns 1997: 90–1).

Nevertheless, this level of acceptance for fuller figures cannot be taken at face value. Studies point to the fact that advertisers seem to pay little regard to weight control issues in black-oriented magazines, despite the growing concern about health issues connected with the traditional African American diet (Pratt and Pratt 1996). Disordered eating exists also in minorities. Even if thinness is not considered a criterion of beauty, "women may use eating to numb pain and cope with violations of their bodies." There is a "wide range of traumas that women associate with the origins of their eating problems, including racism, sexual abuse, poverty, sexism, emotional or physical abuse, heterosexism, class injuries, and acculturation" (Wangsgaard Thompson 1992: 452).

Contemporary pop culture, which tends to prefer slimmer female figures, is clearly exerting a strong influence on the traditional attitude towards large bodies in the African American community (Hesse-Biber 1996: 109). Scholar Susan Bordo, in her seminal *Unbearable Weight*, states that in the 1980s and 1990s "an increasingly universal equation of slenderness with beauty and success has rendered the competing claims of cultural diversity even feebler" (Bordo 1993: 103).

Middle-class black women seem to have adopted similar attitudes on body sizes as middle- and upper-class white females. Excess body weight is increasingly perceived as a reflection of class status within the black community, as the trendy, slim female characters in popular TV shows such as *Girlfriends* and *Soul Food* seem to indicate. For overweight middle-class black women, often able to react actively against racism, it is increasingly more difficult to defend themselves against the discrimination they suffer because of their body size. As literary critic Margaret Bass observes, "With fat there is the element of will. You are black because you have to be – you can't change that, but the culture says you are fat because you want to be" (Bass 2001: 223). The debate has spilled beyond academia and the health sector into the public debate within the black community.

Former top model and now TV hostess Tyra Banks has made the acceptance of different body types a main topic of her shows. In the 2007 edition of the reality show *America's Next Top Model* she selected not one, but two plus-size young women to compete for the coveted title. She dedicated an episode of her afternoon talk show to re-create the same photos that in 1997 made her the first black woman to appear on the cover of the swimsuit issue of *Sports Illustrated*. She proudly displayed her fuller, more mature body as an accomplishment, eliciting an enormous response from the audience, both black and white. Queen Latifah, the voluptuous recording artist, actress, and producer, has become the spokesmodel for Cover Girl beauty products. Singer and actress Jennifer Hudson, winner of the 2007 Oscar award as best supporting actress for her work in the 2007 movie *Dreamgirls*, has never shied away from displaying her curves and her abundant body.

The positions and attitudes towards female bodies, however, vary according to age, class, education, place, and style, revealing increasing differences within the black community. In this context, the female body, and in particular the booty, plays an important role in being depicted as a tease for men, but in reality as a means of self-affirmation for women. At the same time, the frequent connection between the booty and food seems to aim at reassuring men, emphasizing the traditional nurturing role of women.

In the movie *The Queens of Comedy* (2001), the comedian Sommore launches herself in praise of big behinds.

> I have this one prayer I say all the time, every night, for my ass to swell up. ... I want an ass so big that when I'm walking through the club, a man could just take his drink and lay it up on my ass, and I don't even know it's there. I'm just movin' on through the club and shit; knocking drinks off the tables and shit, movin' tablecloths over and shit. I want me a big ol' ign'ant ass. The kind of ass you just frown up, you be like, dayum! I want an ass so big that if I'm on top, he roll me over, I'm still on top. It's a wrap-around ass.

In Sommore's skit, the connection between food and the derrière is both subtle and disquieting. A big booty can be used as a table to lay food, but at the same time it creates mayhem, destroying all accoutrements usually deemed necessary for a civil meal. French photographer Jean-Paul Goude used a similar image – actually much more problematic, being the fruit of the imagination of a French white man: a black woman balancing a glass of champagne on her behind, and holding a bottle with champagne gushing from it (Goude 1981). At any rate, the booty becomes a site of self-affirmation in the face of men, rather than a cause for self-deprecation.

The other comedian in *The Queens of Comedy*, Mo'nique, is the more direct in connecting the large body, sexuality, and food.

> You'd better represent, fat girls. I love you baby girls. You handle your shit. Fuck you skinny bitches. Now! Fuck you skinny, anorexic, bulimic motherfuckers! Big women, it's our goddamn time, baby. Look at her shaking, bitch. 'Cause you're hungry! Get a motherfuckin' two piece and a biscuit, humm? Big women handle your shit! Y'all look good from the top of your head to the bottom of your motherfuckin' feet. ... Fuck these skinny bitches! You're some hateful bitches! Skinny women are evil and they need to be destroyed!

In Mo'nique's comedy, as it is also expressed in the successful sitcom *The Parkers* and in her book *Skinny Women are Evil*, the large body is clearly acknowledged as sexy and desirable. Her choreographies on Beyonce's songs at the 2004 and 2007 BET Awards and her appearance in the soul singer Marc Hamilton's "Sista Big

Bones" video are just a few occurrences where the comedian has shown how a big body can be attractive, even when its sexiness comes directly from a pleasurable yet often guilty connection with food (Mo'nique and McGee 2004). The same concepts became the theme for the low-budget 2006 movie *Phat Girlz*, where an overweight black woman ends up meeting a gorgeous African man who falls for her and says: "In Africa, a woman's body size is a reflection of her social status." The painful social issue gets diluted into a fantasy. However, Mo'nique has also been publicly bringing forth wellbeing concerns, making the point that a woman can be big, healthy, and classy. Her role as the dean in the *School of Charm* reality show has confirmed her as spokesperson for big, sexy, and *classy* women: one of the ten commandments of the show was precisely "Thou Shalt Work What Thou Art Working With." By her looks and style, Mo'nique underlines that there is a difference between fat and "phat" (to use a hip hop neologism), between obscenely flaunted obesity and tasty, healthy, and appealing fleshiness.

Caring and Nurturing

The articulations between female flesh, sex, and food are complex. A large body is often identified with a woman who expresses her affection for her family by cooking large, if unhealthy, meals. The archetype of the "Big Mama," so present in African American culture, would seem to represent the positive and non-exploitative counterpart of the Aunt Jemimas who haunted white imaginations. But are "Big Mamas" so free from exploitation?

In the 1997 movie *Soul Food*, the matriarch who keeps her family united by cooking large Sunday dinners together with her daughters, burns herself while preparing the meal, without even realizing it because of the diabetes that has numbed her extremities. The same food that nurtures a whole family is the cause of the disease that leads to Big Mama's self-immolation on the stove. We have a quasi-identification of the female body with the food it prepares, not only because food is the source of flesh, but also because the flesh becomes the nourishment that has to be offered to keep the family together.

We can see another example in *Waiting to Exhale*, adapted for the silver screen in 1995 from the bestselling book by Terry McMillan. Marvin, a widower played by Gregory Hines, is moving into a middle-class area in a Southwestern town. He immediately catches the eye of hefty single mother Gloria, played by Loretta Devine. She welcomes Marvin while he unloads his moving truck and ends up inviting him over for dinner.

> *Gloria*: It's just leftovers. Collard green and corn bread ... some candied yams, a little
>   potato salad ... Fried chicken peach cobbler, few slices of ham.
> *Marvin*: Yum yum! I would love to, Gloria, but I just got too much work to do here.
>   Maybe another time.

Gloria: Yeah, well, to be honest, I don't have no business eating it myself, big as I am.

Marvin: Well, my wife was a big woman. I like that. I like a woman with a little meat on her bones.

Gloria: Well, I could send a plate over by my son Tarik for you.

She goes back to her house, sashaying her rear. The camera goes from the transfixed look on Marvin's face to her behind, while she coyly thinks to herself (but audible to the audience): "Oh God, I hope he's not watching me walk away…" She turns and she realizes he is watching, to her evident satisfaction, while her swinging becomes even more evident.

Here the triangle between a fleshy body (booty in particular), sexiness, and food – and not just any food, but soul food – generates itself in the presence of a man. As a matter of fact, the man himself would seem to be the main reason for this performance, to the point it actually becomes the fulcrum of the triangle.

The direct connection between the black female flesh and food, especially soul food, bridging pleasure and nurturance, desire and culture, acts as a valid counterbalance against the sexist identification between the black female flesh and the unruly and threatening sexuality that was attributed to it first by white culture, then by the misogynistic streak in some expressions of young black male culture. Young black women seem to have found in the connection between fleshy body (booty), food, and sexiness the key to affirming their femininity and their agency without exacerbating the lingering tension between the sexes that many feel mounting within the community. Yet this phenomenon does not happen in a void, but within the field of the mass media industry, run mostly by non-blacks. Commodifying minorities, even when giving them a certain creative freedom, mainstream culture can find new and discreet ways to reaffirm its power. These elements risk vilifying the creative, positive impact that the public appreciation of the fleshy black female body could have on white culture, whose obsession with thinness in the female body still reveals deep patriarchal traits.

Black Men in Fat Drag

It is also in pop culture that we find a set of characters that can shed a different light on this issue, blurring and repositioning the ongoing negotiations involving gender, power, desire, and sexual politics both within the black community itself and in the often tense relations between blacks and other Americans.

Particularly in comedy, men have always worn women's clothes to solicit laughter by playing on stereotypes, bending social rules, and generally provoking audiences. Of course, black comedians have also often walked on the same path as their white counterparts in this respect: Jamie Foxx created the loud and ignorant Wanda in the comedy show *In Living Color*, while Martin Lawrence gave life to the slightly wiser Shenehneh in his show *Martin*. More recently, Shawn and Marlon Wayans dressed as unlikely white high society young women in the 2004 movie *White Chicks*. All of these characters are quite stereotyped: curvy, often foul-mouthed, and street-savvy. Male comedians obviously try to poke fun at recognizable types that audiences are supposed to be familiar with. However there are some comedians who have embodied another kind of black woman: older, wiser, wider, heavier, big bosomed, and often in the kitchen, or at least around food. Big mamas are such a relevant presence in the black community, including in the lives of many black men, that they embody a crucial archetype appearing in many forms of contemporary comedy.

The advances in make-up techniques and prosthetics now allow slim men to transform themselves into overweight, older women. They are never completely credible, also because they often appear in the same movie or show out of drag, but that is not the point. The fact that they are still recognizable as males is actually part of the act and definitely one of the fun factors the comedians have recourse to.

Sometimes the fat drag is just that, a disguise that plays a relevant role as a narrative device in the plot, like in the *Big Momma's House* blockbuster flicks, with Martin Lawrence. In the first movie, a policeman (Lawrence himself) in an effort to find a dangerous criminal disguises himself as Big Momma, the grandmother of the criminal's girlfriend, a young single mother played by Nia Long. As an effort to not be discovered as a fraud by the young woman, Lawrence/Big Momma is forced to prepare a nice dinner – of course, soul food – as if a good meal would be enough to cover the ruse and to make him credible. As expected, during the preparations the padding in the fake huge breasts catches fire. Still he goes on until a pitiful and almost inedible meal is ready. Here we have a strange rendition of the same dramatic scene as in *Soul Food*, where the grandmother burns herself while cooking without even realizing it, because of the loss of sensitivity caused by the diabetes closely connected precisely with the heavy diet that keeps the family together. Here it is an artificial padding being burnt: self-sacrifice turns into a parody of nurturing. However, the fake Big Momma will learn how to cook, while the policeman who lives inside her body discovers his own nurturing qualities with Nia Long character's son. In the second movie, Big Momma is hired as a nanny in a well-off but dysfunctional white family where the breadwinner is involved in an illegal business that the policeman is investigating. Strong with newly acquired culinary skills, Big Momma manages to wow everybody and convince them to keep her by cooking an amazing soul food breakfast. Once again the policeman develops a nurturing attachment towards the family's three children, helping them to grow and become more self-assured. This time what saves the day is not only the domestic qualities of the fat drag, but also her very blackness, with her savvy and her no-nonsense attitude. Big Momma translates these traits also into material food, with a move that in pop culture is often perceived as feminine. However, this caring attitude does not strictly depend on gender, since in the movie it is shared both by the policeman and by his older female double.

A nurturing and large black woman appears also in the *Nutty Professor* series, where comedian Eddie Murphy plays all the roles in the whole heavy, loud, and rude family of the clumsy and lovable professor Sherman Klump. The main character of the series, gentle and soft-spoken, Sherman is always represented fighting with his weight and his frustration, which he expresses by binging on food. Sherman's feminine traits literally expand in his mother Anna, also played by Eddie Murphy, a large, overbearing, hypersensitive woman, always dealing with her rude and obnoxious husband, and a whole set of voracious mouths to feed. While cooking is her way to express affection and attachment, as her son's body reveals, she also tries to acquire a certain refinement, often with hilarious results. During an elegant evening event, her attempts to go beyond the heavy and abundant soul food fare to enjoy dainty finger food provoke her husband's worst mockery.

At the opposite end of the spectrum from the Nutty Professor's mother, we find Ms. Peachez, a character who has become infamous through youtube.com and the viral videos that people now exchange on their cell phones. According to his web home page on myspace.com, Ms. Peachez, whose real name remains unknown, hails from Shreveport, Louisiana. A slightly overweight and bow-legged man sporting long fake fingernails in flashy colors and even flashier wigs, often wearing oversized T-shirts, sweatpants with faded floral motifs, and house slippers, he is the embodiment of all the worst stereotypes about rural Southern black people. Ms. Peachez's videos shine for sheer offensiveness and total lack of political correctness. In "Try That Chicken," a group of children sings and dances with her while she fries chicken in what seems to be the back of a junkyard. The sign "Peachez Ghetto Fried Chicken" welcomes viewers at the beginning of the video, with the chorus "Everybody wants a piece of my chicken, southern fried chicken, finger-licking. You hear me?" Ms. Peachez definitely plays on the stereotype of the underprivileged black woman feeding scores of children, relatives, and various unrelated people.

A similar environment provides the background also for the "From da Country" video, which opens on an almost toothless old black man in a blond wig and cowboy hat stuffing his face with watermelon in a sort of barn among hay and tractors. The song goes on listing all the dishes they like "down here," like cornbread, neck bones, chitterlings, pig feet, candied yams, and so on, all shown in cracked and dirty dishes, covered with flies. The debate raged on the web if Ms. Peachez's videos are actually racist or, rather, employ what cultural critic José Muñoz defines as "disidentification," the ruse where victims and outsiders perform the traits of their identity that are socially perceived as negative by the mainstream, and by doing this they actually take control of their image and social role (Muñoz 1999). Within the dynamics of disidentification, these performances constitute survival strategies that at the same time reinforce and resist the stereotypes imposed on those who do not conform to the mainstream. The complexity of Ms. Peachez's performances increases if we consider them as forms of the specific African American tradition that literary critic Henry Louis Gates, Jr. defined as "signifying": a difference between what is said for the benefit of those outside the community and what is meant for insiders (Gates 1988). The effectiveness of the comical outcome becomes even more controversial when we add in the factor that the actors impersonating the various avatars of the matriarch archetype are actually black men. Are we facing what scholar Psyche Williams-Forson considers as "gender malpractice," that is to say, "instances where black women have been intentionally misrepresented by white people and ambiguously misrepresented by blacks" (Williams-Forson 2006: 166)? Especially in the case of Ms. Peachez, we are reminded of the antics of the white performers in black face of the minstrelsy era. If irony and parody are key elements in any kind of comedy, the ideological elements that are evoked and reinforced in these specific cases have often troublesome implications at the cultural and political level.

However, the most popular Big Mama character in recent black pop culture is certainly Madea, played by the 6'4" Tyler Perry. Despite her house dresses with floral patterns, her dainty eyeglasses, and the nicely coiffed white hair, Madea sports a daring masculinity in her attitude, fast in using her hands and the gun she always keeps close. Madea, short for Ma' dear, is an expression sometimes used to address older ladies, whose nurturing role in the community is undisputed and to whom respect and affection are due. Perry's Madea does embody these elements: she is the one whom everybody counts on, especially children and women in the most vulnerable positions. She puts up with her vulgar and unkind brother (also played by Mr. Perry), she acts as a foster mother and offers consolation, but at the same time she is always ready to "whop some ass" when necessary. Although many key scenes in the movies happen in the kitchen, where Madea's guests are provided with physical nourishment and emotional protection, we never see her actually cooking. As a matter of fact, in these movies food reveals a certain ambiguity: if it is reassuring and nurturing for the weak, it can become a tool of offense and violence against those who take advantage of the weak. In the first movie, *Diary of a Mad Black Woman* (2005), a battered and abused woman takes revenge on her violent husband, when a gun shot paralyzes him, by sitting him in front of food without feeding him and eventually beating him with a baseball bat and almost drowning him. In the second movie, *Madea's Family Reunion* (2006), Madea instructs another battered woman about how to hurt her abusive fiancé by throwing scalding grits in his face (maybe inspired by the 1974 incident involving the famous singer Al Green) and hitting him repeatedly and systematically with a frying pan. It is ironic that grits, one of the most iconic soul food items, becomes the weapon used by a black woman to assert herself. Among the black comedians in fat drag, Tyler Perry has managed to elicit laughter without debasing women, especially big women and their traditional role in the community, even if using formulaic situations and characters. His character actually plays on the ambiguous mix of stereotypical traits commonly projected on black men and women by mainstream culture, but also by black pop culture itself. As a matter of fact, Perry's male figure becomes an important element in Madea, further complicating the issue of black edible masculinities.

Powerful Juices

The nurturing aspects of the black men in fat drag, as predictable and sometimes questionable as they are, constitute an interesting counterpoint to another contemporary performance of black masculinities, embodied by the hypersexual stars of hip hop. However, even the latter have shown some involvement in food: as a matter of fact, in the past few years we have witnessed some rap artists banking on their image and their appeal to promote energy or sport-related drinks. Nelly sold the Pimp Juice, Lil' Jon advertised Crunk, and even 50 Cent got his own line of Vitaminwater. These performers would probably have been happy to endorse more mainstream drinks (like Kanye West's commercial for Pepsi, which was not discontinued despite the artist's declarations after Katrina about President Bush "hating black people"). But because of their controversial public image they might have settled for lesser-known "niche" beverages.

The crossover between the world of hip hop and business is no longer limited to fashion, design, and entertainment endorsements. However, the discourse exploited by marketers, publicists, and – last but not least – the stars themselves hinges on a set of markers and stereotypes that has haunted American culture since its beginning, shifting in meaning according to the changing environment. It is evident that what is for sale is masculinity, and a peculiar brand of it: brash, in your face, and very sexualized. Why are audiences – especially young, often white and suburban – willing to metaphorically ingest this staged black maleness? Is this a new phenomenon, or are there other occurrences where black masculinities and the energy and power they are supposed to embody were perceived as edible in the pop culture arena?

The launch release for Pimp Juice, the new beverage introduced in 2003 by the platinum grilled star from St. Louis, together with Fillmore Street Brewing Company, also based in Nelly's hometown, stated: "When it gets hot in 'herre,' you can cool down and hype up with Pimp Juice." The quote from Nelly's most famous hit song immediately connects the celebrity to the product, placing it in an aura of coolness and sexual heat ("It's getting hot in here, so take off all your clothes," goes the chorus).

Nelly had dedicated a song to the Pimp Juice in an anthem that hit the streets in 2002, long before his drink. This miraculous substance is described as color blind, good for all kinds of people.

The meaning of the word "juice" shifts during the song: from money, to fame and straight intellect. However, what counts is that the "juice" attracts the opposite sex: it has very sexual qualities to it, qualities which, nevertheless, are color blind, just like the drink he promotes. The beverage had an immediate audience in the black club party crowds, but was also widely adopted by young white consumers.

The song plays with the wide variety of meanings of the word "juice." According to the popular website www.urbandicitonary.com, the on-line dictionary where definitions are given by users, who also vote and rank them, besides "1) power 2) gun 3) outpace 4) alcoholic beverage," the word also means "respect and credibility on the street" and "nutrition or lifeblood," sometimes indicating fuel for a car or steroids, electricity, semen, and female vaginal secretions (Westbrook 2002: 80).

The trademark "Pimp Juice" somehow suggests that the physical ingestion of the beverage could give access to the metaphorical qualities it embodies, whatever the race of the consumer may be. Many voices in the black community lamented and condemned the merchandising move from Nelly (Page 2003). Cultural critic Mark Anthony Neal reports that "groups like Project Islamic Hope, the National Alliance for Positive Action, and the National Black Anti-Defamation League, along with ministers Michael Pfleger and Paul Scott, quickly called for a national black boycott of Pimp Juice" (Neal 2005: 136). The pimp whose magical juice hit the streets is a mythical character of the ghetto, respected because he thrives despite harsh conditions, even if his survival implies the exploitation of women. Author Michael Eric Dyson notices that for the hip hop generation: "Pimping has been seen more in its metaphorical intensity; that is to say it's an analogy for how black men who are on the underside of society catch on, get over and engage in practices that may be seen outside of traditional orthodox society and yet allows them to get over" (Dyson and Smiley 2003, cited in Neal 2005: 137). As Mark Anthony Neal states: "Whereas the old guard can only see literal pimps, many within the hip hop generation have redefined the word to suit the needs of the post-civil-rights era world." (Neal 2005: 137)

The pimp, a mainstay in blaxploitation movies, is inherently voracious, consuming others to affirm himself. As often happens, he becomes the object of a strong ambivalence: he is loathed, but at the same time his inherent power and sexual energy are envied. Many would love to be able to incorporate that aura. Hence the power drink "Pimp Juice," something tasty and nourishing that one can drink. It is not by chance that in a satirical movie-length cartoon feature, the 2004 *Little Pimp* by Peter Gilstrap and Mark Brooks, the main character – a young fatherless white boy ("a tender white cracker") – is educated in the ways of the pimp by a short, street-smart, but all in all well-meaning man known, interestingly enough, as "Fruit Juice."

In the fall of 2004 it was the turn for another very visible rapper, Curtis Jackson, a.k.a. 50 Cent (or Fiddy, as it is commonly pronounced), to launch his energy drink, Formula 50, in a joint venture with Glacéau Vitaminwater, bought in 2007 by the Coca-Cola Company. On the industry website bevnet.com we read:

> For him drinking Vitaminwater makes as much sense as wearing a bulletproof vest. Whether he's gulping a power-c during his daily workout or drinking a revive after a long night in the recording studio, Vitaminwater works to support his active lifestyle. "Being as healthy as I am – I don't drink alcohol – Vitaminwater helps me live a healthier lifestyle and control what goes into my body," says 50 Cent. "The nutrients give me the energy that I don't always get from my diet, and certainly can't get from any other beverage."

The levels of discourse here get quite complex. The controversial ex-gangster, whose life story inspired Jim Sheridan's 2005 movie *Get Rich or Die Tryin'* , plays with different elements of his success: the lingering violence, complete with shootings and gang battles, his muscular, ripped, and tattooed body, of which he clearly takes great care, and his appeal to large audiences. By ingesting the beverage, consumers do not directly incorporate the "juice" that they long for, but they rather participate in the source of what provides the celebrity with his body and his energy.

The beverage Crunk, launched by the southern rapper Lil' Jon in February 2004, adds a new layer to this discussion. At the same time the artist issued an album by the same title, whose opening song was precisely "Crunk Juice," an invite to sit back, smoke joints, and listen to music.

Urbandictionary.com defines the expression "crunk juice" as "a combination of an energy drink, and hard liquor (it is said to have unusual results when consumed); a popular one is Hennessy and Red Bull."

Reportedly created by Conan O'Brien in the 1995 season of *Late Night with Conan O'Brien* as a replacement of all the curse words that could not be aired on TV, the word "crunk" (also spelled krunk) had assumed different meanings over the years. Used by Outkast in their infamous 1998 song "Rosa Parks," it is now a mainstay of Southern hip hop, meaning "1) crowded 2) hyped 3) exciting 4) fun" (Westbrook 2002: 32). Urbandictionary.com explains it as "a mixture of the words crazy and drunk." Lil' Jon himself defines it as "a state of heightened excitement." It also indicates a specific style of rap, based in the Southern part of the country. The official website for the drink, crunkenergydrink.com, states:

> Letting loose, feeling free, and expressing yourself is crunk. … Crunk is a bi-product of Hip-Hop and southern pride and resilience. The significance of family, be it biological or community and uninhibited pride for your city or 'hood is central to the appeal of crunk on a youthful southern generation. With its global influence, the Hip-Hop community is not only defined by its music, but also by its fashion, culture, and language.

Crunk juice tastes like pomegranate, a tart substance that is becoming more and more popular among health-conscious consumers. Among other ingredients, we find guaranà, horny goat weed (*sic*), and ginseng, which are often used to enhance energy and sexual potency. What is ingested with the drink is not only male sensuality, sexual potency, party energy, but the whole Southern mystique that plays such an important role, for instance, in the cultural construction of soul food.

This connection between the male body and some power that can be ingested and consumed is apparently not limited to American pop culture. Similar expressions can be found in British urban slang. We can point to the lyrics of a famous song by the Rolling Stones, "Some Girls": "Black Girls just wanna get fucked all night/I just don't have that much jam" (Poulson-Bryant 2005: 80). Mick Jagger seems to use the term "jam" as a black girl would use it to tell her partner he hasn't got enough potency and skill. Urbandictionary.com indicates various meanings to the word "jam" that are not used in American English:

> Jam: to relax. Used by black people in London, to have sex with a girl. Jam strangler: jam is another name for seman [*sic*] and strangler comes from the action that the man does whilst mastubating [*sic*] like he is strangling someone hence jam strangler! Jam rag: a garment of clothing or a hand towel used to wipe up one's wank juice after a five-knuckle shuffle.

Once again, in a different Anglo-Saxon environment, we find a food metaphor to indicate black male potency. Is this a new phenomenon, or does it tap into undercurrents that have haunted U.S. pop culture since its beginnings?

A History of Edible Bodies

In the past decades, black masculinities have played an important role in the world of international entertainment, especially when it comes to sports, dance, and music. It is almost to state the obvious to point out that black male stars are the objects of ambivalence: they embody natural skills, raw power, elegance, and flamboyance, qualities that are considered almost genetically inherent in their bodies. Author Scott Poulson-Bryant affirms: "It could be argued that almost everything the world knows about black men it has learned by watching black men in these most presentational of modes: dribbling, defending, or spiking a ball; strutting, shooting, or grinning across cinema screens: crooning, toasting or rhyming into microphones" (Poulson-Bryant 2005: 105).

The old stereotype of the black man who's got game around the hoop, and who's got rhythm in his blood are too expansive to be discussed in this chapter (Eversley 2001; Harper 1996; Mailer 1994). On the other hand, black males are also often perceived as powder kegs ready to go off, unleashing unspeakable violence. Without getting into the merit of the judicial cases, the way the media dealt with the O.J. Simpson, Mike Tyson, and Kobe Bryant scandals is indicative (Williams 2002).

Since the beginning of American pop culture, when it came to black male sexuality, the stakes were always high when white male domination was perceived to be at risk. Historian David Roediger claims that by asserting their whiteness, poorer workers could find an outlet for the frustrations born of exploitative class relationships (Roediger 1991: 13). The black male, made into a hypersexualized monster, had to be kept under control and emasculated, symbolically and, often, physically. At the same time this threat could not be made public and freely discussed, as in the case of black women: the supposed black male's sexual potency was something men could comment on among themselves, but no self-respecting lady could even refer to it in a social setting. The black male body became something to fear for its power, energy, and fully expressed sexuality; for the same reason, it was something to desire (Kimmel 1996: 50; Mercer 1994).

Literary critic Robert Reid-Pharr, in his book *Once You Go Black*, notices that in the American context we find the idea of a universal, eternal blackness that would stay the same though time and space, from slavery to the contemporary urban experience.

> Blackness itself, that telltale color, is always a sort of sexual crime regardless of how it is articulated. The presence of the black in any location represents precisely the failure of American and European eugenicist projects, a failure that has occurred precisely because the black is not only threatening but appealing, not only the monster that the policeman must beat into submission, but also the beauty without whom he cannot seem to live. ... Once you go black, you never go back. The myth of our potent sexuality has, I would argue, not only been a great burden but one of the most powerful means by which we have resisted – or at least adapted – racist and racialist oppression. (Reid-Pharr 2007: 31–2)

Already in the nineteenth century, the black body became a controversial element in American culture, and its visible presence as a worker, and in particular as a food producer, exerted a long-lasting influence on white culture, at that time very busy in defining itself after the separation from England and very determined to distinguish itself from other strong ethnic realities on American territory, particularly blacks and natives. Discussing antebellum black novels, Reid-Pharr notices how racial boundaries were still uncertain in the developing colonial society, so the diffusion of certain images and stereotypes helped define not only the black body as a stable element, but also whiteness itself (Reid-Pharr 1999: 5–6).

The tension often acquired very tangible qualities. Slaves were often left hungry, even when they were forced to accomplish most strenuous activities. This situation was often the cause of tension between master and slaves, as literary critic Andrew Warnes argues.

> The narratives of former slaves refer repeatedly to slave traders' and slaveholders' attempts to monitor, regulate, and circumscribe both the literacy and the diet of their human property. ... Equally often, they refer to acts of resistance – to moments of food theft and foraging, to surreptitious self-education, and to other individual rebellions that challenged such circumscription. ... What these acts suggest is that, within the plantation, the almost constant ability of slaveholders to control access to food and words coincided with the occasional ability of slaves to disrupt this calculated distribution. (Warnes 2004: 1–3)

Against this background, it was almost natural that racial tensions were often expressed in terms of food and edibility (Tompkins 2007). The actual consumption through physical exhaustion of black bodies that sustained the plantation and later the post-Civil War economy, where black men reclaimed their manhood at the economic and social level, often took the metaphorical tone of symbolic incorporation. It is in the horrifying phenomenon of lynching that we find clear traces of this transition (Perloff 2000).

In one of the most disturbing books published on the subject, a collection of lynching photographs, Leon Litwack explains:

> Newspaper reporters dutifully reported the events under such lurid headlines as "COLORED MAN ROASTED ALIVE," describing in graphic detail the slow and methodical agony and death of the victim and devising a vocabulary that would benefit the occasion. The public burning of a Negro would soon be known as a "Negro Barbecue," reinforcing the perception of blacks as less than human. (Allen et al. 2000: 10)

What Litwack misses, probably in the subconscious refusal to acknowledge the patent cannibalistic drive of these popular expressions, are precisely the food metaphors. We have to keep in mind that most lynching victims were black males, often accused of "not staying in their place" and, more specifically, disrespecting, touching, or even raping white women, revealing the uncontrollable sexual depravity that was considered typical of the race. The images from Griffith's *Birth of a Nation* summarized and voiced these lingering fears (Bogle 2003). Although lynching had always been a fast method of imposing extra-legal justice in the Far West, it is not by chance that a peak in this practice was recorded between 1890 and 1920, a reaction of white Americans to free African American communities that were striving to find a new place in society after the Reconstruction and often constituted also an economic threat to the lowest classes of white blue-collar workers. Litwack also gives us specific details that seem to corroborate the element of symbolic consumption of lynching.

> If execution is by fire, it is the red-hot poker applied to the eyes and genitals and the stench of burning flesh, as the body slowly roasts over the flames and the blood sizzles in the heat. ... Whether by fire or rope, it is the dismemberment and distribution of severed bodily parts as favors and souvenirs to participants and the crowd: teeth, ears, toes, fingers, nails, kneecaps, bits of charred skin and bones. Such human trophies might reappear as watch fobs or be displayed conspicuously for public viewing. The severed knuckles of Sam Hose, for example, would be prominently displayed in the window of a grocery store in Atlanta. (Allen et al. 2000: 14)

The presence of pieces of black bodies in a grocery store would seem to indicate the need for white communities to exorcize the perceived threat of these powerful and sexually potent males by breaking them down into more controllable and almost magical fragments. We witness a sort of symbolic cannibalism whose rituals are supposed to enhance the strength of the white community. This elusive element, often ignored by scholars and historians, was perfectly perceived by one of the greatest, and most tormented, jazz vocalists of all times: Billie Holiday. When performed in 1938, her signature song "Strange Fruit" created havoc even in the most progressive circles, to the point that her recording label, Columbia, refused to produce it. The song actually began as a poem by Abel Meeropol, a Jewish schoolteacher and union activist from the Bronx who later set it to music. Disturbed by a photograph of a lynching, the teacher wrote the stark verse and brooding melody under the pseudonym Lewis Allan in the late 1930s. In the song, the trees of the pastoral South, thriving on blood both on the leaves and in the root, are described as producing unusual fruits with bulging eyes and twisted mouths, swinging from the trees to the Southern breezes.

The food metaphors are right in your face: the black body who used to produce food in the South has been transformed into a horrific crop, whose smell of burning flesh reminds us of the quasi-cannibalistic elements of lynching.

Sometimes the connection between food and black males has been taken to its extreme: the 1975 movie *Mandingo* offers one of the most disturbing examples in recent times. As the title already suggests, it is a sort of plantation fantasy built around a slave from the Mandingos, an African tribe supposedly particularly gifted with courage, strength, and sexual potency. The film was adapted from a 1957 novel by Kyle Onstott, a work written during the Civil Rights movement, arguably as an expression of regret for the demise of the last remnants of plantation society. Former boxer Ken Norton plays Mede, a slave who is bought and trained by his owner as a bare-knuckle fighter. His name, short for Ganymede – the cupbearer of the Gods on Mount Olympus according to Greek mythology – already points to a connection between the slave, with his impressive but controlled power, and food. During the movie, Mede is literally cooked twice, in a huge iron cauldron placed in the front of the house. The first time he is brined in hot salt water to harden his skin and enhance his resistance during the fights. He stands up to the quasi-torture bravely, with his master observing him complacently. The second time, Mede is thrown into the cauldron filled with actual boiling water by the son of his master, whose wife had enticed him into her bed to get revenge against her husband and his black slave lover.

The images, in their unflinching rawness, present us with a weird inversion of the usual fantasy concerning African cannibals, often depicted boiling the innocent white explorer in their cauldrons. Here is the slave owner who seems to exorcise his deepest fears about his male slave and the actual humiliation suffered because of the slave's sexuality, not by destroying him but by truly cooking him, making him symbolically ready for consumption and, maybe, ingestion.

However, the fantasy of the edible black body can be turned against the power structure, or at least exploited to make money from white customers, like in the case of the rappers who are cashing in on their appeal by selling energy drinks that metaphorically transmit their aura. Trey Parker and Matt Stone, the creators of the satirical cartoon show *South Park*, anticipating the same business move, exposed and made fun of the fantasies about the black male body through the character of Chef, the burly African American manning the canteen of the town's elementary school.

In the 1998 episode "Chef's Chocolate Salty Balls," the well-meaning and artsy crowd of the Sundance Film Festival, feeling that their location is getting too crowded and commercial, decide to move their event to South Park. While the excess of granola consumption of the new horde of visitors indirectly creates an overflow in the sewer system, Chef decides to organize a little side-hustle by selling the visitors his cookies, which he aptly calls "Chocolate Salty Balls." The song that accompanies Chef's entrepreneurial effort is a long *double entendre* based on identification of the chocolate salty balls with the chef's genitalia, used as the symbol for his unbridled masculinity. The impact of the song is enhanced by the fact that Chef's voice belongs to Isaac Hayes, a sexy icon since his interpretation of the *Shaft* movie soundtrack. (For the record, Isaac Hayes has not lent his voice to Chef since the 2006 season: the artist decided to quit the cast of *South Park*, mentioning the show's "intolerance and bigotry towards religious beliefs of others" (Sisario 2006).) After listing the ingredients and the directions to make the cookies, Chef describes his chocolate balls as "big and salty and brown," so powerful that anybody in need of a little boost should pop one in their mouths.

The identification of Chef's body with the food he cooks is complete. But the authors of the show, known for their irreverent critique of American society, distort the normal use of these metaphors. The desire for the black body is exposed in all its cannibalistic undertones, but this time it is a black man taking advantage of it to make some money at the expense of the white radical chic intelligentsia, in a move similar to that accomplished by the rappers we discussed. However, in real life this kind of success is limited to very few exceptions, becoming myths for many young men and women in black communities who consider show business or sports as the only viable escapes from difficult environments. In the meanwhile, little effort is made to actually change the power structures that might limit their access to successful careers; unfortunately, a few happy (*very* happy) endings distract many from examining and opposing the actual situations and the power relations behind their reality.

Black Men Cooking

Naturally the connection between food and masculinity is represented in completely different ways in movies by black filmmakers. The examples are endless. In a scene from John Singleton's *Baby Boy* (2001), the main character, played by singer and model Tyrese, is having a hard time accepting his mother's new boyfriend, who is becoming the woman's center of attention. Early in the morning, the two men meet in the kitchen, where the younger man has been attracted by an appetizing smell: the older man, played by Ving Rhames, is making breakfast in the nude, just wearing his slippers. We see tattoos all over the massive body of the actor, who is scrambling eggs to add to sausages. Besides the *double entendre*, we see the actor from the back, so that it seems that his crotch is actually at the same level as the stove, almost *in* the frying pan. At any rate, the affectionate move of cooking breakfast for his lover does not feminize the character in the least; on the other hand, it gives him more depth, makes him less threatening.

Movies and TV shows written, directed, and produced by black artists and creative movers and shakers often present characters whose masculinities connect to food in healthy, caring, and nurturing ways, against the stereotyped images frequently offered by mainstream media. The American male tradition of the backyard BBQ is embraced with gusto, reinforcing the presumably common division between the everyday indoor cooking that is the domain of women and the festive outdoors grilling that is perceived as an acceptable masculine activity, where men who do not tinker with stoves can proudly display their skills with friends and families on special occasions. In movies like the *The Cookout* or *Barbershop 2: Back in Business* (both released in 2004) we have lively scenes of family and neighborhood reunions where the men are busy at the grill while entertaining their peers. In this context, the main distinction is between the soul food items, prepared in the kitchen by the women and constituting the core and the bulk of the event, and the BBQ, a male contribution that has visible elements of performance.

However, at times, black men seem open to take on more feminine aspects, not only as food providers, but also as actual everyday cooks. In *Everybody Hates Chris*, the show written by comedian Chris Rock, food plays a key role in the family dynamics. Julius, the father played by Terry Crews, is so involved with grocery shopping and preparation that he is able to say what exactly is in the fridge at any given moment, and the exact value of all items, especially when food is wasted or go spoiled. Always worried about the family finances, he comes up with all sorts of schemes to save money, including choosing products with no brand, buying sausages in bulk from the back of a car, and selling food stamps to get extra cash. In the episode "Everybody Hates Fat Mike," first aired on October 20, 2005, Julius is at home for a few days because of a strike and decides to help his wife by taking on the cooking. Eventually the children end up preferring his meals to the mother's, creating friction in the family that ebbs down only when he goes back to work.

In Spike Lee's 1994 movie *Crooklyn*, Delroy Lindo plays Woody Carmichael, a musician whose career is faltering, forcing him to count on his wife's income. With his masculinity threatened by the situation, he tries to express his affection to his unruly and noisy five children through food, especially the sweets and treats that they are otherwise not allowed to eat; he prepares lemonade adding lots of sugar in it and carries ice cream home while his wife, the real bread-winner, takes care of the children's actual nutritional needs.

Jesse (the strapping Henry Simmons), the boyfriend of Queen Latifah's character Belle in *Taxi* (2004), where she plays a taxi driver involved in a bank robbery investigation, offers another example of a black man as food provider and caregiver. While she is into motors and NASCAR, driving a cab and building her career, he prepares romantic dinners at home that she misses without even calling, and gets stood up in a fancy restaurant where he wants to propose. Although we never see Jesse actually cooking, the inversion between the expected masculine and feminine roles is definitely provoking, and the effect is enhanced by the sheer physicality of the actor, often shown in tight tank tops and T-shirts.

In all these examples, just a handful of the black male characters in many black-produced and -written works, food is a narrative device used to convey acceptable, protective, and caring models of masculinity, a black masculinity that mainstream pop culture seems unable to recognize.

The social and political implications of this lack of positive representations cannot be ignored. On the other hand, there is an abundance of perceptions and images that confirm the underlying assumptions about black bodies as consumable, expendable, and even edible matter. These images tend to make one of the historically most visible "Others" within Western societies even more different, less normalized, and inevitably external to the mainstream, perfect for entertainment and leisure. A similar approach to the "Other," perceived as different in terms not only race but also of culture, nationality, and religion, has become the backbone for mass tourism, a contemporary phenomenon that is providing Western pop culture with rich material in terms of representations, practices, but also social and political ideology.

–6–

Tourism and Taste
Exploring Identities

To live together in the world means essentially that a world of things is between those who have it in common, as a table is located between those who sit around it; the world, like every in-between, relates and separates at the same time.

Arendt 1958: 48

Keep Your Hands Off My Espresso

The sun was rising over a crisp morning in Inner Mongolia, the People's Republic of China. As an exchange student in Beijing, I decided to spend a weekend in Inner Mongolia with a few foreign friends, not too far from the provincial capital, Huhehot. Although we considered ourselves quite adventurous and attuned to all kinds of hardships and unusual experiences, we opted for a "regular" tourist hotel, a cluster of kitsch, cement replicas of the traditional wood and felt Mongol yurts (with a comfortable bathroom). Our hosts were waiting for us to go to breakfast. We were ready for the usual Chinese fare: rice porridge with pickled vegetables, warm soymilk, maybe a hard-boiled egg; something I was not particularly fond of, but had grown used to. Even after almost two years in China, the simple thought of a steaming cup of espresso was likely to make me salivate; as a matter of fact, I had brought a tiny espresso machine from Italy, and I received the coffee grinds by mail … None of that here: we were served a hot, greasy boiled sheep knee, accompanied by hot tea mixed with melted rancid butter and fried millet. The meal ended with a tiny glass of extremely strong – and mysteriously undefined – liquor. In my head, the food I was facing could not really fit under the title "breakfast," a category that at any rate had already been quite stretched in the previous months of my stay in China. The set of rules through which I approached and interpreted my meals was to be revised once again. I knew I was having breakfast, because it was early morning and the first meal of the day, but any other clue was pointing to a different, more substantial kind of meal. My culinary competence – my patrimony of food-related knowledge – was clearly insufficient to face the challenge. Why was I finding the experience disturbing? Wasn't it food, after all? Why was I enduring that breakfast as a threat to my wellbeing, to what I had so far considered my fairly enlightened and tolerant worldview, to my identity, to the very order of things?

Tourism has grown to be a common leisure activity in affluent Western societies (Löfgren 1999; MacCannell 1999; Veblen 2001). Travelers, each endowed with a specific culinary competence, are forced to acknowledge and take into account the existence of different foodways in a more or less conscious fashion. Indirectly, the analysis of tourism can uncover the political, social, and cultural relevance of food – foreign food in particular – as captured in a network of symbols, images, practices, and beliefs that occupy an important space in pop culture. Meals unite and divide. They connect those who share them, confirm their identities as individuals and as a collectivity, and reinforce their mutual bonds. At the same time, meals exclude those who do not participate in them, threatening and negating their very humanity.

Examining travelers' behaviors can shed a revealing light on the role of food in constituting and reinforcing personal and shared identities, a factor that acquires particular relevance at a time of globalization and swift technological changes. In this chapter I will adopt a wandering approach as homage to the ever-moving tourist – my subject at hand, but also as a methodological ruse to touch on very different and very distant environments and situations. The study of food-related behaviors from tourists is still developing: we are moving from empirical observations to theoretical analysis. Without aiming at any definitive conclusion, my travel notes are meant to draw attention to different aspects of the phenomenon, in order to prod the reader to further research and reflection on the uninterrupted changes of pop culture and consumption.

Fueled by the media and the growing presence of various ethnic groups in all large Western cities, curiosity for all things foreign has also sustained a certain interest in the so-called "exotic" cuisines. Ethnic products fill many shelves in large supermarkets and stalls in outdoor markets; ethnic restaurants are multiplying also in Western countries notoriously impermeable to foreign food, such as Italy; and ethnic recipes are the object of TV shows and magazine articles. This form of culinary tourism allows us to momentarily "travel" to far-away lands without leaving our everyday space (Long 2003). However, the attitude towards the "exotic" cuisines raises plenty of questions about our relationship with otherness: is it the outcome of a real interest in different cultures, or is it rather another, more modern and discreet, form of exploitation (Heldke 2003)?

Wanderlust as Appetite

Growing attention has recently been paid to the role of gastronomy and culinary traditions to sustain and, at times, even to initiate tourism. This trend has captured the interest of tour operators, restaurateurs, local administrators, and national governments. Food has come to the forefront, together with art, history, and landscape: the physical involvement of travelers with the places they visit has reached new and unexpected heights. Symbolically, economically, and materially, tourists consume and ingest the communities they visit. There is no better example to examine these behaviors than the resorts, now widespread all over the world, where visitors are allowed to enjoy a domesticated version of the local culture, prepackaged and predigested to avoid culture shock, while enjoying a period of carefree fun in a different environment that embraces without threatening. When it comes to food, all-inclusive deals offer guests various restaurants and eateries that frequently propose what the foreign guests are supposed to perceive or expect as "local" food. Within the gated compound of the resort, all sort of places to eat a quick bite are also available, some inspired by local street traditions, but others modeled after Western fast-food, often offering the same kind of fare. It is not rare to find menu items like hamburgers, French fries, hot dogs, pizza, and spaghetti in places where temperature and humidity would recommend any sane tourist to avoid heavy meals.

The Caribbean, a playground for both Americans and Europeans, provides some of the best examples of this kind of tourism, but a similar analysis could apply to the Red Sea beaches of the coasts of Mauritius in the Indian Ocean. We cannot read the stereotyped imagery we find on brochures, commercials, and other promotional material for the Caribbean, such as palm-fringed beaches and verdant forests, as mere meaningless clichés and marketing tools. These representations build on longstanding cultural perceptions that somehow equate tropical islands to a Paradise on earth (Sheller 2003: 36). As scholar Gregory Strachan points out,

> At various periods in the past five hundred years, paradise has been associated with notions of the primitive, innocence, savagery, and a lack of civilization, as well as of ignorance and nakedness, health and happiness, isolation from the rest of the world and humanity, timelessness, nature's beauty and abundance, life without labor, human beings' absolute freedom and domination over nature as God's stewards on earth, and connections of paradise with concepts of wild pleasure, perpetual sunshine, and leisure. (Strachan 2002: 5)

These images are so strong that they erase the events following Columbus's arrival in the area: the conquest, the introduction of new species and the export of others to the outside world, the destruction of the natives, the creation of colonies, the arrival of slaves, the establishment of plantation economies, and, more recently, the damage inflicted on the environment (forests, coral reefs, and soil). In fact, tourism imagery can be interpreted just as another form of consumption, the last in a long history of exploitation: an act of symbolic cannibalism against those lands that gave birth to the cannibal myth in Western culture in the first place.

At times, even the locals working in the Caribbean resorts and in the tourism sector in general are sucked into the fantasy landscape, just as are the palm trees and the sandy beaches. Quite often they are required to wear uniforms that echo their role as colonial subjects in subordinate positions: women in traditional – and out-of-context – garbs and hairdos, men in plantation-house-style pants and coats, or old-fashioned uniforms of all kinds. In promotional pictures, they are shown smiling, dancing, or otherwise giving a performance of happy and content service. In this sort of imagery, "when they are not producing the exotic, Caribbeans are cultivating a colonial past that adds to the visitor's sense of a quaint island atmosphere" (Strachan 2002: 2). These representations seem to have a certain appeal also for Western citizens of African descent, although many of them perceive the Caribbean as a region that historically has maintained closer ties with Africa (Rahming 1986).

The presence of resorts and foreign visitors, both traveling in groups and as individuals, exerts a heavy influence on the whole food scene of the destinations, shaping their material cultures and their national identities, as we can observe in other former European colonies in Africa and Asia. Even Thailand, a country that managed to maintain its independence from Western powers throughout its history, has conformed to the demands and the business requirements of contemporary tourism. Nevertheless, the worldwide popularity of Thai cuisines strongly enhances its status as a culinary attraction: tourists are often familiar with the dishes and the cooking techniques behind them, even if the actual flavors may startle visitors, usually accustomed to tamed and domesticated versions.

In the Caribbean, aware of the potential of tourism to generate investment, employment, and foreign exchange, the governing bodies of several countries have encouraged their citizens to create and maintain the fantasy that foreigners expect. However, they contribute to re-create a modern version of the plantation economy, similar to the old one in its inherent fragility as a productive system. In fact, tourism often favors the growth of foreign-owned and -managed businesses, reserves stretches of land (in this case beaches) for the sole use of the industry, and increases dependency on imports and on foreign consumption (Strachan 2002: 9). When it comes to food, data seem to show that high-end hotels and resorts are heavily dependent on food imports, while low-end establishments rely largely on local networks of producers (Belisle 1984). At the same time, the presence of tourists exposed to Caribbean restaurants in their place of origin can stimulate curiosity and appreciation in the locals for their own food. Anthropologist Richard Wilk has shown how in Belize, after centuries of widespread preference for foreign foods perceived as superior and more refined, the return of many emigrants who had somehow affirmed the existence of a Belizean cuisine in foreign lands, especially the U.S., has rekindled interest in local culinary ingredients and traditions. Observing the development of a Belizean national identity relating to food, Wilk wonders whether "maybe there is something about globalization itself that produces local culture, and promotes the constant formation of new forms of local identity, dress, cuisine, music, dance, and language" (Wilk 2006: 10). This hypothesis would seem to explain contemporary tourism trends that refuse the logic of the resort and focus instead on the local, the original, and the unspoiled, especially in environmentally friendly locations and receptive structures. All over the Caribbean, culinary expressions that had not been considered as part of the "typical" national identity have been re-evaluated. This is the case of the Garifuna in Nicaragua and Honduras, and the Afro-Caribbean populations of the Boca del Toro Islands in Panama. Their dishes and customs, which do not conform to the supposed prevalence of the Spanish influence as the core trait of the national character, have been rediscovered by foreigners, always looking for something different and new. As a consequence, the local government is also now presenting them as a vital part of the national heritage and appealing for tourists (Guerrón-Montero 2004).

All over the world, food has acquired full status as a tourist attraction, as proved by the growing popularity of markets, especially outdoor and street markets, as destinations. Centuries-old markets, like those of Samarkhand and Bukhara in Uzbekistan or Kashgar in Xinjiang, China, are now promoted as hot attractions, in a new trend that highlights so-called "cultural heritage tourism," which has been defined as "travel concerned with experiencing the visual and performing arts, heritage buildings, areas, landscapes, and special lifestyles, values, traditions and events" (Jamieson 1998: 65; see also Blake 2000). New markets have been established as the result of efforts to gentrify city neighborhoods in full decay, like the Granville Island market in Vancouver (Black 2006). Others that have been around for decades have now been included in tourist tours, with positive or negative impacts on the local economies and community life: we can mention the Damnoen Saduak floating market near Bangkok, the night markets in Beijing, and the Jemaa el Fna in Marrakesh, the suq in Istanbul or Damasco, and the green or farmers' markets all over the world. All of them have been more or less domesticated and sanitized to welcome tourists. The real marketplaces are either displaced towards the urban periphery (this was the fate of the original Marché des Halles in Paris and the Mercati Generali in Rome) or closed to visitors. The core sections of the Tsukiji fish market in Tokyo are accessible only to professionals, with the general public and the tourists confined to certain areas at the outer limits (Bestor 2004). Some food fairs are temporary, connected with special occasions and specific specialties: this is the case for the Day of the Dead in Mexico, the Caribbean Carnivals, or the Tuesday's Blessing in Pelourinho, the baroque neighborhood of Salvador da Bahia. Some of these events have changed over time after the local authorities realized their value as tourist attractions. Nowadays, Carnivals take place in the Caribbean at various times of the year, and not only in the traditional periods around Christmas or before Lent. The Tuesday's Blessing is repeated every Tuesday, becoming a huge party with Afro-Brazilian street food and live music that attracts thousands of tourists to Salvador.

The Typical and the Local

Tourism, including that which takes place within one's country or even one's region, has turned into a quest for the ever-fleeting dimension of the "local" and the "typical," for otherness anchored in "tradition" and "authenticity," the perfect antidote for the threatened identities of many citizens of Western countries. The restaurant business has also discovered local traditions as a solution to differentiate the options in an increasingly demanding market. Gastronomy is precisely one of the aspects of the travel experience where tourists can get in close contact with different realities: ingestion, after all, is a very intimate act. For this reason, food has acquired an increasingly growing relevance in the travel and leisure sector. Many destinations have acquired popularity precisely because of specific products that cannot be found anywhere else, due to their limited availability, or that can supposedly be enjoyed at their best in their place of production. In many Western countries, for instance, national and local governments are promoting itineraries in specific wine-growing regions where tourists can visit estates, taste the wines together with local products and traditional dishes, and even participate in grape harvesting and wine making. Similar initiatives have been organized around olive oil, cheese, oysters, and other specialties (Hall et al. 2003; Hjalager and Richards 2002).

Tourists often have romantic and idealized expectations of the food they will find. At a time when identities are continuously challenged and reshaped under the unrelenting thrusts of supranational homogenization and hybridization, the search for authenticity appears to be one of the main reasons to travel to unfamiliar environments. But regional gastronomic specificities, deprived of their connection with society and culture, risk often being reduced to local color, produced for the sole amusement and consumption of tourists (Feierman 1999).

> Modernization simultaneously separates these things from the people and the places that made them, breaks up the solidarity of the group in which they originally figured as cultural elements, and brings the people liberated from traditional attachments into the modern world where, as tourists, they may attempt to discover or reconstruct a cultural heritage or a social identity. (MacCannell 1999: 13)

What defines certain customs, products, and dishes as "local" or "typical"?

For instance, when traveling to Louisiana, one cannot help finding dishes like gumbo or jambalaya on most restaurant menus (Harris 2003). For an American traveler, these dishes already carry the connotation "Creole/Cajun food," as vague as this definition is for many. Foreigners usually perceive them as exotic, totally extraneous to their culinary competence as consumers, and have to refer to their travel guide and to the information acquired through the media or the Internet to decide whether they want to try them. By so doing, they acquire a more complete competence after ordering and tasting them. If they like the dishes, both American and foreign travelers may even want to learn how to make them, in order to relive at home the same experiences they enjoyed on vacation, or to entertain (and impress) friends with their newly enhanced cultural capital. By being taught how to prepare and to properly taste certain dishes, tourists enrich their knowledge with practical information about ingredients, preparation, and modality of serving. A whole industry of trips focused on cooking classes has developed, offering all kinds of educational experiences in different settings and environments.

Consumers, including tourists, need to be taught to acknowledge a dish or a product as "local" or "typical." In the case of French champagne, for instance, several elements are necessary to fully appreciate its cultural value and its role in the local identity. Its place of origin and methods of production, ingredients, history, and marketing are strongly defined as distinct or opposed to other sparkling wines – say German *Sekt*, Italian *spumante* or even American "champagne." The more or less deep understanding of what French champagne is, how it is produced and where, its cultural and social signification as a symbol of affluent consumption, and how and when to enjoy it, can help define an individual as French (and as part of a specific social class) or, in different contexts, as a Francophile, as a worldly gourmet, or simply as a snob. These elements may affect the image that members of a certain culinary community nurture of themselves and of their social position in the ongoing negotiations that define and redefine food.

The concepts of "tradition" and "authenticity" both play a crucial role in constructing what is "typical" and in defining local, regional, or even national identities. Since these qualities are supposed to catch the "essence" of a certain food or a culinary custom, they develop into the core for the construction of all sorts of identification and exclusion processes.

The same categories operate in an increasingly abstract way as we pass from the local to the regional and national levels. For instance, the local population of the Basque provinces in Spain could mention many typical elements differentiating, say, the traditional foods from Bilbao and San Sebastian. Nevertheless, the average non-Basque Spaniards would perceive these distinctions as secondary, and they would rather focus on the more general elements defining Basque cuisine as opposed to the rest of Spain. So, for instance, Basques could debate the most authentic recipe for pil pil sauce to accompany salted cod, mentioning ingredients, techniques, traditions, and so on. On the other hand, the average Spaniard would probably find these same elements too complicated or detailed, focusing instead on the fact that pil pil sauce is totally different from other sauces accompanying salted cod in other parts of the country. To define these differences, non-Basque Spaniards would refer to the same set of elements – ingredients, techniques, history – but would use them at a level of higher abstraction. Going from the regional to the national level, a Portuguese person would find even more abstract categories to define the typicality or the authenticity of pil pil sauce, opposing its supposed Spanish flavor and character to more familiar sauces used with salted cod in Portugal.

Eatymologies

Various elements of language, practices, and meaning may help identify as "typical" products, dishes, or eating customs and norms that constitute part of a specific identity. These elements do not reflect scientific definitions, but, rather, semiotic and cultural categories that function in different ways within a given community and in the exchanges among different communities. We may call these repertoires of meaning "eatymologies," borrowing this neologism from novelist Salman Rushdie (Rushdie 1999: 61). Just like etymology deals with the origin and development of words, tracing their diffusion through different places and cultures, these "eatymologies" refer to information concerning the origin and development of specific products, norms, and dishes, their diffusion and hybridization through commerce, cultural expansion, colonization, migration, and tourism, their interpretation in different cultures, the meanings and practices attached to them, and even their ideological value in different political and social contexts.

We can now point out some of the aspects contributing to these "eatymologies." We will not linger on several elements that can be listed under the heading of "social interactions," such as gender and sex, race, ethnicity, age, body images, nationality, social status, and so on, which have already been the topic of the previous chapters.

Ingredients

Some ingredients, as we have already mentioned, are especially important in the recognition of a specific dish as "typical" or "local." In the case of gumbo, for instance, andouille, okra, and filé are required in most versions of the recipe. Yet, okra was probably introduced to the U.S. by the slaves coming from Africa, while andouille is connected to the French heritage that emerges in Creole and Cajun cultures. The true Neapolitan pizza, according to some purists, should only be made using mozzarella made of water buffalo milk and San Marzano tomatoes: San Marzano tomatoes need the Mediterranean climate of the countryside around Naples to grow at their best, and water buffaloes are common herds in the marshy areas between the Italian regions of Lazio and Campania. We can also mention, for example, smoked reindeer manufactured in Lapland, northern Finland, or caviar produced along the coasts of the Caspian Sea.

The task of defining a "local" ingredient is not always easy. For instance, to ensure the survival of their vineyards after the phylloxera epidemic raged throughout Europe at the end of the nineteenth century, wiping out most of the local production, wine makers had to graft many European plants onto American roots, which were immune to the pest. Growers tend to ignore the powerful symbolism of the use of American roots – the part of the plant that conveys to the grapes the character of the local soil – in making Spanish, Italian, or French wines (Laudan 2004). At the same time, wine makers are investing time and money to develop native grape varieties that have been virtually lost for decades. Such is the case of Sagrantino di Monte-falco, in the Italian region of Umbria, which, after near-total extinction, in less than a decade has become a highly appreciated wine. Stimulated by these accomplishments, and by the fact that local varieties can offer wider choices to the educated wine lover who wants to try something new beyond the ubiquitous chardonnays and merlots, many producers are investing in the promotion and marketing of these newly rediscovered wines. Similarly, a few Eastern European countries are trying to change the image of their wines, to give them more exposure and international appeal: among them we can mention Bulgaria, Romania, Moldavia, Georgia, and Slovakia. In this case, the rediscovery and promotion of these local ingredients are the result of recent developments, although their historical origins date to a far, almost forgotten past.

Techniques

Many dishes and specialties are characterized by specific techniques that, in the case of artisanal products, are transmitted in very codified ways through generations, constituting a coherent and structured heritage that often plays an important role in the definition of the identity of a local community. This is the case, just to mention a few examples, for the production of Beijing roast duck (*kaoya*), foie gras in France, Jerez wine in Spain, and *lardo* (cured pork fat) in Italy (Leitch 2000). In a not so remote past, the secrets connected with specific products were often protected by guilds regulated by strict rules and quite difficult to access. Nowadays, many of those techniques are not what they used to be even a few decades ago. The food industry is undergoing an uninterrupted process of modernization and innovation. For instance, even some among the most traditional wine producers use pneumatic presses, or other kinds of time-saving and quality-enhancing machinery. However, although procedures tend to be industrialized, the production of many handmade products cannot easily be automated without losing certain specific traits such as nuances in flavor and texture. Besides, well-off and discriminate consumers often prefer a traditionally made product, even if it is more expensive. They are willing to pay higher prices for authenticity, or at least for what they assume an authentic dish or product should be (even when this does not necessarily correspond to its perception within the community that actually created it). Despite the existence of a high-end market, excessive industrialization could ultimately cause the disappearance of certain artisanal products, very labor-intensive and often not in line with modern hygiene requirements – as in the case of cheese made of raw milk.

Location/Place

Unlike Cartesian space, where every point is qualitatively equal to the next, place is not neutral. Every point is different because it has been lived and experienced differently by its inhabitants, and still is. Place generates concepts connected with rootedness, such as *terroir* in France or *territorio* in Italy, which nevertheless also include traits such as soil, climate, and other geographical elements. These ideas yield the concept of "origin," included in the legal definition of "geographical indication," a key element in current international trade negotiations (Parasecoli 2004: 36–9).

Besides influencing the character of local products, place is particularly important because it provides a foundation for identities – individual and social, local and national. The category of place has recently been the focus of theoretical works that connect space and meaning, defining place as a cultural dimension. "The whole of (social) space proceeds from the body," affirms scholar Henri Lefebvre (Lefebvre 1991: 405).

The connection between place and identities is jeopardized by what critic Frederic Jameson defined as the "postmodern hyperspace," which "has finally succeeded in transcending the capacity of the individual human body to locate itself, to organize immediate surroundings, perceptually and cognitively to map its position in a mappable external world" (Jameson 1984: 83). This tendency has been read as the ultimate triumph of Western universalism and cultural imperialism.

> At work as well in the obscuration of place is the universalism inherent in Western culture from the beginning. This universalism is most starkly evident in the search for ideas, usually labeled "essences", that obtain everywhere and for which a particular somewhere, a given place, is presumably irrelevant. ... The Age of Exploration had begun, an era in which the domination of native people was accomplished by their deplacialization: the systematic destruction of regional landscapes that served as the concrete settings for local cultures. (Casey 1997: xii)

The sameness-of-place on a global scale has its highest and most recent expression in the growing importance of the "virtual places" created by the Internet, where it is possible to buy products and food from all over the world. Also, many food corporations seem to operate in a different space dimension that has been called "glocal," where the global and the local are intermingled so that localities are promoted in the frame of transnationalization, where the very concept of national border, which defines nation-states, is threatened by the homogenization of political space in every continent (Lacoste 1988). Many international fast-food chains, for instance, rely on local products to assemble dishes that are the same all over the planet.

Trade/Economy

A dish, to be considered "local" or "typical," must also be included in trade and exchange. Until a product is consumed exclusively in its place of origin, it is not perceived as unique or specific to that particular location; it is just common food for those who produce it. On the other hand, when it becomes available to travelers or it is distributed elsewhere, its local and traditional traits acquire visibility for other communities. In turn, the producers themselves end up acknowledging its distinctive elements, turned into important economic and commercial pluses. When it comes to bread, for instance, each type is recognized as typical of a certain place only when it is sold where the common sort of bread is different.

> Identity is also defined as difference, as its relationship with otherness. This is evident in the particular case of gastronomy: a local identity is generated by exchange, when and insofar as a product or a recipe meets different cultures and regimes. ... Cooking is the locus of exchange and contamination, besides and more then the locus of origin. If a product can be considered the expression of a territory, its use in a recipe or a menu is almost always the result of hybridization. (Capatti and Montanari 1999: viii–ix)

The notion of identity moves thus from production to exchange, from point to network. Each community acknowledges certain elements of its culinary tradition as typical and special, enhancing its identity only when exposed to other communities that produce different kinds of food.

Time

Also time can be part of many cultural networks and established practices that help define the character of a specific food or custom. We can list cosmological time (night and day, seasons, years), which determines the growth and the development of many products; biological time, connected with the phases of human life (different foods are eaten at different ages) and biorhythms; anthropological time, which directs which part of the day, on what occasions, on which part of the year one would eat certain dishes; history, the time of human societies (the consumption of certain products varies in time); and psychological time, where "the memory-trace is nothing more or less than a signifier amongst others, in complex and mobile relations with other signifiers," and it is more or less accessible to consciousness (Burgin 1996: 216–18). Also time, like place, is under attack due to what has been defined dromocentrism, which "amounts to temporocentrism writ large: not just time but speeded-up time (*dromos* connotes 'running,' 'race,' 'racecourse') is of the essence of the era" (Casey 1997: xiii). Western food culture seems to be caught up in a new dimension of time that is determined by necessities of capitalist production, transnational financial exchange, and high-speed information highways. The only form of resistance to these phenomena would seem to be the construction of a conscious counter-culture that can start at the dining table, as the increasingly popular Slow Food association proposes (Kummer 2002).

> We are enslaved by speed and have all succumbed to the same insidious virus: Fast Life, which disrupts our habits, pervades the privacy of our homes and forces us to eat Fast Foods. ... May suitable doses of guaranteed sensual pleasure and slow, long-lasting enjoyment preserve us from the contagion of the multitude who mistake frenzy for efficiency. Our defense should begin at the table with Slow Food. Let us rediscover the flavors and savors of regional cooking and banish the degrading effects of Fast Food. (Bonilli et al. 1987: 1)

The association considers tradition in terms of its connections with material culture, labor, territory, and human time, as opposed to the obsessive rhythm of modern economies that deprive us of our leisure time. Nevertheless, this approach has been labeled as "culinary luddism," whose goal would be "to turn back the flood tide of industrialized food in the First World, and to prevent such foods from engulfing traditional ethnic foods elsewhere" (Laudan 1999: 136; see also Chrzan 2004; Donati 2005; Laudan 2001). This criticism points to the danger that the rediscovery of tradition might be captured within a discourse hinging on conservative moral values, reconstructing the ideological myth of a time which knew neither disruptions nor crises. In fact, the appeal of tradition has already been largely exploited in this sense by the advertising industry: many products are marketed bearing an image of the "good old days."

Media

In a book about food and pop culture, we can never underline enough how the growing impact of media on contemporary societies has generated autonomous fields of meaning where facts, events, and trends are largely determined by the media themselves, in a phenomenon the French sociologist Pierre Bourdieu called "the circular circulation of information" (Bourdieu 1998: 23). The relevance of a piece of news or of a show does not lie in what they refer to, but to the fact that they simply exist, creating a wide-spread effect of auto-referentiality where images and information bear little or no connection with what used to be called reality. (Baudrillard 1983b: 93–109; Baudrillard 1988: 12). Images and information heavily influence other aspects of culture. In the case of food, TV networks and magazines affect our perception of what good eating is supposed to be. Recipes created by famous chefs can become so glamorous, perceived as "high end," that a middle-class housewife might want to try them to impress her friends. Advertising tries to differentiate food in order to induce new needs in the consumers and to boost sales. The average American supermarket patron is used to choosing among various brands of the same kind of products, each of them connoted as "designer food," "family food," "diet food," "organic food," "luxury food." Similarly, a certain product or dish can be converted into the "marker" of a place or a culture for the media, creating a new perception. You don't really experience Louisiana if you don't eat gumbo or jambalaya. Balsamic vinegar was little known in Italy (outside Emilia Romagna, the region where it is produced) until the media connoted it as refined and rare, and famous chefs started using it instead of normal vinegar. Now it is one of the markers for "high-end Italian cuisine," even if you can buy cheap versions. Something similar happened to Prague ham slowly cured in brine, then smoked with birch wood and left to age. Only recently has this exquisite meat gained international recognition, owing to the increase in tourism to the Czech Republic, and the attention of the media, which is always on the lookout for new products and trends.

Administrative Regulations

The rekindled interest in wine and food, in culinary traditions and local produce, as promoted and exploited by the media, is reaching new heights while Europe is undergoing major political changes aimed at increasing integration among the member states, not only administratively but also economically. The process is not painless, with the political leaderships in different countries trying to cling to their power and their dominant role against these transformations. Food is not excluded from this evolution. Many countries are trying to gain advantage from the introduction of regulatory systems that derive from the one France invented in 1855 to exert state control over its agricultural production: a classification that ranked 60 wine makers (or châteaux) on the basis of their wine price and quality. In the 1930s, the system developed into the Controlled Appellation of Origin (AOC, Appélation d'Origine Controlée) (Guy 2002). In time, each area created rules to regulate the production of local wines. Wine makers had to meet specific requirements in order to receive the coveted denomination, which was perceived as a guarantee of higher quality and had proved to be a very effective marketing device. The system paid off. Wine quality was actually enhanced, and consumers were willing to pay more for wines that had received some sort of recognition from the state. Similar wine classifications have been adopted all over Europe. Food manufacturers were aware that a similar mechanism, applied to their production, would increase the value of their goods and protect them from people selling similar products of lesser quality under the same name. Now the European Union is able to defend its marks of quality within the World Trade Organization under the international law of intellectual property.

We have to consider also other political connotations of the concept of "local" that are increasingly relevant in Western societies and that connect local with "just," "sustainable," "organic," and such. For certain categories of consumers, the fact that their consumption choices can actually have an impact on the social and political arrangments of their communities increases their sense of involvement in production and distribution issues. Interestingly, freshness and taste often are not the highest priorities for these consumers. However, initiatives such as cooperatives of farmers and consumers, community-supported agriculture, and organic produce markets are adding new political meaning to the concept of local as opposed to national and international, in a framework that opposes "big business" to "human relations," "democracy" to "control," "participation" to "passivity."

The elements to be considered in any definition of "local" or "typical" appear countless, most impossible to assess in their totality. Yet, when it comes to our own culinary tradition, we are able to point out many defining elements of our identity and culinary competence. The existence of generally accepted "local" dishes, practices, and widespread disgusts within any given community seems to point to the fact that all the layers of meaning we have described interact with each other to form some sort of "nodal points," such as generally acknowledged recipes or widely practiced food customs. In fact, as we discussed in the Introduction, these may change in time or be interpreted in different ways according to the situation and the context. Nevertheless, the presence of stable elements providing permanent clusters of meaning allows individuals within a group to share the same information and the same interpretive grids about culinary traditions. If I mention *pasta e fagioli* (pasta and bean soup) in Italy, or shepherd's pie in England, members of the community that considers those dishes as theirs are likely to understand the reference immediately. Yet, within the same community, the *pasta e fagioli* could be perceived either as a symbol of long-lasting tradition or merely as a simple, uninteresting, almost vulgar dish; shepherd's pie is considered by some to be a nutritious, substantial comfort food, by others a cheap pub food. These perceptions are not casual or serendipitous, but they respond to precise and structured interpretations. Within broad limits, the meaning we attribute to food reveals itself as intrinsically plural and subject to interpretation and negotiations by different and competing agencies. This introduces politics into the communication and the customs related to food, where by politics we intend the expression of the efforts by specific actors to articulate the fluid field of meaning and practice in a way that might be beneficial for their own goals. The "super foods" that acquire a special status in the definition of the identity of a community, both from within and from without, reveal enormous political relevance. If, as I propose, we interpret food as a signifying network, an interconnected web of systems of signs, these identity foods at the same time play different roles in various layers of meaning. As we mentioned, the gumbo might mean something specific to the Louisiana community from which it originated, something different to the larger American community, and something else to foreigners. Gumbo is a sign that lives and functions concurrently in different signifying networks. It plays a role similar to what historian Lydia Liu calls a "super sign."

We are catapulted in the realm of what I call the super-sign – a linguistic monstrosity that thrives on the excess of the presumed meanings by virtue of being exposed to, or thrown together with, foreign etymologies and foreign languages. The super-sign escapes our attention because it is made to camouflage the traces of that excess through normative etymological procedures and to disavow the mutual exposure and transformation of the language. ... Properly speaking, a super-sign is not a word but a hetero-cultural signifying chain that crisscrosses the semantic fields of two or more languages simultaneously and makes an impact on the meaning of recognizable verbal units. ... The super-sign can thus be figured as a manner of metonymical thinking that induces, compels, and orders the migration and dispersion of prior signs across different languages and different semiotic media. (Liu 2004: 13)

If we substitute culinary system for language, we can see that the definition actually works very well. Certain foods, ingredients, or dishes acquire worldwide notoriety and a certain status precisely because they are signs shared by various signifying networks, carrying different meaning in each environment but somehow maintaining bits and pieces of all those interpretations.

Traveling Food

These shifts in meaning could not take place if we did not live in times of global exchanges of people, money, and goods, with tourism playing a key role in stimulating these phenomena. In the past few decades, human masses have been moving all over the planet, creating unprecedented contacts between different cultures. The modern technopolis, the updated version of the global village that McLuhan had imagined decades ago, engenders various forms of nomadism, a result that escapes any logic aiming at establishing controlled and contained social structures (Ferrara 1990). Political refugees, immigrants, tourists, global managers, exploited workers, find themselves facing new food habits, unfamiliar dishes, even unknown ingredients. At the same time, they carry with them their own foodways, recipes, and flavors, introducing elements of novelty in the culture that welcomes (or does not welcome) them.

As we discussed, travelers have their own food competence. We all have very clear ideas about what certain recipes should taste like. When we are within our own culture, we do not necessarily have to know how to cook to say what we are eating, and if it is good. It does not matter how developed and conscious it is, this food competence turns out to be very relevant when travelers encounter unfamiliar culinary environments, constituting a loose interpretive grid through which experience gets sifted. When they arrive in another country or another region in their country, tourists find themselves in a position quite different from immigrants. They do not have to adapt themselves to the new environment, if they so choose; they have paid for their trips and they want to have fun. They might experience various feelings: anxiety, elation, curiosity, annoyance, or fear. They can either be adventurous, challenging each other to eat whatever seems more exotic and dangerous, ordering from the menu the very dishes they are not familiar with, or they might try to avoid as much as possible the contact with the unknown, with what does not fit within their categories and as a consequence is perceived as polluting or disgusting. The latter attitude is at the origin of tourist enclaves where foods from different countries are guaranteed. Claude Fischler, building on the work of psychologist Paul Rozin, noticed how human beings are pulled by two opposite attitudes, neophobia and neophilia: the curiosity to try new food, based in humans' omnivorous nature, and the concurrent fear of being poisoned (Fischler 2001; Rozin, 1988). This ambivalence seems to be intrinsic to food itself: here it may be useful to refer to the concept of *pharmakon*, the medicine that must enter our body to be effective, singled out by the French philosopher Jacques Derrida (Parasecoli 2001): "There is no such thing as a harmless remedy. The *pharmakon* can never be simply beneficial. ... It partakes of both good and ill, of the agreeable and the disagreeable" (Derrida 1981: 99). In the same way, human beings are aware that food can be both a source of nourishment (and pleasure) and a very dangerous substance, if taken in excessive quantities, or badly cooked, or just clumsily chosen.

Beside this basic factor and many others, such as social position or spending capacity, two key elements affect the attitude of all newcomers towards local food: their knowledge and familiarity with it, and their capacity to engage with otherness. They can situate themselves on a continuum whose extremes are an advanced knowledge of the local gastronomic system and, on the opposite end, a total ignorance. In the case of Western travelers, these extremes are quite theoretical, and travelers would probably find themselves at some intermediate point. Owing to the abundance of information available through the media, the presence of immigrants and exotic restaurants, and the enhancement of the average education level, travelers are likely to have some basic competence; at least, they expect to find unfamiliar food. Travelers' knowledge and competence can vary widely, especially if their experience is based uniquely on the exotic restaurants in their country of origin, which probably offer a choice of dishes selected to please the local patrons, adapted to local taste and habits, and made with available products. Culinary tourism is a way to explore difference, but we cannot forget that the notion of what constitutes this difference is personal and cultural, in the sense that one person's "unfamiliar" is another's "familiar." In many ways, tourism and the restaurant business are trying to discover always new "unfamiliar" elements to keep the most sophisticated travelers and patrons intrigued.

Although massive exchange of alimentary products has always been very important, determining commercial trends and even the rise and decadence of empires, in recent years culinary traditions throughout the world have become less and less isolated. Beside the more or less wide knowledge of local gastronomy, all kinds of newcomers situate themselves on another continuum going from a total refusal of anything unfamiliar to a total acceptance of whatever might land on their tables: the tension between neophobia and neophilia. The same range of attitudes can be found, as if reflected in a mirror, in those who have to deal with them at their arrival.

Applying the Lacanian categories of analysis that we introduced in Chapter 4, travelers finding themselves in a new environment with foreign foods sometimes feel that their cultural identity is threatened. Facing alien culinary customs and unknown flavors equates to an encounter with the Real, that which resists symbolization and that cannot be recognized as part of culture and of any understandable signifying system. In other words, the Real is all that we cannot wrap our minds around and disturbs our comprehension of reality. It is a situation that reveals the fundamental gap in the structured and shared practices, ideas, and values in which subjects try to anchor their identities as individuals. This constitutive lack of coherence in culture hinders any attempt at achieving definitive, fixed, and reassuring meanings, as hard as we try to suture these gaps to achieve a more stable self (Stavrakakis 1999: 45–6).

Travelers also realize that their identity is based on a specific and limited cultural system, which cannot be considered as absolutely objective and natural. As a consequence, they might decide to face the Real to expand and enhance their subjective experience. In a very common narrative of travel, often cunningly exploited by high-end tour operators catering to worldly and often jaded travelers, the tourist experience is supposed to enrich them, to broaden their vision, to the point of offering a new, sutured identity to the subject, where the Real is somehow tamed and reduced to a controllable presence, ceasing precisely to be the Real and fitting nicely within the symbolic network. This amounts to a politically correct, more modern version of colonialism, based on stereotypes that reflect a specific hierarchical perception of the world and society, and a fantasy of control over otherness (hooks 1995: 38).

The Politics of Culinary Encounters

Culinary fusion, gastronomical curiosity, and mutual enjoyment are not the obvious outcome of every food culture encounter. Emphasis on food as a social and cultural practice often constitutes a very effective antidote to the damage suffered by traditional identities or, better, to the painful disclosure of the fundamentally cultural and historical character of any identity. Various political instances often carefully conceal the constructed nature of these elements, employing food-related issues as weapons to implement their attempt at cultural hegemony in a given society. Food often assumes "the function of ideological fantasy to mask this inconsistency ... and thus to compensate us for the failed identification" (Žižek 1989: 27). We must never forget that food, although a highly symbolic and cultural phenomenon, remains closely connected with desire, pleasure, and the fullness of personal enjoyment, a dimension that escapes the symbolic universality and the historical certainty of any political project.

In this sense, politics must be distinguished from the political, the open field of negotiation of meaning in its fluid and shifting aspect, prior to any specific fixation, but already belonging to the symbolic, not to any supposed pre-cultural reality.

> It [the political] appears in the sense that the process whereby society is ordered and unified across its divisions becomes visible. It is obscured in the sense that the locus of politics (the locus in which parties compete and in which a general agency of power takes shapes and is reproduced) becomes defined as particular, while the principle which generates the overall configuration is concealed. (Lefort 1985: 11)

The political reveals the unavoidable and hidden gap at the heart of the cultural dimension, which our quest for identity constantly tries to conceal and suture. The relevance of these phenomena is not secondary, as Roland Barthes already demonstrated in his work on mythologies, denouncing connotations that are universalized for the whole society to become dominant and hegemonic (Barthes 1972; Camargo Heck 1980). As in the recent debates over genetically modified crops, the presence of hormones in meat, or the increasing opposition to fast-food in certain European political circles, food can become a nodal point condensing symbolic networks and connecting various heterogeneous elements, which somehow, in their political neutrality, could have been absorbed in all kinds of discourses, and get their meaning from them (Parasecoli 2003b). In the case of Western tourism, food may be used as a metaphor for otherness and to affirm cultural superiority. In this sense, the political value of tourism in constructing perceptions of otherness when facing foreign systems of meaning cannot be overlooked. The economic and social impact of Western tourism on developing countries, including culinary tourism, is all but negligible, which adds to its political importance. For lack of information, or because of deeply encroached identifications, the food of strangers can be looked upon as barbarian, uncouth, dirty, even disgusting. Tourists can totally refuse it, sticking to the "international cuisine" catered by many hotels; they may try it as a sign of bravery and, again, superiority; or they can adopt a more tolerant attitude and accept otherness as such. A semiotic analysis of these phenomena connected to culinary tourism, and to tourism in general, can allow each subject to acknowledge his or her specific location within communication, perceived as a cultural construction connected with race, national identity, class, gender, and other determining factors. A deeper awareness of the political, non-neutral nature of semiotic processes defining codes and modalities of cultural exchange can help tourists to shift their location not only physically, but also culturally. Having a better grasp of the various signifying networks that make tourists define a phenomenon, in our case a dish or a product, as "typical" or "local" might help them learn how to occupy the subject position of the otherness, without losing the awareness of their own location. This would constitute the ultimate travel experience, providing effective tools to enhance diversity and open-mindedness in increasingly larger strata of society. And could there be a better place than the table, considered in many cultures as the locus for pleasure and conviviality, to undergo these often troubling and unsettling processes leading to a critical awareness of one's identity?

Afterword: A Plea for Pleasure

In the end, that's what this election is about. Do we participate in a politics of cynicism or a politics of hope?

Obama 2007

Food studies is a developing discipline. An enticing feature of this new field of study is that it can encompass many approaches and different topics that range from history to sociology, from anthropology to women's studies, and nutrition. However, in the search of recognition from more established academic quarters, little attention has been paid to aspects that would fall under the heading of cultural or media studies, especially those belonging to popular culture. We cannot underestimate the impact of communication on the ways we perceive, consume, and produce food. On the other hand, food plays such an important role in human life that it emerges in many aspects of our culture, as well as in those apparently less connected with it. Developing an analytical framework to handle these topics is an important task for food studies and this book aims to be a contribution in that direction. I hope readers have enjoyed giving a second, maybe fresher look to everyday objects and facts, including our own practices and ideas, to achieve a better grasp of how much food shapes our lives, our mental worlds, and our cultural identities.

However, as useful as these critical tools prove to be, they might not be enough, if we want to turn intellectual understanding into action, from everyday choices at the grocery shop to wider social and political issues.

In the past few years I have been teaching some very stimulating courses about food in pop culture and in movies (at least stimulating for me to teach, but I think the students liked them too). I thoroughly enjoy the whole experience. I must admit that I get a kick out of pop culture, including the campy, slapstick, and over-the-top varieties. Being involved with the media, it was only natural for me to look for food in all its expressions, especially those where the connection with food is less evident. Many movies have food at their core: it is enough to mention *Babette's Feast*, or *Like Water for Chocolate*. These films have already become the objects of research and reflection for academics and movie critics. But what about cartoons, or B-movies? These genres have not been included in the literature and arts canons (at least not yet), and consequently they have often been left out of classrooms and serious discussions, even if they are the object of a wide interest that surfaces in magazines, blogs, and talk shows. The same goes for literary genres such as horror

147

or science fiction, or forms of visual expression like advertising, packaging, and tourism brochures. A similar fate befalls popular music and television shows, and even less respectable forms of expression like pornography. Although cultural studies has often turned its attention to these phenomena, food studies, still in its initial stage, has usually maintained a more dignified attitude, concentrating on artistic or mainstream movies, visual arts (painting and sculpture above all), and respectable works of literature. Traditional customs and the objects related to them have long been the focuses of study for ethnologists, anthropologists, and folklorists.

My work as a journalist for *Gambero Rosso*, a very well-established Italian food and wine magazine, has offered an outlet for my interests in material culture, entertainment, and leisure, not only from the participative point of view, but also as a topic for reflection and discussion. Nevertheless, this pleasure of mine has always been spoiled to a certain extent by a subtle, lingering sense of guilt. Somehow, probably due to my upbringing and education in the not-so-flexible Italian academic system, wasting energy and time on trivial subject matter does not sit too well with the internalized expectations of what serious scholarly and intellectual work should be.

The issue is, of course, a complex one. As academics and intellectuals – and, I should add, as journalists and often as informed readers – we are the heirs of the tradition initiated by Aristotle that blossomed with the Enlightenment. It is a tradition that underscores the rationality of human beings and their capacity to make informed decisions based on facts, in an incessant effort to achieve objective truths. We are trained to stick to the evidence and to develop rational and critical analyses of the world that surrounds us, looking for unbiased and verifiable realities; a very honorable activity indeed, of which I am a proud practitioner and defender.

Yet, as this book has tried to illustrate, we should realize that we live in a "society of spectacle", using Guy Debord's definition, a culture based on that hyperreality and lack of solid points of reference that Jean Baudrillard scathingly criticizes in his work. When it comes to market-oriented culture, we cannot limit ourselves to analysis and disapproval: whether we accept it or not, we are all part of the consumer society. New methods and tools to deal with it are in order, particularly if we want to play any role in today's reality instead of limiting ourselves to be informed spectators. This necessity has been outlined, among others, by political scientist Stephen Duncombe in his *Dreams: Re-imagining Progressive Politics in an Age of Fantasy* (2007). Duncombe's argument develops from the quite obvious observation of the Bush administration's grip on much of middle America. In the book he quotes a *New York Times* article, where writer Ron Suskind reported the words of a senior advisor to the president, whose name remains unknown. In an interview, the officer told Suskind, to his utter dismay: "We're an empire now, and when we act, we create reality. And while you are studying that reality – judiciously as you will – we'll act again creating other new realities, which you can study too, and that's how things will sort out. We're history actors ... and you, all of you will be left to just study what we do" (Suskind 2004). The interview, published right before the election of George W. Bush to his second term as a president, proved prophetic. As Duncombe points out:

> The problem, as I see it, comes down to reality. Progressives believe in it, Bush's people believe in creating it. The left and right have switched roles – the right taking on the mantle of radicalism and progressives waving the flag of conservatism. The political progeny of the protestors who proclaimed, "Take your desires for reality" in May of 1968, were now counseling the reversal: take reality for your desires. Republicans were the ones proclaiming, "I have a dream." (Duncombe 2007: 3)

A hilarious exposé of this new cultural and political climate was provided the host of Comedy Central's *The Colbert Report*, Stephen Colbert, when he was invited on April 29, 2006, to deliver the keynote speech for the White House Correspondents Dinner, at the Hilton Hotel in Washington. D.C. The event, broadcast live on C-SPAN and MSNBC, showed an increasingly uncomfortable audience of journalists and correspondents listening to Mr. Colbert's very special homage to a visibly puzzled George W. Bush.

> We're not so different, he and I. We both get it. Guys like us, we're not some brainiacs on the nerd patrol. We're not members of the factinistas. We go straight from the gut, right Sir? That's where the truth lies: right here, in the gut. Do you know you've got more endings in your gut than you have in your head? You can look it up. Now I know some of you will say: I did look it up and it's not true. That's because you looked it up in a book. Next time, look it up in your gut. I did. My gut tells me that's how our nervous system works. Every night on my show, *The Colbert Report*, I speak straight from the gut. I give people the truth unfiltered by rational argument. I call it the "No Fact Zone". Fox News, I want the copyright on that term. ... Guys like us, we don't pay attention to the polls. We know that polls are just a collection of statistics that reflect what people are thinking in "reality." And reality has a well-known liberal bias.

Needless to say, the long tirade became a major hit on youtube.com that has grown to be – I must admit – a priceless mine of material for my recent research. In the months preceding the 2008 presidential elections in the United States, Democratic candidate Barack Obama built his political discourse on words such as "hope" and "change," presenting himself as the alternative to politics as usual, embodied by his opponent Hillary Clinton. The reactions of the huge crowds who gathered to welcome him all over the countries seem to confirm that there is a need for passion and emotion, a desire to believe in momentous projects and in epochal overhauls.

These phenomena are certainly not limited to the United States. In Italy, the former Prime Minister Silvio Berlusconi cajoled public opinion and created a strong basis of political support through his media empire, which includes three national TV channels, various papers, magazines, and radios. Berlusconi managed to channel the dreams of many Italians, embodying the myth of the entrepreneur who is able to take advantage of any situation for his economic advantage. The following center-left government, more attuned to reality, had a very hard time communicating with Italians.

The point of this excursion into politics is that it is clear that a deep and practical understanding of the mechanisms of pop culture and the society of spectacle in general can become a very effective tool for political hegemony. The capacity of creating and spreading narratives that communicate in terms not only of rational priorities, but also of emotions, desires, and fantasies becomes a crucial weapon to have any impact on reality. Most of the time, we engage with market-driven culture in order to make its critique, to uncover its tight connection with consumerism, to debunk fads and fashions, or to demonstrate how pop culture actually fosters, solidifies, and naturalizes concepts and perceptions that sometimes hinder the development of free and thinking subjects. We all acknowledge that contemporary imagination is heavily based on consumption and commoditization. Nevertheless, there can be ways to ensure that somehow passive consumption becomes active enjoyment and then participation and choice.

To reach this goal in the field of food and food choices, it might not be enough to focus on what is good and right for the single citizen and for society at large, on what is nutritious and healthy for the body, and on what can help the environment in order to ensure the future of humanity. Although these are important objectives to which we should adhere in our everyday choices, there is one aspect that very often is left out in our intellectual discourse: personal pleasure. I am not implying that pleasure is not cultural and context-sensitive, just like desires and even fantasies are. Neither am I referring to any pre-symbolic dimension of our inner life, purely emotional and instinctive, that can act as an antidote to rationality. However, we often end up focusing on all those aspects of food that are connected with its function as fuel (for the body, for society, for the economy, for the planet), and we forget that subjective experiences play a key role in everyday life. Unfortunately, in the academic, intellectual, and even activist environment we are often very good at leaving the fun out of food. That is too bad, because I do believe with anthropologist Arjun Appadurai that "where there is pleasure, there is agency" (Appadurai 1996: 7). Pleasure is powerful, anarchical, self-centered, irrational, and emotional. It can constitute a very disruptive and subversive element in any social structure, as all past and present totalitarian propaganda machines have proven, since it can become a very effective tool to create consent. What if it were used not to bamboozle but to stimulate? The question is: How do we harness pleasure? How do we redirect desires and fantasies towards positive, constructive goals?

Twenty years ago a group of Italian intellectuals figured out that maybe, just maybe, food could represent a way to reaffirm one's identity, to generate a different sense of community based on shared consumption, and to decelerate the rhythm of modernity. The Slow Food movement began in a small town in northern Italy, far from the places inhabited by the movers and shakers of pop culture, yet its powerful, simple concepts proved to be immediately and intuitively accessible to a vast audience. The core ideas refer to people's daily experience, in particular the relaxed enjoyment of food in good company, with all those connotations of authenticity, nostalgia, and cultural heritage that stubbornly insist on being part of who we are, as hard as we try to debunk them. Over time, at least in Italy, the public mission of Slow Food has become so relevant, its involvement in big-time politics and economy so intense and visible, that sometimes pleasure seems to be forgotten. Now the goals are sustainability, the protection of the environment, and social justice, to be achieved through different structures of production and consumption. Many used to criticize the movement for being an expression of a certain kind of bourgeois sensibility, concentrating on private enjoyment and blind to the grim realities that clutch our world. Now it has redirected its operations towards new objectives, gaining wider recognition and more respect on the international scene. But is pleasure still there? Or has it become too low of a priority, when compared to more serious matters?

As intellectuals and citizens trained in a tradition based on empiricism, rationalism, and scientific principles, we get uncomfortable when it comes to desires, fantasies, and pleasure. We need to acquire new tools that allow us to stay relevant in the society of spectacle – possibly without making a spectacle of ourselves – by creating narratives based not on lies but on facts and truths.

Where could we get these new tools? I think we can actually learn quite a bit from pop culture. Being commercially savvy, mass-produced, and geared towards consumption, it *has* to relate to people's imaginations, sometimes to capture elements from them and transform them into new forms, sometimes to spread or impose practices and discourses, sometimes simply to generate and negotiate new meanings at an exponentially faster speed. Market-driven culture has transformed not only our minds, but also our bodies, into an arena of an uninterrupted struggle for the heart and soul of consumers, an arena where interconnected webs of communication codes, practices, and ideas are formed, transformed, and destroyed.

By acquiring a better grasp of the dynamics of commercial culture we could redirect its mechanisms towards different goals. Are we capable of putting pleasure at the forefront, not to numb the intellect, but to let the mind participate more intensely in the life of the body? Are we ready to use our bodies and our senses as hermeneutic tools?

After all, most of our daily choices are definitely based not only on accurate pondering of pros and cons, but also on our mood, wishes, and even drives. As a matter of fact, our irrational modes of operation often trump the rational ones. As we discussed, the most recent research in neuroscience seems to point in that direction: even the decisions that we feel are most rational, the ones that are derived from our frontal lobes, are heavily influenced by those parts of the brain in charge of emotions and passions. Some marketers are fully aware of this: consumption-driven economies seem to turn increasingly into "experience economies," whose goal is not only to provide commodities and goods, but also to ensure high added-value services and experiences (Pine and Gilmore 1999). Politicians know very well that, in contemporary democracies, truth and power belong to those who tell the better story (Duncombe 2007: 8). In other words, voters follow whoever is able to articulate their aspirations and their desires through symbols, images, and associations that make sense to them. Unfortunately, these elements are used at times to convey lies. Too often they have been used as propaganda by regimes that eventually strangle democracy.

However, narratives appear to be a great political and social tool. Warren Belasco, in his 2006 book *Meals to Come*, has shown how different ideas about the future of food have actually shaped much larger political debates for at least a couple of centuries. In those debates, scientists transformed their arguments into scenarios of possible realities to get their points through. "We need to get better at story telling," declared rock star Bono to explain his decision to take on the challenge of acting as guest editor of the July 2007 issue of *Vanity Fair*, about poverty and AIDS in Africa (Carr 2007).

Many programs, such as the Urban Nutrition Initiative in Philadelphia, Spoons Across America, and the numerous initiatives started by chef Alice Waters, are trying to introduce children of all ethnic, racial, and class background to fresh food and cooking by facilitating situations where they can work together in gardens, familiarize themselves with unusual ingredients, learn how to prepare new dishes, and consume them together. Through these practical experiences, young men and women also acquire a different outlook on social and political issues concerning production, distribution, and consumption of food, the environment, and the urban realities they inhabit.

Through food and the body, we can stimulate ourselves and others to think about our actual material physicality in time and space and to gain a sense of a lived place. Adopting Spanish sociologist Manuel Castell's terminology, we can integrate the somehow abstract, often homogenized, and always economy-driven "space of flows" with a more personal, more aware "space of places," our local environment where we make choices that influence not only our eating habits, but also our involvement with the economic and political aspects of food systems, with the cultural system that proposes various body ideals, and with contrasting social and political systems (Castells 1996).

I hope the reader has enjoyed the ride. I have tried to make it as pleasurable and as engaging as I could. I think it was the only way to tackle topics such as food and pop culture, both at times too close for comfort.

References

Adams, Douglas. 1995 (1980). *The Restaurant at the End of the Universe*. New York: Ballantine Books

Adema, Pauline. 2000. "Vicarious Consumption: Food, Television, and the Ambiguity of Modernity." In *Journal of American & Comparative Cultures* 23(3): 113–23

Adolphs, Ralph. 2003. "The Cognitive Neuroscience of Human Social Behavior." In *Nature Reviews Neuroscience* 4(3): 165–78

Allen, James, Hilton Als, John Lewis, and Leon F. Litwack. 2000. *Without Sanctuary: Lynching Photography in America*. Santa Fe: Twin Palms Publishers

Appadurai, Arjun. 1996. *Modernity at Large*. Minneapolis: University of Minnesota Press

Arendt, Hannah. 1958. *The Human Condition*. Garden City, NY: Doubleday Anchor Books

Asimov, Isaac. 1984 (1972). *The Gods Themselves*. New York: Ballantine Books

Atkins, Robert. 2002. *Dr. Atkins' New Diet Revolution*. New York: Avon

Bakhtin, Mikhail. 1984 (1965). *Rabelais and His World*. Bloomington: Indiana University Press

Barthes, Roland. 1972. *Mythologies*. New York: The Noonday Press

Bartolovich Crystal. 1998. "Consumerism, or the Cultural Logic of Late Cannibalism." In *Cannibalism and the Colonial World*, ed. Francis Barker, Peter Hulme, and Margaret Iversen. Cambridge: Cambridge University Press

Bass, Margaret K. 2001. "On Being a Fat Black Girl in a Fat Eating Culture." In *Recovering the Black Female Body: Self-representations by African American Women*, ed. Michael Bennet and Vanessa Dickerson. New Brunswick: Rutgers University Press

Baudrillard, Jean. 1983a. *Simulations*. New York: Semiotext(e)

Baudrillard, Jean. 1983b. "The Implosion of Meaning in the Media." In *The Shadow of Silent Majorities*. New York: Semiotext(e)

Baudrillard, Jean. 1988. *The Ecstasy of Communication*. New York: Semiotext(e)

Belasco, Warren. 2006. *Meals to Come: A History of the Future of Food*. Berkeley and Los Angeles: University of California Press

Belisle, François J. 1984. "Tourism and Food Imports: The Case of Jamaica." In *Economic Development and Cultural Change* 32(4): 819–42

Bellafante, Ginia. 2004. "Now Serving: Serena, Warrior Princess." In *New York Times*, September 5

Bentley, Amy. 2005. "Men on Atkins: Dieting, Meat and Masculinity." In *The Atkins Diet and Philosophy*, ed. Lisa M. Heldke, Kerri Mommer, and Cynthea Pineo. Chicago: Open Court

Bestor, Theodore C. 2004. *Tsukuji: The Fish Market at the Center of the World.* Berkeley and Los Angeles: University of California Press

Black, Rachel. 2006. "Acquirenti di Autenticità." In *Slow Food* 22(November): 133–6

Blake, Janet. 2000. "On Defining the Cultural Heritage." In *The International and Comparative Law Quarterly* 49(1): 61–85

Blakemore, Sarah-Jayne and Jean Decety. 2001. "From the perception of action to the understanding of intention." In *Nature Reviews Neuroscience* 2(8): 561-67

Bodin, Ron. 1990. *Voodoo: Past and Present.* Lafayette, LA: University of Southwestern Louisiana

Bogle, Donald. 2003. *Toms, Coons, Mulattoes, Mammies, and Bucks: An Interpretive History of Blacks in American Films.* New York: Continuum

Bolasco, Marco. 2000. "Il Cuoco dai Nervi Saldi." In *Gambero Rosso* 107(December): 117–26

Bonilli, Stefano, Carlo Petrini et al. 1987. *Slow Food. Gambero Rosso* 11(3 November): 1

Bordo, Susan. 1993. *Unbearable Weight.* Berkeley and Los Angeles: University of California Press

Bordo, Susan. 1999. *The Male Body: A New Look at Men in Public and in Private.* New York: Farrar, Strauss and Giroux

Bourdieu, Pierre. 1984. *Distinction: A Social Critique of the Judgment of Taste.* Cambridge, MA: Harvard University Press

Bourdieu, Pierre. 1998. *On Television.* New York: The New Press

Braudel, Fernand. 1982. *The Wheels of Commerce, Volume 2, Civilization and Capitalism, 15th–18th Century.* New York: Harper and Row

Bronski, Michael. 1998. "The Male Body in the Western Mind." In *Harvard Gay and Lesbian Review* 5(4): 28–32

Bryson, Norman. 1990. *Looking at the Overlooked: Four Essays on Still Life Painting.* Cambridge, MA: Harvard University Press

Buchan, Mark. 2001. "Food for Thought: Achilles and the Cyclops." In *Eating Their Words: Cannibalism and the Boundaries of Cultural Identity*, ed. Kristen Guest. Albany: State University of New York Press

Burgin, Victor. 1996. *In/different Spaces.* Berkeley and Los Angeles: University of California Press

Burton, Richard D.E. 1997. *Afro-Creole: Power, Opposition, and Play in the Caribbean.* Ithaca, NY: Cornell University Press

Butler, Judith. 1993. *Bodies That Matter.* New York: Routledge

Butler, Octavia E. 1993. *Parable of the Sower.* New York: Warner Books

Butler, Octavia E. 2005. *Fledgling.* New York: Seven Stories Press

Bynum, Caroline Walker. 1984. "Fast, Feast, and Flesh: The Religious Significance of Food to Medieval Women." In *Representations* 11: 1–25

Bynum, Caroline Walker. 1987. *Holy Feast and Holy Fast: The Religious Significance of Food to Medieval Women*. Berkeley and Los Angeles: University of California Press

Camargo Heck, Marina. 1980. "The Ideological Dimension of Media Messages." In *Culture, Media, Language*, ed. Stuart Hall, Dorothy Hobson, Andrew Lowe, and Paul Willis. London: Unwin Hyman

Camerer, Colin. 2005. "Behavioral Economics." Paper presented at World Congress of the Econometric Society. London, August 18–24

Canetti, Elias. 1984 (1960). *Crowds and Power*. New York: The Noonday Press

Capatti, Alberto and Massimo Montanari. 1999. *La Cucina Italiana*. Bari: Laterza; 2003. *Italian Cuisine: A Cultural History*. New York: Columbia University Press

Carby, Hazel. 1987. *Reconstructing Womanhood*. New York: Oxford University Press

Carr, David. 2007. "Citizen Bono Brings Africa to Idle Rich." In *New York Times*, March 5

Casey, Edward. 1997. *The Fate of Place*. Berkeley and Los Angeles: University of California Press

Cassidy, John. 2006. "Mind Games: What Neuroeconomics Tells Us about Money and the Brain." In *The New Yorker*, September 18, 30–7

Castells, Manuel. 1996. *The Information Age: Economy, Society and Culture. Volume I: The Rise of the Network Society*. Oxford: Blackwell

Chodorow, Nancy. 2000. Foreword. In Sigmund Freud, *Three Essays on the Theory of Sexuality*. New York: Basic Books

Chrzan Janet. 2004. "Slow Food: What, Why, and to Where?" In *Food, Culture & Society* 7(2): 117–32

Classen, Constan. 1994. *Aroma: The Cultural History of Smell*. New York and London: Routledge

Cockburn, Alexander. 1977. "Gastro-porn." In *New York Review of Books* 24 (20), December 8, 15–19

Connell, R.W. 1995. *Masculinities*. Berkeley: University of California Press

Connell, R.W. 2000. *The Men and the Boys*. Berkeley: University of California Press

Copjec, Joan 1991. "Vampires, Breast-Feeding, and Anxiety." In *October* 58: 25–43

Curry, Timothy, Paula Arriagada, and Benjamin Cornwell. 2002. "Images of Sport in Popular Nonsport Magazines: Power and Performance versus Pleasure and Participation." In *Sociological Perspectives* 45: 397–413

Curtin, Deane W. and Lisa M. Heldke. 1992. "Introduction." In *Cooking, Eating, Thinking*, ed. Deane W. Curtin and Lisa M. Heldke. Bloomington and Indianapolis: Indiana University Press

Cytowic, Richard. 2003. *The Man Who Tasted Shapes*. Cambridge, MA: MIT Press

Davis, Angela. 1998. *Blues Legacies and Black Feminism: Gertrude "Ma" Rainey, Bessie Smith, and Billie Holiday*. New York: Vintage

Debord, Guy. 1977 (1967). *Society of the Spectacle*. Detroit: Black & Red

de Certeau, Michel. 1984. *The Practice of Everyday Life*. Berkeley and Los Angeles: University of California Press

Deck, Alice A. 2001. "Now Then – Who Said Biscuits? The Black Woman Cook as Fetish in American Advertising, 1905–1953." In *Kitchen Culture in America*, ed. Sherrie A. Inness. Philadelphia: University of Pennsylvania Press

Delany, Samuel R. 1985. *Stars in My Pocket Like Grains of Sand*. New York: Bantam Books

Delany, Samuel R. 1996 (1975). *Dahlgren*. Hanover, NH: Wesleyan University Press

Derrida, Jacques. 1981. "Plato's Pharmacy." In *Dissemination*. Chicago: University of Chicago Press

Descartes, René. 2003 (1648). *Treatise of Man*. Amherst, NY: Prometheus Books

Dick, Philip K. 1992 (1962) *The Man in the High Castle*. New York: Vintage Books

Dinnerstein, Dorothy. 1976. *The Mermaid and the Minotaur: Sexual Arrangements and the Human Malaise*. New York: Harper and Row

Donati, Kelly. 2005. "The Pleasure of Diversity in Slow Food's Ethics of Taste." In *Food, Culture & Society* 8(2): 227–42

Douglas, Mary. 1969. *Purity and Danger*. London: Routledge and Kegan Paul

Duncombe, Stephen. 2007. *Dreams: Re-imagining Progressive Politics in an Age of Fantasy*. New York: The New Press

Dundes, Alan. 1998. *The Vampire: A Casebook*. Madison: University of Wisconsin Press

du Plessis, Eric. 2005. *Advertised Mind: Ground-Breaking Insights Into How Our Brains Respond To Advertising*. London: Kogan Page

Dyson, Michael Eric and Tavis Smiley. 2003. "Rebirth and Fascination with Pimp in Hip-Hop Culture." *National Public Radio*, October 2

Edelman, Gerald and Giulio Tononi. 2000. *A Universe of Consciousness*. New York: Basic Books

Evans Braziel, Jana. 2001. "Sex and Fat Chicks: Deterritorializing the Fat Female Body." *In Bodies Out of Bounds*, ed. Jana Evans Braziel and Kathleen LeBesco. Berkeley and Los Angeles: University of California Press

Eversley, Shelly . 2001. "The Source of Hip." In *The Minnesota Review: A Journal of Committed Writing* 55–7 (Spring/Fall): 257–70

Feierman, Steven. 1999. "Colonizers, Scholars and the Creation of Invisible Histories." In *Beyond the Cultural Turn*, ed. Victoria E. Bonnell and Lynn Hunt. Berkeley and Los Angeles: University of California Press

Fernàndez Olmos, Margarite and Lizabeth Paravisini-Gebert. 2003. *Creole Religions of the Caribbean*. New York: New York University Press

Ferrara, Pasquale. 1990. *L'Uno plurale*. Roma: Città Nuova

Fischler, Claude. 2001. *L'Homnivore*. Paris: Éditions Odile Jacob

Flanagan, Owen J., Jr. 1984. *The Science of the Mind*. Cambridge, MA: Bradford Books

Fodor, Jerry. 1983. *The Modularity of the Mind*. Cambridge, MA: Bradford Books

Forster, Laurel. 2004. "Futuristic Foodways: The Metaphorical Meaning of Food in Science Fiction Film." In *Reel Food: Essays on Food and Film*, ed. Anne Bower. London and New York: Routledge

Foucault, Michel. 1988. *The History of Sexuality, Vol. III: The Care of the Self*. New York: Vintage Books

Foucault, Michel. 1990. *The History of Sexuality, Vol. I: An Introduction*. New York: Vintage Books

Frankiel, R.V. 1993. "Hide-and-Seek in the Playroom: On Object Loss and Transference in Child Treatment." In *Psychoanalitic Review* 80: 351–9

Freedman, Carl. 2000. *Critical Theory and Science Fiction*. Hanover, NH: Wesleyan University Press

Freud, Sigmund. 1998 (1913). *Totem and Taboo*. Mineola, NY: Dover Publications

Freud, Sigmund. 2000 (1905). *Three Essays on the Theory of Sexuality*. New York: Basic Books

Frith, Christopher and Daniel Wolpert. 2004. *The Neuroscience of Social Interaction: Decoding, Imitating, and Influencing the Actions of Others*. New York: Oxford University Press

Gates, Henry Louis. 1988. *The Signifying Monkey*. New York: Oxford University Press

Gerschick Thomas J. and Adam S. Miller 1994. "Gender Identities at the Crossroads of Masculinity and Physical Disability." In *Masculinites* 2: 34–55

Geurts, Kathryn Linn. 2002. *Culture and the Senses: Bodily Ways of Knowing in an African Community*. Berkeley and Los Angeles: University of California Press.

Girard, René. 1979. *Violence and the Sacred*. Baltimore: Johns Hopkins University Press

Goleman, Daniel. 2006. *Social Intelligence: The New Science of Human Relationships*. New York: Bantam

Goude, Jean-Paul. 1981. *Jungle Fever*. New York: Xavier Moreau

Gramsci, Antonio. 2000. *The Antonio Gramsci Reader*, ed. David Forgacs. New York: New York University Press.

Greene, Bob. 2006. *The Best Life Diet*. New York: Simon and Schuster

Grimm, Jacob Ludwig Karl and Wilhelm Karl Grimm. 1898 (1812–15). "Little Snow White." In *Grimm's Fairy Tales*. London: Ernest Nister.

Guerrón-Montero Carla. 2004. "Afro-Antillean Cuisine and Global Tourism." In *Food, Culture & Society* 7(2): 29–47

Guy, Kolleen M. 2002. "Wine, Champagne and the Making of French Identity in the Belle Époque." In *Food, Drink and Identity*, ed. Peter Scholliers. Oxford and New York: Berg

Hall, C. Michael, Liz Sharples, Richard Mitchell, and Niki Macionis. 2003. *Food Tourism around The World: Development, Management and Markets*. London: Butterworth-Heinemann

Hardt, Michael and Antonio Negri. 2001. *Empire*. Cambridge, MA: Harvard University Press

Harper, Philip Brian. 1996. *Are We Not Men? Masculine Anxiety and the Problem of African-American Identity*. New York: Oxford University Press

Harris, Jessica. 2003. *Beyond Gumbo: Creole Fusion Food from the Atlantic Rim*. New York: Simon and Schuster

Harrus-Révidi, Gisèle. 1994. *Psychanalyse de la Gourmandise*. Paris: Payot

Haugeland, John. 1981. "Semantic Engines: An Introduction to Mind Design." In *Mind Design*. Cambridge, MA: Bradford Books

Hebb, Donald. 1949. *The Organization of Behavior*. New York: Wiley

Heldke, Lisa M. 1992 "Foodmaking as a Thoughtful Practice." In *Cooking, Eating, Thinking*, ed. Deane W. Curtin and Lisa M. Heldke. Bloomington and Indianapolis: Indiana University Press

Heldke Lisa M. 2003. *Exotic Appetites: Ruminations of a Food Adventurer*. London and New York: Routledge

Hesse-Biber, Sharlene. 1996. *Am I Thin Enough Yet?* New York: Oxford University Press.

Higgs, Catriona, Karen Weiller, and Scott Martin. 2003. "Gender Bias in the 1996 Olympic Games." In *Journal of Sport and Social Issues* 27: 52–64

Hjalager, Anne-Mette and Greg Richards, ed. 2002. *Tourism and Gastronomy*. London: Routledge

Hobbes, Thomas. 1982 (1651). *Leviathan*. New York and London: Penguin Classics

Hobson, Janell, 2003. "The 'Batty' Politic: Toward an Aesthetic of the Black Female Body." In *Hypatia* 18(4): 87–105

Hobson, Janell. 2005. *Venus in the Dark: Blackness and Beauty in Popular Culture*. New York: Routledge

Holmes, Rachel. 2007. *African Queen: The Real Life of the Hottentot Venus*. New York: Random House

hooks, bell. 1995. *Killing Rage, Ending Racism*. New York: Henry Holt and Co.

Howes, David. 2003. *Sensual Relations: Engaging the Senses in Culture and Social Theory*. Ann Arbor: University of Michigan Press

Islam Muhammad, Nisa. 2004. "Spelman Students Cancel Rapper's Charity Event." In Finalcall.com news, April 19. *http://www.finalcall.com/artman/publish/article_1380.shtml.*. Accessed March 11, 2008

Jackson, Janet. 2004. Acceptance Speech at the Soul Train Awards, Sunday, March 21

Jackson, Linda. 1992. *Physical Appearance and Gender: Sociobiological and Sociocultural Perspective*. Albany: New York State University Press

Jameson, Frederic. 1984. "Postmodernism, or the Cultural Logic of Late Capitalism." In *New Left Review* 146 (July–August): 52–92

Jamieson, Walter. 1998. "Cultural Heritage Tourism Planning and Development: Defining the Field and its Challenges." In *APT Bulletin* 29(3/4): 65–7

Jeffords, Susan. 1989. *The Remasculinization of America: Gender and the Vietnam War*. Bloomington: Indiana University Press

Kilgour, Maggie. 1990. *From Communion to Cannibalism: An Anatomy of Metaphors of Incorporations*. Princeton: Princeton University Press

Kimmel, Michael. 1996. *Manhood in America: A Cultural History*. New York: The Free Press

King, Stephen. 1991 (1978). *The Stand*. New York: Signet

King, Stephen. 2000 (1975). *'Salem's Lot*. New York: Pocket Books

King, Stephen. 2003. *Everything's Eventual*. New York: Pocket Books

Klaniczay, Gàbor. 1990. "The Decline of Witches and the Rise of Vampires under the Eighteenth-Century Hapsburg Monarchies." In *The Uses of Supernatural Power: The Transformation of Popular Religion in Medieval and Early Modern Europe*. Princeton: Princeton University Press

Klein, Melanie. 1987a (1926). "The Psychological Principles of Infant Analysis." In *The Selected Melanie Klein*, ed. Juliet Mitchell. New York: The Free Press

Klein, Melanie. 1987b (1955). "The Psycho-analytic Play Technique: Its History and Significance." In *The Selected Melanie Klein*, ed. Juliet Mitchell. New York: The Free Press

Kristeva, Julia. 1982. *Powers of Horror*. New York: Columbia University Press

Kumanyika, Hiriku, Judy Wilson, and Marsha Guilford-Davenport. 1993. "Weight-Related Attitudes and Behaviors of Black Women." In *Journal of the American Dietetic Association* 93: 416–22

Kummer, Corby. 2002. *The Pleasures of Slow Food: Celebrating Authentic Traditions, Flavors, and Recipes*. San Francisco: Chronicle Books

Lacan, Jacques. 2002 (1966). *Écrits: A Selection*. New York and London: W.W. Norton & Company

Laclau, Ernesto and Chantal Mouffe. 1985 *Hegemony and Socialist Strategy*. London and New York: Verso

Lacoste, Yves. 1988. *Questions de Géopolitique*. Paris: La Découverte

Laudan, Rachel. 1999. "A World of Inauthentic Cuisine." Paper presented at the conference *Cultural and Historical Aspects of Foods*. Oregon State University, April 9–11

Laudan, Rachel. 2001. "A Plea for Culinary Modernism: Why We Should Love New, Fast, Processed Food." In *Gastronomica* 1(1): 36–44

Laudan, Rachel. 2004. "Slow Food: The French Terroir Strategy, and Culinary Modernism." In *Food, Culture & Society* 7(2): 133–44

LeDoux, Joseph. 1998. *The Emotional Brain*. New York: Touchstone

LeDoux, Joseph. 2002. *The Synaptic Self.* New York: Viking Books

Lee, Jonathan Scott. 1990. *Jacques Lacan.* Amherst: University of Massachusetts Press

Lefebvre, Henri. 1991. *The Production of Space.* Oxford: Basil Blackwell

Lefort, Claude. 1985. *Democracy and Political Theory.* Cambridge: Polity

Leitch, Alison. 2000. "The Social Life of *Lardo.*" In *The Asia Pacific Journal of Anthropology* 1(1): 103–18

Lévi-Strauss, Claude. 1968. *L'Origine des manières de table.* Paris: Plon.

Liu, Lidia. 2004. *Clash of Empire: The Invention of China in Modern World Making.* Cambridge, MA: Harvard University Press

Löfgren, Orvar. 1999. *On Holiday: A History of Vacation.* Berkeley and Los Angeles: University of California Press

Long, Lucy M. ed. 2003. *Culinary Tourism.* Lexington: University Press of Kentucky

Lyotard, François. 1984. *The Postmodern Condition: A Report on Knowledge.* Minneapolis: University of Minnesota Press

MacCannell, Dean. 1999. *The Tourist.* Berkeley and Los Angeles: University of California Press

Mailer. Norman. 1994 (1959). "The White Negro." In *Advertisements for Myself.* Glasgow: Flamingo Modern Classic

Marx, Karl. 1990 (1867). *Capital, Vol. I.* Harmondsworth: Penguin

Matheson, Richard. 1995 (1954). *I Am Legend.* New York: Orb Edition

Mauss, Marcel. 1973 (1935). "Techniques of the Body." In *Economy and Society* 2(1): 70–85

Meltzoff, Andrew and Wolfgang Prinz. 2002. *The Imitative Mind: Development, Evolution and Brain Bases.* Cambridge: Cambridge University Press

Mercer, Kobena. 1994. "Reading Racial Fetishism." In *Welcome to the Jungle*, ed. Kobena Mercer. London: Routledge

Messner, Michael, Margaret Carlisle Duncan, and Kerry Jensen. 1993. "Separating the Men from the Girls: The Gendered Language of Televised Sports." In *Gender and Society* 7: 121–37

Métraux, Alfred. 1972. *Voodoo in Haiti.* New York: Schocken Books

Mo'nique and Sherri McGee. 2004. *Skinny Women Are Evil: Notes of a Big Girl in a Small-Minded World.* New York: Atria Books

Mongai, Massimo. 2000. *Memorie di un Cuoco d'Astronave.* Milan: Publigold

Morgan, Jennifer. 1997. "Some Could Suckle Over Their Shoulder: Male Travelers, Female Bodies and Gendering of Racial ideology, 1500–1770." In *The William and Mary Quarterly* (Third Series) 36(1): 167–92

Muñoz, José Esteban. 1999. *Disidentifications: Queers of Color and the Performance of Politics.* Minneapolis: University of Minnesota Press.

Neal, Marc Anthony. 2005. *New Black Man.* London and New York: Routledge

Neisser, Ulrich. 1966. *Cognitive Psychology.* New York: Appleton-Century-Crofts

Nestle, Marion. 2002. *Food Politics*. Berkeley and Los Angeles: University of California Press.

Norman, Donald. 1989. *The Design of Everyday Things*. New York: Doubleday

Norman, Donald. 2004. *Emotional Design: Why we Love (or Hate) Everyday Things*. New York: Basic Books

Obama, Barack. 2007. Keynote address, Democratic National Convention, Boston, July 27

O'Neill, Molly. 2003. "Food Porn." In *Columbia Journalism Review* 42(3): 38–45

Onfray, Michel. 1995. *La Raison gourmande*. Paris: Grasset

Orwell, George. 1983 (1949). *Nineteen Eighty-four*. New York: Signet

Page, Clarence. 2003 "Why Nelly Pimp Juice is Nothing but Poison." In *New York Newsday*, September 16.

Parasecoli, Fabio. 2001. "Deconstructing Soup: Ferran Adriá's Culinary Universe." In *Gastronomica* 1(1): 61–73

Parasecoli, Fabio. 2003a. "*La Cocina de los Sentidos.*" In *Gastronomica* 3(1): 110–11

Parasecoli, Fabio. 2003b. "Postrevolutionary Chowhounds: Pleasure, Food and the Italian Left." In *Gastronomica* 3(3): 29–39

Parasecoli, Fabio. 2004. *Food Culture in Italy*. Westport, CT: Greenwood

Parasecoli, Fabio. 2005. "Feeding Hard Bodies: Food and Masculinities in Men's Fitness Magazines." In *Food & Foodways* 13(1–2): 17–37

Parasecoli, Fabio. 2007. "Bootylicious: Food and the Female Body in Contemporary Pop Culture." In *WSQ: Women's Studies Quarterly* 35(1–2): 110–25

Peirce, Charles Sanders. 1966. *Selected Writings*. New York: Dover

Pels, Peter. 1992. "Mumiani: The White Vampire. A Neo-diffusionist Analysis of Rumor." In *Ethnofoor* 5(1–2): 166–7

Perloff, Richard M. 2000. "The Press and Lynchings of African Americans." In *Journal of Black Studies* 20(3): 315–30

Pine, B. Joseph and James Gilmore. 1999. *The Experience Economy*. Cambridge, MA: Harvard Business School Press

Pope, Harrison G., Katharine A. Phillips, and Roberto Olivardia. 2000. *The Adonis Complex*. New York: Touchstone Books

Poulson-Bryant, Scott. 2005. *Hung*. New York: Doubleday

Pratt, Charlotte and Cornelius Pratt.1996. "Nutrition Advertisements in Consumer Magazines: Health Implications for African Americans." In *Journal of Black Studies* 26(4): 504–23

Proust, Marcel. 1984 (1913). *Du Côté de Chez Swann*. Paris: Gallimard

Rahming, Melvin B. 1986. *The Evolution of the West Indian's Image in the Afro-American Novel*. New York: Associated Faculty Press

Ravaldi, Claudia, Alfredo Vannacci, Teresa Zucchi et. al. 2003 "Eating Disorders and Body Image Disturbances among Ballet Dancers, Gymnasium Users and Body Builders." In *Psychopathology* 36: 247–54

Ray, Krishnendu. 2007. "Domesticating Cuisine." In *Gastronomica* 7(1): 50–63

Reid-Pharr, Robert. 1999. *Conjugal Union*. New York: Oxford University Press

Reid-Pharr Robert. 2007. *Once You Go Black: Desire, Choice and Black Masculinity in Post-War America*. New York: New York University Press

Rice, Anne. 1977. *Interview with the Vampire*. New York: Ballantine Books

Rice, Anne. 2000. *The Vampire Armand*. New York: Ballantine Books

Rigaud, Milo. 1985 (1953). *Secrets of Voodoo*. San Francisco: City Lights Books

Roediger, David. 1991. *The Wages of Whiteness: Race and the Making of the American Working Class*. New York: Verso

Rose, Steven. 2005. *The Future of the Brain*. New York: Oxford University Press

Rouby, Catherine, Benoist Schaal, Danièle Dubois, Rémi Gervais, and André. Holley, ed. 2005. *Olfaction, Taste, and Cognition*. Cambridge: Cambridge University Press

Rozin, Paul. 1988. "Cultural Approaches to Human Food Preferences." In *Nutritional Modulation of Neural Function*. New York: Academic Press

Rozin, Paul. 1998. "Food is Fundamental, Fun, Frightening, and Far-reaching." In *Social Research* 66(Winter): 9–30

Rushdie, Salman. 1999. *The Ground beneath Her Feet*. New York: Picador USA

Salaam, Kalammu ya. 1997. "Do Right Women: Black Women, Eroticism, and Classic Blues." In *Dark Eros*, ed. Reginald Martin. New York: St. Martin's Press

Sánchez Romera, Miguel. 2001. *La Cocina de los Sentidos*. Barcelona: Planeta

Saussure, Fernand de. 1983 (1916). *Course in General Linguistics*. London: Duckworth

Scheper-Hughes, Nancy. 1992. *Death without Weeping: The Violence of Everyday Life in Brazil*. Berkeley and Los Angeles: University of California Press

Schick, Irvin. 1999. *The Erotic Margin: Sexuality and Spatiality in Alterist Discourse*. London: Verso

Sheller, Mimi. 2003. *Consuming the Caribbean*. London and New York: Routledge

Singer, Tania, Ben Seymour, John O'Doherty, Holger Kaube, Raymond J. Dolan, and Chris D. Frith. 2004. "Empathy for Pain Involves the Affective But Not Sensory Components of Pain." In *Science* 303(20): 1157–62

Sisario, Ben. 2006. "Citing Religion, Isaac Hayes Is Leaving 'South Park'." In *New York Times*, March 14

Stade, George. 1982. *Dracula: Introduction*. New York: Bantam Books

Stavrakakis, Yannis. 1999. *Lacan and the Political*. London and New York: Routledge

Stearns, Peter N. 1997. *Fat History*. New York: New York University Press

Stoker, Bram. 2003 (1867). *Dracula*, introduction by Brooke Allen. New York: Barnes & Nobles Classics

Strachan, Ian Gregory. 2002. *Paradise and Plantation: Tourism and Culture in the Anglophone Caribbean*. Charlotsville and London: University of Virginia Press

Sudi, Karl, Karl Öttl, Doris Payerl, Peter Baumgartl, Klemens Tauschmann, and Wolfram Müller 2004. "Anorexia Athletica." In *Nutrition* 20(7–8): 657–61

Suskind, Ron. 2004. "Without a Doubt." In *New York Times Magazine*, October 17, 51

Sutton, David. 2001. *Remembrance of Repasts: An Anthropology of Food and Memory*. Oxford: Berg

Suvin, Darko. 1979. *Metamorphoses of Science Fiction*. New Haven: Yale University Press

Thagard, Paul. 2005. *Mind: Introduction to Cognitive Science*. Cambridge, MA: MIT Press

Thomsen, Steven, Danny Bower, and Michael Barnes. 2004. "Photographic Images in Women's Health, Fitness, and Sports Magazines and the Physical Self-concept of a group of Adolescent Female Volleyball Players." In *Journal of Sport and Social Issues* 28: 266–83

Tompkins, Kyla Wazana. 2007. "Everything 'Cept Eat Us: The Antebellum Black Body Portrayed as Edible Body." In *Callaloo* 30(1): 201–24

Veblen, Thorstein. 2001 (1899). *The Theory of Leisure Class*. New York: The Modern Library

Visser, Margaret. 1992. *The Rituals of Dinner*. New York: Penguin Books

Wallerstein, Immanuel. 1980. *The Modern World-System, II: Mercantilism and the Consolidation of the European World-Economy, 1600–1750*. New York: Academic Press

Wangsgaard Thompson, Becky . 1992. "A Way Outta No Way: Eating Problems among African-American, Latina and White Women." In *Gender and Society* 6(4): 546–61

Warnes, Andrew. 2004. *Hunger Overcome? Food and Resistance in Twentieth-Century African American Literature*. Athens: University of Georgia Press

Watchel, Nathan. 1994. *God and Vampires: Return to Chipaya*. Chicago: University of Chicago Press

Welch, Evelyn. 2005. *Shopping in the Renaissance*. New Haven and London: Yale University Press

Wells, H.G. undated (1904). *Food of the Gods*. Mannford, OK: University Publishing House

Westbrook, Alonzo. 2002. *Hip Hoptionary*. New York: Harlem Moon Broadway

White, Luise. 2000. *Speaking with Vampires: Rumor and History in Colonial Africa*. Berkeley and Los Angeles: University of California Press

Wienke, Chris. 1998. "Negotiating the Male Body: Men, Masculinity, and Cultural Ideas." In *The Journal of Men's Studies* 6(3): 255–82

Wilk. Richard. 2006. *Home Cooking in the Global Village*. Oxford and New York: Berg

Williams, Linda. 2002. "Melodrama in Black and White: *Uncle Tom* and *The Green Mile*." In *Film Quarterly* 55(2): 14–21

Williams-Forson, Psyche A. 2006. *Building Houses out of Chicken Legs: Black Women, Food, and Power*. Chapel Hill: University of North Carolina Press

Willis, Deborah and Carla Williams. 2002. *The Black Female Body: A Photographic History*. Philadelphia: Temple University Press

Witt, Doris. 1999. *Black Hunger*. New York: Oxford University Press

Wolf, Naomi. 1991. *The Beauty Myth: How Images of Beauty Are Used Against Women*. New York: W. Morrow.

Žižek, Slavoj. 1989. *The Sublime Object of Ideology*. London: Verso

Žižek, Slavoj. 1992. *Looking Awry*. Cambridge MA: MIT Press

Index

12 Monkeys 19
301/302 59
50 Cent 116, 117–118
6ᵗʰ Day, The 20

Adriá, Ferran 2, 17
advertising 2, 5, 6, 12, 32, 33, 34, 35, 99, 100, 109, 138, 148
Alien 80
Appadurai, Arjun 3, 74, 150
Arendt, Hannah 60
Asimov, Isaac 77
athletes 99–101
Atkins, Robert C. 87–88, 90, 91–95

Babette's Feast 28, 147
Baby Boy 123
Bakhtin, Mikhail 78–79
Banks, Tyra 109
Barthes, Roland 6–7, 144
Baudrillard, Jean 7, 148
Beauty Shop 104
Belasco, Warren 64, 68, 152
Bentley, Amy 88
Big Momma's House 113
Big Night 30
Blade 65–66
Blues 105, 107
body 5, 10, 13, 16, 45, 73–75, 78–79, 83, 94–96, 98, 101–102, 103–105, 109–110, 118, 122–124, 136, 142, 150, 152
body-builder 88, 97–100
body image 13, 42, 51, 85–94, 97–98, 101, 103–104, 108–113
booty 104, 105–108, 110, 112
Bordo, Susan 45, 102, 109
Bourdieu, Pierre 11, 34, 73, 74, 138

brain 12, 16–17, 23–25, 31–32, 40, 151
breast 49–50, 51, 54
Butler, Judith 57
Butler, Octavia E. 45, 69

Canetti, Elias 60
cannibal 39, 42, 56–59, 62, 65, 81, 122, 129
cannibalistic desire/drive 12, 39–40, 50, 51, 54, 70, 72, 121, 123
Carby, Hazel
Caribbean 55, 57, 129–131
Castell, Manuel 152
celebrity chef 2–3, 27, 30
Chocolat 27
cognitive psychology 23
Colbert, Stephen 149
computer 19–21, 23–24, 31, 40
connotation 7, 10, 82, 105, 132, 139, 144, 151
consumption 2, 11, 15, 32, 33, 40, 45, 48, 52, 60, 63, 68, 73, 93, 105, 108, 121, 122, 129, 132, 140, 150
Cook, The Thief, His Wife and Her Lover, The 59
cooking 3, 16–18, 25–31, 43, 59, 72, 75, 101, 111, 113, 123–124, 133, 152
Crooklyn 124
crunk 118
cultural capital 2, 34, 132

Dahlgreen 70–72
Debord, Guy 3, 148
de Certeau, Michel 34
Delany, Samuel R. 70, 80
Delicatessen 59
Demolition Man 68–69
denotation 7, 106

Derrida, Jacques 142
desire 8, 12, 15, 35, 41, 50–51, 55, 61, 66,
    90, 102, 106, 112, 123
diachronic analysis 6
Diary of a Mad Black Woman 115
Dick. Philip K. 61
diet 13, 42, 86–88, 91, 94–96, 100–101,
    109, 113, 139
disidentification 114
Dona Flor and Her Two Husbands 26
Douglas, Mary 57
Dracula 44
drag 112–116
Duncombe, Stephen 148
Dyson, Michael Eric 117

Eat Drink Man Woman 29
eating disorders 42, 99, 101
Eating Raoul 59
Edelman, Gerard, 24
emotion 16, 24, 32–35, 40–41, 45, 66, 77,
    81, 98, 149–150
Everybody Hates Chris 124
Everything is Illuminated 103
Everything's Eventual 38–39

Facing Windows 30
faith 86, 94, 96
Fischler, Claude 142
fitness magazines 97–103
Food of the Gods, the 76
food studies 2, 11, 147–148
food TV 1–3
Foucault, Michel 74
Freedman, Carl 64
Freud, Sigmund 41–42, 48–49, 59–60

Gates, Henry Louis Jr. 114
gay 30, 97–98, 103
gender 2, 5, 11, 12, 46, 70, 74, 83, 91, 101,
    103, 112, 113, 115, 134, 144
Ghosts of Mars 80
Girard, René 57
God of Cookery, The 30

Gods Themselves, The 77–78
Gramsci, Antonio, 9
Grande Bouffe, La 59

habitus 73–74
Harrus-Révidi, Gisèle 86
hegemony 9–10, 79, 98–99, 144, 150
high brow 5, 9
hip hop 106, 108, 111, 116, 118
His Secret Life 30
Hitchhiker's Guide to the Galaxy, The
    37–38
Hobbes, Thomas 40
Holiday, Billie 122
horror 12, 39, 65, 66, 147
hunger 13, 15, 17, 39, 41, 48–49, 51,53, 66,
    70, 79, 92, 93, 105, 106

I Am Legend 46–47
identification 32, 46, 48, 51, 55, 87–91,
    111, 112, 123, 133, 143, 144
identity 11, 29, 57, 64, 69, 78, 98, 106, 114,
    130, 133, 135, 137, 140, 143–145, 150
imaginary (Lacanian) 89–90, 95
incorporation 2, 12, 15, 41, 50, 57, 121
infants 39, 41–43, 45, 47, 49–50, 89, 94
ingestion 2, 10, 12, 15, 25, 39, 41, 45, 48,
    50, 55, 60, 62–63, 75, 103, 117, 122, 132
ingredient 5, 8, 11, 18, 23, 29, 32, 65, 76,
    100, 123, 133–135, 141
Interview with the Vampire 42–43
Island, the 22

Jameson, Frederic 136
Johnny Mnemonic 19

King, Stephen 38, 47, 69
Klein, Melanie 41, 49–50, 79
Kristeva, Julia 57

Lacan, Jacques 8, 41, 51–52, 88–89, 91,
    93, 95
Laclau, Ernesto 9–10, 88
LeDoux, Joseph 24–25

Like Water for Chocolate 27, 147
Lil' Jon 116, 118
Little Pimp 117
local food 129–144
Lynching 121–122

Madea's Family Reunion 115
Mandingo 122
Man in the High Castle, The 61–63
Marvel Comics 65, 75
Marx, Karl 58
masculinity 13, 28–31, 97–102, 116, 119,
    122–123, 124–125
Matrix, The 20–22, 65
Matrix Reloaded, The 22
Mauss, Marcel 73
media 1, 2, 3, 5, 7, 10, 11, 34, 86, 97, 112,
    119, 128, 132, 138–139, 142, 147
Memoir of a Starship Cook 79–80
memory 12, 15–18, 25, 34, 137
memory and food 17–18, 25–27, 29, 67
memory in science fiction 19–22
metaphor 8, 12, 23, 28, 48, 71, 76, 79, 81,
    98, 99, 105–107, 122, 123, 144
mirror stage 89
molecular gastronomy 2
Mongai, Massimo, 79
Mo'nique 110–111
Morgan, Jennifer 106
Mostly Martha 29–30
Mouffe, Chantal 9–10, 88
Ms. Peachez 114
Muñoz, José 114

Neal, Mark Anthony 117
Nelly 13, 108, 116–117
neuroscience 12, 16, 18, 24, 31, 151
Nineteen Eighty-Four 66–68
Norman, Donald 32
nutrition 6, 11, 41, 77, 92–94, 97, 99–100,
    147, 152
Nutty Professor, the 113–114

Orwell, George 66, 68

Parable of the Sower 69–70
Peirce, Charles S. 8
performance 6, 11, 32, 33, 82, 99, 101, 103,
    112, 114, 116, 124, 130
Perry, Tyler 115
Phat Girlz 111
pimp 116–117
pleasure 16, 18, 28, 33, 42, 44, 45, 49–50,
    92, 93, 106, 144, 150
politics 9, 13, 58, 63, 70, 75–76, 79, 82,
    103, 112, 140, 143–145
pop culture, definition 3–5
Poulson-Bryant, Scott 119
power 2, 12, 13, 35, 40, 58–60, 62, 63, 65,
    74, 83, 98, 103, 106, 112, 117, 120, 123,
    139, 152

Queen Latifah 104, 109, 125
Queens of Comedy, The 110

race 15, 56, 64, 70, 80–81, 103, 121, 125,
    134, 144
Ratatouille 28
Real (Lacanian) 95, 143
recipe 2, 8, 18, 23, 26, 72, 128, 133, 134,
    137, 138
Reid-Pharr, Robert 120
Rice, Anne 42–43
Robocop 19
Roediger, David 119
Rozin, Paul 142

Salem's Lot 47
Sánchez Romera, Miguel 16–18
Saussure, Ferdinand de 8
science 76, 94, 97, 100, 102
science fiction 12–13, 19–22, 28, 61–72,
    75–83, 148
self-help literature 87
semiotics 6, 8, 11, 23, 144
sex 11, 13, 18, 26, 45, 46, 48, 57, 67, 70,
    74, 79, 91, 101, 105–112, 116–122,
    134
sign 6, 7, 8, 73, 93, 106, 140–141

signifier 6–8, 137
signifying network 9–10, 143–144
Silence of the Lambs, The 59
slave 8, 55–56, 103, 106, 120, 122, 129, 134
Slow Food 138, 150, 151
Sommore 110
soul food 8, 13, 111–115, 124
Soul Food 109, 111, 113
South Park 13, 53, 123
Soylent Green 65
Spanglish 30
Stand, The 69
Stars in My Pocket like Grains of Sand, 80–83
Strachan, Gregory 129
Strange Days 20
street markets 131
Sweeney Todd 59
symbolic (Lacanian) 51, 63, 91, 95, 143, 144, 150
synchronic analysis 6
system 8–10, 14, 24, 25, 31, 66, 70, 73, 79, 91, 93, 94, 96, 141, 142, 152

Tampopo 27
Taxi 125
technology 63, 65–66, 75–76
Tortilla Soup 29
tourism 13–14, 125, 128, 130, 131, 141–144, 148
typical food 131–134, 137, 144

vampire 12, 39, 42–47, 54–56, 65
Vatel 29
voodoo 55–56

Waiting to Exhale 111
Warnes, Andrew 120
Wedding Banquet, The 30
Wells, H.G. 68, 76
Wild, Richard 130
Williams-Forson Psyche, 115
Winfrey, Oprah 88
Woman on Top 26
women 13, 25–28, 45, 59, 101–102, 103–115, 121, 124, 129, 147, 152

Žižek, Slavoj 88